Pedagogical Responses to the Changing Position of Girls and Young Women

Academics and professionals working with young women face a series of paradoxes. Over the last 20 years, the lives of young women in the UK and Europe have been transformed. They have gained considerable freedom and independence, but at the very same time, new, less tangible forms of constraint and subordination now play a defining role in the formation of their everyday subjectivities and identities. Young women have come to exemplify the pervasive sensibility of self-responsibility and self-organisation. This new 'gender regime' demands both conceptualisation and practical response, drawing on educational research, social and cultural theory and contemporary feminist thought.

Within the overarching theme of pedagogical responses to these trends, through work in schools and within young women's online and face-to-face communities, this book interrogates the field of sexuality and its visualisation across new and old media in the context of often predictable and endemic 'moral panics' about teenage pregnancy rates, sexually transmitted diseases and internet pornography. In exploring how girls and young women respond to increasing expectations of them as the vanguard of economic, social and cultural change, contributors to this volume interrogate the ways in which social and educational aspiration interact with young women's developing and embodied identities.

This book was originally published as a special issue of *Pedagogy, Culture & Society*.

Carrie Paechter is Professor of Education at Goldsmiths, University of London, UK. Her research centres on the intersection of gender, power and knowledge, the construction of gendered, spatialised and embodied identities, and the processes of curriculum negotiation. She is particularly interested on how children construct themselves as gendered, embodied, social actors.

Rosalyn George is Professor of Education and Equality at Goldsmiths, University of London, UK. Her research is in the areas of social justice, education and schooling, especially with regard to gender and race. Her current work focuses on recent forms of migration and its impact on the promotion of non-colour-coded racism.

Angela McRobbie is Professor of Communications at Goldsmiths, University of London, UK. Her fields of expertise are young women and popular culture, feminist theory, the new creative economy and the rise of 'cultural labour process'. Her current research includes an investigation of the working lives of young fashion designers in London, Berlin and Milan.

Pedagogical Responses to the Changing Position of Girls and Young Women

Edited by
Carrie Paechter, Rosalyn George and Angela McRobbie

LONDON AND NEW YORK

First published 2016
by Routledge
2 Park Square, Milton Park, Abingdon, Oxon, OX14 4RN, UK

and by Routledge
711 Third Avenue, New York, NY 10017, USA

Routledge is an imprint of the Taylor & Francis Group, an informa business

© 2016 Pedagogy, Culture & Society

All rights reserved. No part of this book may be reprinted or reproduced or utilised in any form or by any electronic, mechanical, or other means, now known or hereafter invented, including photocopying and recording, or in any information storage or retrieval system, without permission in writing from the publishers.

Trademark notice: Product or corporate names may be trademarks or registered trademarks, and are used only for identification and explanation without intent to infringe.

British Library Cataloguing in Publication Data
A catalogue record for this book is available from the British Library

ISBN 13: 978-1-138-65492-1

Typeset in Times New Roman
by RefineCatch Limited, Bungay, Suffolk

Publisher's Note
The publisher accepts responsibility for any inconsistencies that may have arisen during the conversion of this book from journal articles to book chapters, namely the possible inclusion of journal terminology.

Disclaimer
Every effort has been made to contact copyright holders for their permission to reprint material in this book. The publishers would be grateful to hear from any copyright holder who is not here acknowledged and will undertake to rectify any errors or omissions in future editions of this book.

Contents

Citation Information vii
Notes on Contributors ix

Introduction: Pedagogical responses to the changing position of girls
and young women 1
Carrie Paechter, Rosalyn George and Angela McRobbie

1. Changing times, future bodies? The significance of health in young women's imagined futures 5
Emma Rich and John Evans

2. From DIY to teen pregnancy: new pathologies, melancholia and feminist practice in contemporary English youth work 23
Fin Cullen

3. A girl is no girl is a girl_: Girls-work after queer theory 43
Mart Busche

4. 'Too pretty to do math!' Young women in movement and pedagogical challenges 57
Ulrike Graff

5. Becoming accomplished: concerted cultivation among privately educated young women 75
Claire Maxwell and Peter Aggleton

6. Dissident daughters? The psychic life of class inheritance 95
Valerie Hey and Rosalyn George

7. Young women online: collaboratively constructing identities 111
Carrie Paechter

8. Growing-up challenged and challenging: gender and sexuality norms in referential research on 'internet risks' and in children 129
Renata Šribar

9. Trainee hairdressers' uses of Facebook as a community of gendered literacy practice 147
Julia Davies

CONTENTS

10. 'Not girly, not sexy, not glamorous': primary school girls' and parents' constructions of science aspirations 171
    Louise Archer, Jennifer DeWitt, Jonathan Osborne, Justin Dillon, Beatrice Willis and Billy Wong

    Index 195

Citation Information

The chapters in this book were originally published in *Pedagogy, Culture & Society*, volume 21, issue 1 (March 2013). When citing this material, please use the original page numbering for each article, as follows:

Introduction
Pedagogical responses to the changing position of girls and young women
Carrie Paechter, Rosalyn George and Angela McRobbie
Pedagogy, Culture & Society, volume 21, issue 1 (March 2013) pp. 1–3

Chapter 1
Changing times, future bodies? The significance of health in young women's imagined futures
Emma Rich and John Evans
Pedagogy, Culture & Society, volume 21, issue 1 (March 2013) pp. 5–22

Chapter 2
From DIY to teen pregnancy: new pathologies, melancholia and feminist practice in contemporary English youth work
Fin Cullen
Pedagogy, Culture & Society, volume 21, issue 1 (March 2013) pp. 23–42

Chapter 3
A girl is no girl is a girl_: Girls-work after queer theory
Mart Busche
Pedagogy, Culture & Society, volume 21, issue 1 (March 2013) pp. 43–56

Chapter 4
'Too pretty to do math!' Young women in movement and pedagogical challenges
Ulrike Graff
Pedagogy, Culture & Society, volume 21, issue 1 (March 2013) pp. 57–73

CITATION INFORMATION

Chapter 5
Becoming accomplished: concerted cultivation among privately educated young women
Claire Maxwell and Peter Aggleton
Pedagogy, Culture & Society, volume 21, issue 1 (March 2013) pp. 75–93

Chapter 6
Dissident daughters? The psychic life of class inheritance
Valerie Hey and Rosalyn George
Pedagogy, Culture & Society, volume 21, issue 1 (March 2013) pp. 95–110

Chapter 7
Young women online: collaboratively constructing identities
Carrie Paechter
Pedagogy, Culture & Society, volume 21, issue 1 (March 2013) pp. 111–127

Chapter 8
Growing-up challenged and challenging: gender and sexuality norms in referential research on 'internet risks' and in children
Renata Šribar
Pedagogy, Culture & Society, volume 21, issue 1 (March 2013) pp. 129–145

Chapter 9
Trainee hairdressers' uses of Facebook as a community of gendered literacy practice
Julia Davies
Pedagogy, Culture & Society, volume 21, issue 1 (March 2013) pp. 147–169

Chapter 10
'Not girly, not sexy, not glamorous': primary school girls' and parents' constructions of science aspirations
Louise Archer, Jennifer DeWitt, Jonathan Osborne, Justin Dillon, Beatrice Willis and Billy Wong
Pedagogy, Culture & Society, volume 21, issue 1 (March 2013) pp. 171–194

For any permission-related enquiries please visit:
http://www.tandfonline.com/page/help/permissions

Notes on Contributors

Peter Aggleton is Scientia Professor at the Centre for Social Research in Health at the University of New South Wales, Sydney, Australia. He is the editor-in-chief of the international peer reviewed journals *Culture, Health & Sexuality*, *Health Education Journal* and *Sex Education*. His most recent edited book is *Elite Education: International Perspectives* (with Maxwell, 2015).

Louise Archer is Professor of Sociology of Education at King's College London, UK. She is interested in identities and inequalities of 'race', and gender and social class within compulsory and post-compulsory education. She is the author of *Urban Youth and Schooling* (with Hollingworth and Mendick, 2010).

Mart Busche is a Researcher in the Department of Sociology at the University of Kassel, Germany, and a member of the research group, 'Dynamics of Space and Gender'. Mart's current research is concerned with the sociology of diversity with special reference to gender dimension.

Fin Cullen is a Lecturer in Youth and Community Work at Brunel University, London, UK. Her research interests include drugs and alcohol issues; sex and relationship education; youth and community work, practice and evaluation; and sexuality and gender. She is the author of *Research and Research Methods for Youth Practitioners* (with Bradford, 2011).

Julia Davies is a Senior Lecturer in the School of Education at the University of Sheffield, UK. She researches language and literacy in relation to digital text making practices. She is the editor of *New Literacies around the Globe: Policy and Pedagogy* (with Burnett, Merchant & Rowsell, 2014) and *Virtual Literacies: Interactive Spaces for Children and Young People* (with Gillen, Merchant & Marsh, 2012).

Jennifer DeWitt is a Research Associate in the Department of Education at King's College London, UK. She is a Researcher on the Science Aspirations and Career Choice: Age 10–14 (ASPIRES) project, examining factors that contribute to, or hinder, children's interests and aspirations in science across the 10 to 14-year-old age range.

Justin Dillon is Professor of Science and Environmental Education and Head of the Graduate School of Education at the University of Bristol, UK. His research focuses on science learning outside the classroom, particularly in museums, science centres and botanic gardens in the UK, Europe and elsewhere. He is the editor of the *International*

NOTES ON CONTRIBUTORS

Handbook of Research on Environmental Education (with Stevenson, Brody & Wals, 2013).

John Evans is Professor of Sociology of Education and Physical Education at Loughborough University, UK. His research interests include the politics of the curriculum, pedagogy, equity and identity, and embodiment, education and health. He is the editor of *New Directions in Social Theory, Education and Embodiment* (with Davies, 2013).

Rosalyn George is Professor of Education and Equality at Goldsmiths, University of London, UK. Her research is in the areas of social justice, education and schooling, especially with regard to gender and race. Her current work focuses on recent forms of migration and its impact on the promotion of non-colour-coded racism.

Ulrike Graff is a Lecturer in the Faculty of Education at the University of Bielefeld, Germany. Her research interests include educational theories, gender education, educational ethnography and biographical self-reflection as educational empowerment.

Valerie Hey is Emeritus Professor of Education at the University of Sussex, Brighton, UK. Her interests are in the social, material and psychological construction of identities, and she is intrigued by questions of how the subject is formed between the processes and practices of psychological and social creation and reformation.

Claire Maxwell is a Reader in Sociology of Education at the Institute of Education, University College London, UK. Her current work focuses on private and elite education, and concepts of agency, privilege and affect. Her most recent edited book is *Elite Education: International Perspectives* (with Aggleton, 2015).

Angela McRobbie is Professor of Communications at Goldsmiths, University of London, UK. Her fields of expertise are young women and popular culture, feminist theory, the new creative economy and the rise of 'cultural labour process'. Her current research includes an investigation of the working lives of young fashion designers in London, Berlin and Milan.

Jonathan Osborne is Professor of Science Education at Stanford University, California, USA. He is interested in exploring students' attitudes to science and how school science can be made more worthwhile and engaging, and in the role of argumentation in science education as a means of improving student understanding of the nature of scientific inquiry.

Carrie Paechter is Professor of Education at Goldsmiths, University of London, UK. Her research centres on the intersection of gender, power and knowledge, the construction of gendered, spatialised and embodied identities, and the processes of curriculum negotiation. She is particularly interested on how children construct themselves as gendered, embodied, social actors.

Emma Rich is a Senior Lecturer in the Department of Health at the University of Bath, UK. Her work draws upon the sociology of education, pedagogy, the body and physical culture. She is the editor of *Debating Obesity: Critical Perspectives* (with Monaghan & Aphramor, 2010) and the author of *The Medicalization of Cyberspace* (with Miah, 2008).

NOTES ON CONTRIBUTORS

Renata Šribar is a Lecturer and Researcher in the field of cultural and social anthropology and sociology at the Ljubljana Graduate School of the Humanities, Slovenia. Her research concerns feminist identities, the socio-cultural construction of women's physicality, and issues of gender and language.

Beatrice Willis is the Research Project Administrator for the Science Aspirations and Career Choice: Age 10–14 (ASPIRES) project, examining factors that contribute to, or hinder, children's interests and aspirations in science across the 10 to 14-year-old age range.

Billy Wong is a Researcher for the Science Aspirations and Career Choice: Age 10–14 (ASPIRES) project, examining factors that contribute to, or hinder, children's interests and aspirations in science across the 10 to 14-year-old age range. He is interested in what young people from minority ethnic backgrounds feel about science, education and future careers.

INTRODUCTION

Pedagogical responses to the changing position of girls and young women

Carrie Paechter, Rosalyn George and Angela McRobbie

This Special Issue arises from the UK Economic and Social Research Council-funded seminar series 'Young Women in Movement: Sexualities, Vulnerabilities, Needs and Norms', which took place between 2009 and 2011 at Goldsmiths, University of London. The series focused on girls and young women from ages 10 to 30, considering how recent and current developments affect different aspects of their lives. The papers in this Special Issue arise from the work in the seminar series that was focused on pedagogical approaches to girls and young women from across Europe. Contributors come from a variety of positions and starting points, and their perspectives reflect these.

Academics and professionals working in the field of gender with particular reference to girls and young women are faced with a series of paradoxes. Over the last 20 years, the lives of young women in the UK and Europe have been transformed. They have gained considerable freedom and independence, but at the very same time, new, less tangible, forms of constraint and subordination play a defining role in the formation of their everyday subjectivities and identities. Young women have come to exemplify the pervasive sensibility of self-responsibility and self-organisation. The period of youth is nowadays stretched at both ends. Young women enter teenage social worlds at much younger ages than before, while many young women across Europe are also delaying the age of marriage, partnership and childbirth, extending the period of education and training, then entering the labour market and participating in leisure culture as singles. Consequently, our working definition of 'young woman' is fluid, and spans the age range 10–30. This is reflected in the papers in the Special Issue. While most of them focus on school-aged girls, others, including those by Graff and Davies, discuss the experiences of those who are moving into or already in their twenties. Our understanding of pedagogy is similarly fluid and broad, including youth work as well as school- and college-based approaches.

We were anxious, as part of the seminar series, to interrogate the field of sexuality and its visualisation across new and old media in the context of often predictable and endemic 'moral panics' about teenage pregnancy rates, sexually transmitted diseases and internet pornography. We aimed to dig beneath the surface of media fears to consider the re-positioning of young women as citizens, future mothers, workforce, etc., while also reflecting on empirical research on these topics and its theorisation. The Special Issue reflects this focus, both by discussing new research in how young women construct their identities both online and offline, and in considering pedagogic responses to this situation by both formal and informal educators.

The world in which young women live and learn is rapidly changing. In particular, the proliferation of new communications technologies has resulted in new ways of interacting and identity construction which require a pedagogic response. Questions about how girls and young women respond to online contexts are addressed by several papers in this issue. While young women are happy to be innovative in their use of social media, using it to explore new ways of being social, they are less interested in learning about science and technology itself. Young women's relationship to science and technology education was another key theme of the series. While gender discrepancies in science performance at school have been overcome, female participation remains comparatively low at higher levels of education and in the workplace.

We consider a number of key issues in relation to the current position of young women and formal and informal pedagogic responses to these. We commence with a paper by Emma Rich in which she examines how young women integrate ideas about health into their imagined futures. She explores how the increasing expectations placed on young women as the vanguard of economic, social and cultural change impinge upon young women's understandings of their bodies. She argues that attention is cast specifically towards the central role of embodiment, health and subjectivity in these images of the future.

This is followed by a series of papers focusing specifically on 'girls work' within the youth work tradition. These consider both the theory and practice of youth work with girls. Fin Cullen's paper examines the discourses shaping girls work practice, before focusing more closely on two contrasting examples through which she explores the possibilities for feminist praxis. These ideas are then taken up by two contributions from German writers, Mart Busche and Ulrike Graff, both focusing on specific sites at which such work has taken place, and both arguing for the continuation of single-sex work with girls.

A key aim of such work with girls and young women is the development of social aspiration and the engagement with particular identity formations. The next cluster of papers, from Claire Maxwell and Peter Aggleton, Rosalyn George and Valerie Hey, and Carrie Paechter, take this focus further. Maxwell and Aggleton take the concept of 'concerted cultivation', a process by which middle-class parents invest in their children through the provision of time and resources. They examine how this affects the self-esteem of privately educated young women to reproduce privilege in and through their lives. George and Hey, by contrast, discuss the apparently opposite trajectory of their own daughters who seemed to aspire to return to the social class origins of their upwardly mobile mothers, considering this in terms of both subjectification and resistance. In the third paper in this group, Paechter discusses the ways in which young women collaboratively construct identities in online contexts, examining this in terms of changing notions of privacy, the development and sustaining of identity communities, and questions of authenticity in relation to online identities.

The two subsequent papers remain with this theme of young women and how they are constructed or construct themselves in online contexts. Renata Šribar's paper considers young women's engendering and sexualisation in new media contexts through a dual focus of a critique of recent survey research in the EU Kids Online II framework, and contrasting Slovenian ethnographic research which suggests that girls are themselves critical of some commercial new media contexts. She argues that the large EU surveys are constructed in such a way as to hide gender-related phenomena, and that more detailed research is essential to uncover the complexities of young people's approaches to online pornification and sexualisation. Some of this more detailed work is reported in Julia Davies' study of the use of young British trainee hairdressers' use of Facebook as a site of gendered literacy practices. Davies traces the ways in which her research participants use their mutual participation in Facebook-based practices as a means of community development and identity construction.

Finally, we return to a much-studied but still puzzling theme: the issue of why girls and young women, despite high involvement in some aspects of new technologies, continue to avoid participation in the non-compulsory study of science. In our final paper, Louise Archer, Jennifer DeWitt, Jonathan Osborne, Justin Dillon, Beatrice Willis and Billy Wong argue that careers in science are largely 'unthinkable' for girls, because they do not conform to either their constructions of femininity or their understandings of themselves as learners. Their finding that this is particularly the case for working-class girls brings us back to Maxwell and Aggleton's paper earlier in the issue, inviting the question: how do we support working-class young women to develop the strong sense of self and self-efficacy that is evidenced by those who are more financially and culturally privileged?

Changing times, future bodies? The significance of health in young women's imagined futures[1]

Emma Rich[a] and John Evans[b]

[a]*Education, University of Bath, Bath, UK;* [b]*Loughborough University, Loughborough, UK*

> A growing number of authors recognise the increasing expectations placed on young women as the vanguard of economic, social and cultural change. This paper explores how these imaginings have come to bear upon young women's bodies, as part of a special issue on pedagogical responses to the changing position of girls and young women. In examining how 'girlhood' has been constituted as the vanguard of cultural change, attention is cast specifically towards the central role of embodiment, health and subjectivity in these images of the future.

Introduction: changing social position of young women and girls

> In a time of dramatic social, cultural and political transition, young women are being constructed as a vanguard of new subjectivity. They are supposed to offer clues about the best way to cope with these changes. Power, opportunities, and success are all modelled by the 'future girl', a kind of young woman celebrated for her 'desire, determination and confidence' to take charge of her life, seize chances, and achieve her goals. (Harris 2004, 1)

Harris' (2004) observation above captures some of the key concerns arising from recent theorisations of contemporary girlhood that have endeavoured to make sense of the integral role that young women play in relation to the future of society. As Harris suggests, young women in contemporary western society are constituted through neoliberal discourses as 'agents' ultimately in control of and responsible for their own destinies/futures. Such thinking rarely appreciates or acknowledges the socio-economic, material and regional influences that bear upon young women's opportunities to either develop or achieve normatively sanctioned (usually 'westernised') forms of health and well-being. Over the last two decades, young women have been constituted through new visions of girlhood and womanhood; being placed at the centre of moral panics about the body whilst at the same time being positioned as the 'vanguard of new subjectivity' (Harris 2004, 1) and future change (see McRobbie 2000). It is well recognised that within these contemporary discourses endorsing images of the 'future girl' (Harris 2004), young white middle-class women have been positioned as 'new girls' located at the intersection of cultural change. In this paper, as part of a special issue on pedagogical responses to the changing position of girls and young women, I explore how these imaginings have come to bear upon girls' and young women's bodies. In examining how 'girlhood' has been constituted as the image of cultural change, I cast attention towards the central role of embodiment, health and subjectivity in production of these images of the future.

Elsewhere, cultural studies and childhood studies have already made inroads into explorations of these contemporary visions of girlhood. Part of the narrative accompanying these constructions of girlhood draws specifically on 'celebratory discourses' (Lucey and Reay 2002, 322), whereby girls and young women (middle class in particular) are celebrated for the ostensible progress they have made in various social contexts such as education and employment, as if somehow reflecting a more gender-equitable socio-cultural context. However, a growing body of work recognises the burdens, constraints and expectations accompanying these celebratory discourses. McLeod and Yates (2006, 4), for example, argue that the focus on change has been rather overemphasised and is experienced unevenly by different groups of girls and women. As McRobbie (2000, 200–1) argues, 'young women ... have replaced youth as a metaphor for social change ... are now recognised as one of the stakes upon which the future depends'. One clear example of this is the work required of young women on their bodies as an investment in their future health, not only for themselves but for the sake of the government, private sector, media, schools, etc. Whilst I recognise that expectations and representations of gender and physicality might not necessarily be new (Fisette 2006; Markula 2001), they are made more visible and prevalent via emerging body pedagogies that focus on the particular health crisis of a putative obesity epidemic (Evans et al. 2008). Individuals in neoliberal western societies are increasingly being incited to maintain responsibility for their weight as part of a broader culture of healthism and moral panics about obesity and sedentary lifestyles.

In the UK, as in many other western and westernised societies, something of a crisis has been constructed around the relationships between childhood inactivity, young people's diets and rising obesity levels. This is promoted through various sites of physical culture. This discourse cultivates the idea that reduced activity and poor diets are leading to increased rates of obesity, resulting in an imminent decline in health and increased mortality rates. Fuelled by a moral panic,[2] these concerns have recast attention towards the weight, size shape and lifestyles of young people, intensifying the pressures already on them to regulate their bodies and lifestyles, e.g. alter their eating habits, take more exercise and lose weight. This interest in obesity reflects a biopolitcal shift toward organising, shaping and regulating bodies in particular ways, through a simplistic focus on 'weight' (see Evans et al. 2008; Wright and Harwood 2009) rather than health. Moreover, such fears about the declining future health of current generations of young people are used as justification for intervening in people's lives at an increasingly younger age and on an ever-greater scale. A growing body of work has begun to register the potentially damaging effects of this discourse on the lives of girls and young women (see Halse, Honey, and Boughtwood 2008; Evans et al. 2008). Current imaginings of the 'future girl' (Harris 2004) converge with these 'new health imperatives' (Rich and Evans 2009) to form part of 'the ways in which subjective gender is constituted and mobilised' (Zannettino 2008, 466). In considering the 'changing position of women and girls' in this paper, I consider what kinds of new burdens, expectations and insecurities are brought about by a renewed focus on the body and the accompanying imperative towards self-care (see Armstrong 1995; Crawford 1980).

New pedagogies of health

The emphasis on diet and exercise as health-enhancing strategies, both in public health promotion and public pedagogy, as well as in more localised contexts of school-based practices and pedagogies, has been well documented in recent work (Burrows and Wright 2007; Evans et al. 2008; Wright and Dean 2007; Dinan Thompson 2009). Anti-obesity discourse has resulted in a barrage of policies and initiatives in schools to get children more physically active, slimmer and eating less, fuelled by concerns about the increase in sedentary behaviour (see Evans et al. 2008). In recent years in England and Wales, for example, central Government sought joint action from its agencies, the Department of Health and the Department for Children, Schools and Families (formerly Department for Education and Skills), to address health matters through policy affecting the whole environment of schools. In the UK, a recent Public Health White Paper (Department of Health 2010) identified children in early years settings as a key target group, highlighting the importance of early intervention and prevention as crucial for their future health and well-being. Such is the focus on early intervention that for the first time UK-wide physical activity guidelines have been produced which focus on early years (under fives) (Department of Health 2011).

Reflecting a broader trend towards individualisation (Rose 1999), body pedagogies drawing upon the principles and imperatives of obesity discourse constitute young women as ultimately in control of their own destiny, and as able to shape their future lives and health if only they undertake particular regulative practices (e.g. pursuing 'good' diets, exercising and losing weight). Such thinking reflects the image of 'future girls' (Harris 2004) – in control of their own destiny and able to shape their own life (and health) now celebrated within neoliberal discourse. Like Rail (2009) and Warin et al. (2008, 97), however, I have become increasingly concerned to 'problematise the universality of health promotion messages' of this kind, and alarmed at the way in which exercise and physical activity practices associated with new health imperatives tend to homogenise young people's diverse interests, needs and opportunities across ethnicity, class, age, culture and ability. In this way, obesity discourse may fail to give due attention to the socio-economic contexts which may mediate opportunities and prohibit choices in relation to health. In what follows below, I draw on McLeod and Yates (2006, 3) in asking 'what inequalities are being formed and reformed' through such neoliberal approaches to health.

Moral panics associated with obesity have further intensified the pressures on young people to regulate their behaviours, e.g. alter their eating habits, take more exercise and lose weight. Yet, we know relatively little about how the increased expectation on young women to demonstrate their capacity to be healthy may come to bear upon their subjectivities. McLeod and Yates suggest that this focus on subjectivity alerts us to

> how subjects are formed – the range of influences, practices, experiences and relations that combine to produce a young person and young people. In this way, subjectivity refers to both general and particular processes and patterns in the making of modern lives. (2006, 38)

Further research on how young women are reading and experiencing these discourses in relation to their own bodies and subjectivities is required, not only in school contexts but across myriad social settings. Indeed, whilst these health discourses may dominant contemporary ways of thinking about health and the body, their meanings may be recontextualised, resisted, made meaningful in the lives of girls as they intersect with other categories of experience such as age, family location, social class, sexuality, gender and ethnicity. In this sense, different girls may invest in, resist or negotiate particular discourses of health in the constitution of particular subjectivities (see Atencio and Wright 2009; Skeggs 1997; Hauge 2009; Zannettino 2008).

As Foucault (1972, 46) describes, 'discourse finds a way of limiting its domain, of defining what it is talking about, of giving it the status of an object – and therefore of making it manifest, nameable, and describable'. Obesity discourse not only names and defines how one is to understand the 'problem' of *obesity* through biopedagogies (Wright and Harwood 2009), but through its associated practices of the body may provide certain 'subject positions' (Davies and Harré 1990) which both name and constitute particular ways of being. In what follows below, I examine the effects of pedagogies of health on young women's subjectivities in relation to how they imagine their future lives and choices. In particular, I ask what is being required of young women and girls in fashioning particular subjectivities in relation to health and the body in the constitution of particular forms of citizenship. Whilst there is not space to reveal the complex and multiple ways in which these discourses are mediated and read through particular categories of class, gender, culture, ethnicity, etc., I highlight three key themes which reveal how contemporary discourses of health and the body are appropriated in particular constructions of girlhood. Firstly, following McLeod and Yates (2006), I explore how young people's learning about 'health' is intimately connected to the work young women 'do' to imagine their future lives. In doing so, I examine the possibilities, challenges and dilemmas this might present to the ostensible 'changing position' of women and girls, attending to some of the broader issues which form the focus of this special issue. Secondly, I examine how these 'imagined futures' (McLeod and Yates 2006) shape embodied subjectivities and associated practices of the body. Finally, I suggest that whilst girls and young women may come to imagine their futures in relation to certain health *ideals*, the opportunities available to construct these subjectivities may only be available to some.

Research design

The data are drawn from a UK Economic and Social Research Council-funded project (RES-000-22-2003) exploring young people's experiences of new health imperatives associated with weight loss, examining their manifestation across particular cultural sites and practices. The study has investigated how health imperatives and associated curriculum initiatives are operationalised within and across a range of schools located in English Midlands with parallel studies pursued in Australia and New Zealand. The methodology was designed to explore the relationships between demographic 'resources' (socio-cultural capital) born of age, gender, class, ethnicity and (forms of) schooling; sites and sources of influence on 'body knowledge'; and individuals' relationships to their embodied selves. Data sets were collected across eight schools in England selected to reflect a range of social, cultural and policy contexts enabling the in-depth analysis required to capture the interplay between cultural forces, social institutions and their impact on young people's embodied identities. This paper draws specifically on a combination of quantitative and qualitative data derived from some 1176 questionnaires administered to pupils aged from 9 to 16 years of age, in eight schools

Table 1. School contexts.

School	Type/description (age range)	Groups included in research sample
Bentley Grammar School	Large, independent, secondary school for boys (10–18 years)	12–13- and 15–16-year-olds (Years 8 and 11)
Fielding Community College	Large, co-educational, deprived, multi-ethnic, inner-city college (11–16 years)	13–15-year-olds (Years 9 and 10)
Fraser Preparatory School	Large, independent, co-educational, preparatory school (4–11 years)	9–11-year-olds (Years 5 and 6)
Grange Park High School	Independent secondary school for girls (11–18 years)	12–13- and 15–16-year-olds (Years 8 and 11)
Huntington High School	Large, co-educational, rural, state middle school (11–14 years)	11–14-year-olds (Years 7–9)
Longcliffe High School	Large, co-educational, multi-ethnic, state middle school (11–14 years)	12–13-year-olds (Year 8)
Rosehill Church of England Primary School	Large, co-educational, multi-ethnic, inner-city, state primary school (4–11 years)	9–11-year-olds (Years 5 and 6)
Westwood Church of England Primary School	Very small, co-educational, middle-class, rural/village, state primary school (4–11 years)	9–11-year-olds (Years 5 and 6)

in Middle England, UK (see Table 1), and qualitative data drawn from interviews with 90 pupils and 19 staff. All interview quotes are reported using pseudonyms, school year where appropriate and the school type represented by pseudonym.

Stories of future health: new burdens?

In this first section I report how pedagogies of health inform the constitution of young people's subjectivities and significantly shape the narratives they construct around their 'future selves'. To this end I examine 'the ways various educative dimensions operate in young people's lives to enable the conditions for certain imaginations and subjectivities to emerge' (Savage 2010, 103). Significantly, the data suggest that young people's concerns about weight and health are not simply 'health' or 'medical' worries but are also intimately connected to what McLeod and Yates (2006, 6) refer to as 'imagined futures' and who or what they might become.

Participants across all social categories of age, ethnicity, social class and geographical location made reference to learning about exercise, weight and health in various contexts outside school, revealing the extent to which mediated health practices were part of the broader cultural terrain which informed their everyday lives. Many reported learning about health through various media and cultural artifacts (see Miah and Rich 2010; Rich 2011) via 'public pedagogies' (Giroux 2004).

> I was watching GMTV with my Mum this morning. There's that Inch Loss Island ... I think it's kind of inspiring showing people how you can lose weight if you want to. (Laura)

> Like on the news when they say someone's died from being obese, and all the schools, they switched didn't they and I think that was really good. If someone tries hard enough to get it to stop then I think we will become like non-obese. (Milly, Year 7, Huntington High School)

Body pedagogies and physical culture are mobilised to embody and encourage the neoliberal individual who 'enters into the process of self-examination, self-care and self-improvement' (Petersen 1996, 48–9), to monitor and regulate their body against the future risks of ill health through increased physical activity, weight loss and better diet. These broader socio-political relations of power shape the ways in which ideas around health, physical activity and food are being produced. Indeed, the girls and young women in our research worked on constituting particular subjectivities in relation to obesity discourse. As reflected in Milly's comments above, many recognised the need to be able to shape their future lives and health by undertaking regulative practices to control their weight. This engagement with an ethic of self-care and personal responsibility (Jette 2006; Cole 1998; King 2003) goes some way towards constituting the image of 'future girl' outlined by Harris (2004), i.e. by demonstrating a control over this own lives. As one student described it, exercise and eating well was important 'because it's your *future* health'. The prominence of narrative and storying the future in relation to 'becoming fat' was a feature of constituting the self, undertaken by students from all school contexts. Students storied 'obesity' in such a way that they described their fears of what it would be like to become obese, making reference to social isolation and bullying as a result of one's body size: 'if you just eat junk food all the time you will grow obesity and you won't be able to walk' (Bryony). Thus in storying 'obese futures', these young women are also invoking neoliberal narratives about taking responsibility for who one is and who one might become:

> 'Cause if you're too fat you could not be really fit and walk around as much as you normally do and it would be more unhealthy to be more fat than thin I think it would be hard to exercise and I think I wouldn't really like it 'cause I would just like to be normal like everyone else. (Phillipa, Year 6, Fraser Preparatory School).

This 'fear' of fatness is thus also intimately connected with social differentiation and in part thus reflects 'how pathways and subjectivity [are] closely intertwined' (McLeod and Yates 2006, 11). Thus, it raises the question as to whether neoliberal notions of the choice biography which reframe obesity and health in this way create new burdens associated with the body for some young women and girls. Learning about one's body and thinking about health may for many be an uncomfortable and fearful endeavour, as reflected in the comments of Marie:

> ...Will I *die* because I'm overweight and you won't get any sleep because you'll be thinking about will I die or not. Some people don't sleep at all because they think that they're going to die in their sleep because they're so obese. (Marie, Year 6, Fraser Preparatory School)

> When I think about weight I have dreams yeah, like I become really fat and I can't move. (Dinesh, Year 5, Rosehill Church of England Primary School)

As Probyn (2004, 26) suggests, 'affect amplification makes us care about things'. For Marie and Dinesh, this affective amplification was experienced with such intensity and in such a way that stories about the future tapped into visions of risk of death or immobilisation; a profoundly negative relationality is experienced between their own bodies and the imagery of fatness made available to them. Many of the girls and young women offered up similar explanations as school staff regarding the perceived demise of children's health, blaming TV viewing, fast food culture and inactivity; 'we just keep eating more and more food as a nation', 'Think about your *future*, would you rather look like this person, or this person?' (Louise, author's emphasis). Part of constructing the reflexive self who is the dutiful citizen entailed monitoring the behaviours of their peers/other children and their own family: 'I tell Mum there's too much fat in this'.

Healthy girlhood

As Wright (2009) observes, the 'obesity epidemic' offers one of the most powerful and pervasive discourses influencing ways of thinking about health and the body. In keeping with liberal individualism, this has led to a renewed interest in the need for populations to monitor their own and others' bodies, weight and health against perceived risks associated with deteriorating lifestyles (Rich and Evans 2005). These concerns are driving what might be described as 'new health imperatives' prescribing the choices people should make around lifestyle, in particular relating to physical activity and food (Department of Health 2010). Work elsewhere has begun to explicate the connections between these 'obesity' health imperatives and neoliberal politics (Halse 2009; Halse, Honey, and Boughtwood 2007; Rich and Evans 2005), and demonstrate how they are infused with moral ethics of citizenship where the thin beyond comes to represent the neoliberal individual who makes the right choices. Whilst the making of the self may seem self-evident to many of these young women, I question what is being asked of these young women to demonstrate this, particularly in terms of the pressures to demonstrate a sensibility around self-care and the 'fit' body (Cole 1998; King 2003). To this end, we need be cautious not 'to neglect the losses, discomfort and ambivalences sometimes associated with being somebody' (McLeod and Yates 2006, 77–8) and which may lead to particular expectations and/or burdens on young women's bodies. Understanding contemporary visions of girlhood demands complex explanatory frameworks which avoid monolithic categories and recognise both the pervasive impact of health discourse, but also the *active role* that girls may play in constituting their subjectivities (Davies 1989; Francis and Archer 2005; Skelton and Francis 2009; Susinos et al. 2009; Youdell 2005). Rather than simply reading girls and young women's bodies as being acted upon by global neoliberal discourses, such approaches allow us to explore how different girls and young women invest in, negotiate and/or resist discourses of health (see Atencio and Wright 2009; Skeggs 1997; Youdell 2005; Hauge 2009; Zannettino 2008) and thus come to 'imagine' different selves and 'imagined futures' (McLeod and Yates 2006).

The importance of demonstrating 'healthy girlhood' is particularly significant in terms of the relationship between imagined pathways and the investment in middle-class subjectivity. Students at Fraser Preparatory School, an independent preparatory school, and Grange Park High School, an independent secondary school made up largely of middle-class girls and young women, reported undertaking various regulative practices to monitor their own weight, for example weighing themselves and using pedometers regularly:

> I enjoy swimming and I really enjoy bike riding 'cause it works all of your muscles and so does swimming. I'm trying to work on my thighs at the minute. This morning I didn't have any breakfast … I have, I've got one on my bike. it tells me how many meters I've done in a day and when I clip it on to my belt it will tell me how many steps I've done in a day … I just want to know if I need to do more. I try to improve it, so say if I've done 50 in a day I'd do like 70, and it also tells me how many carbs you've burnt off and how many stones you've lost. (Marie, Year 6, Fraser Preparatory School)

These expressions of health were not simple articulations learnt through health education, but rather an alignment with a broader ethos of the school which concerned making up the middle-class child, as evidenced through teachers' and parents' desires towards the child's future. The school conveyed very specific possibilities for *future lives* which were oriented towards and reflected in one's choices and working hard to 'make' oneself. Health appeared to be taken up as another means through which one could thus demonstrate these orientations towards oneself and the constitution of (middle) class-based subjectivities. In this way, 'such [health] imperatives and school based articulations of the "good student" become part of the self formation and identifications of the student' (McLeod and Yates 2006, 57). For example, many of the students were cognisant of the language of health policy, e.g. advocating '5-a-day' (portions of fruit and vegetables), demonstrating themselves to be the self-improved citizen through 'learning about health'. In this way, they articulated a form of identification salient to their sense of self which drew on 'orientations towards the future' (McLeod and Yates 2006, 166).

Many of the girls and young women in Grange Park High School were physically very active and chose to take part in an extensive extracurricular programme. Participants reported that they often did not get home from extracurricular activities until 9 pm, and would then eat their dinner and complete their homework to retain their A* profiles and sporting success. Working hard was not only tied to the performative (academic) results that this would bring, but intimately connected to being seen to be working on oneself. Students indicated that they often carried the burdens of working this hard, 'I work so hard I make myself ill' (Elizabeth); 'I just want to achieve, I just want to do so well' (Hannah). The school utilised a sticker system with codes and prizes for performance and behaviour. Grange Park High School was clear about the role it played in shaping the future lives of its students to:

> grow to be active citizens of the 21st century, making and taking, political, moral and ethical decisions upon which they have reflected, and in which they have a belief. (Grange Park High School website)

This focus on producing students as citizens was supported by the use of a life coach who was brought into the school to help them 'find their strengths'. This discourse features strongly in the lives of the students who constructed success and health through meritocratic principles, '[It's] my fault because I didn't' revise or do the work' (Tammy), and equally they saw health as the responsibility of 'themselves and people around them' (Sabrina). The pressure to be 'someone' was strong in these contexts where there were 'good people ... and you think you're not as good as them [student]', 'you feel worse next to someone really good looking'. All the students interviewed made reference to the important of 'being someone'. In Grange Park High School, the girls' bodies were intimately part of the school culture and its marketing processes; their bodies inscribed and displayed the civic values the school espouses. Managing one's appearance as an advertisement for the school was not confined to tying ones shoelaces or wearing ones uniform tidily. Read through wider notions of marketisation, such imperatives have impacted on the notion of the healthy body as thin body, as 'good student', through which its students could identify. Thus being thin was as much about being a symbol of the school's distinctive (academic and social) virtues as it was about being healthy.

The school culture of being a 'good citizen' and the desire to both fit in but also stand out meant that many students had to work on their bodies to retain social distinctiveness: 'we do it through school because we don't want to get fat' (Hannah). In extolling the image of the self-directed, neoliberal girl, many of the young women made reference to not simply a 'thin' body, but the 'sculpted lean muscled femininity' (Heywood 2007, 113) that had been worked upon and which circulates in consumer culture (representing a particular expression of fitness). In this sense, it was not enough to just be thin, but to also demonstrate that one had actively worked upon one's body through, for example, a toned physique. Part of constituting a subjectivity of this kind involved demonstrating that one could recognise acceptable and unacceptable physiques in relation to such neoliberal discourses:

Interviewer: What about Victoria Beckham, do you like the way she looks?
Marie: I think she's really pretty and she's got a really good figure but she's just too skinny for me ... hmm the right weight ... well I wouldn't like to be Paula Radcliffe [an international runner].

Abi: Personally I wouldn't like to be that skinny.

Marie: Because she's so skinny. I'd more like to be her really [points to picture of Anna Kourinkova, a tennis player]. (Abi and Marie, Year 6, Fraser Preparatory School)

Many of these girls were therefore navigating physical cultures within which body ideals meant not only demonstrating thinness but also an active working upon oneself and therefore a body which was not 'too thin'. This produced many emotional and identity burdens for those interviewed, who had to constantly manage producing a 'healthy body' and a 'gendered body' but at the same time present themselves as reflexive, active, choosing 'citizens' who were not easily swayed by cultural norms. Thus many of the girls suggested that they did not want to be excessively thin because of its association with negative media imagery and thus did not want to be at all like a 'sheep in the media' (Esther).

The stories above reveal the dilemmas of the neoliberal choice biography through which these girls come to understand health, sport, physical activity and their bodies. For many of them, the opportunities to be physically active, to eat and dress well are plentiful, and the values imbued within family and school life encourage them to become thoughtful active choosing subjects. But in the process, the burdens are many, as they become increasingly introspective and regulative and engage in new forms of reflexivity with and on their bodies which may often be uncomfortable or fail to bring forth much of what these discourses promise (for its focus on working on oneself means health is a limitless status). The emotional burdens and dilemmas which the girls in these school experienced were captured within both survey and interview data. Survey results revealed that 48.8% of participants in Grange Park High School indicated that they had, at some stage, been 'bullied about their weight'. Moreover, interviews with staff revealed that in recent years there had been three or four cases of anorexia or severe eating problems which were dealt with by the School Matron.

Healthism and new girlhood: reformed burdens?

Complex socio-cultural, socio-economic and socio-political dynamics demand a nuanced approach to understanding the relationships between pedagogy, physical culture and female physicality. Elsewhere it has been recognised that within obesity discourse the possibilities for health are often announced through 'one size fits all' policies advocating practices that are deemed appropriate for everyone and fail to give due attention to the socio-economic contexts which may mediate opportunities and come to bear upon choice (see Evans et al. 2008; Rich et al. 2011). However, whilst these structural inequalities may have been registered, less has been written about how mediations of class, gender, ethnicity, socio-cultural context and school culture come to bear upon the 'imagined futures' (McLeod and Yates 2006) these young women construct in relation to health. Moreover, how do future opportunities and possibilities differently constituted and/or identified come to bear upon the particular orientations, opportunities and subjectivities young women of different background have available to them? Whilst contemporary neoliberal health messages may be announced through 'universal' (essentially white, middle class, westernised) *ideals*, their meanings may not be experienced uniformly but are recontextualised, (in some cases) resisted and made meaningful in the lives of girls as it intersects with other categories of experience such as age, family location, social class, sexuality, gender and ethnicity. Fielding Community College is for pupils aged 11–18 from a variety of cultural but mostly working-class backgrounds. Health education in this institution focused on anticipated immediate and projected futures of restricted social and economic opportunity; related to broken relationships, disaffection and poor health.

> They [referring to young women and girls in particular] don't have this concept that they can achieve, that they can go on, that they can do better erm … and it gets very wound up in their self-consciousness and very wound up in, you know … I've got … got to fit in with something. (Samantha, Food Technology teacher)

> They [referring to young women and girls in particular] don't see … very much from the point of view of job role in future life, I think this comes down to the teenage pregnancy as well, it's seen as well that's what everybody does isn't it. (Samantha, Food Technology teacher)

Young people were to be given health knowledge that might help them deal with, avoid or *repair* transgressions/pathologies and in the process announcing particular classed differentiations around absence, pathology and abjection. Health knowledge offered in the school was focused on prevention and protection from specific ills of what was considered to be endemic to local working-class life. Initiatives were configured through classed readings of the assumed preferences and cultures of its students, as described by one teacher:

> catchment area is essentially white, working class and the subcultures that go along with that ... going down to the football and eating your pukka pies ... the fish and chips ... problem we have here is within walking distance of the school we've got a KFC, pizza places ... The kids think it's considered to be quite acceptable.

In this way, class was a significant marker of difference in how new health imperatives were recontextualised, with teachers looking for signs of health/ill health in the everyday lives, dispositions and choices of particular groups (working classes in this instance). 'Looking' for signs of obesity extended well beyond the physiological and was instead tied to identification of class norms as some indication of future ill health or lack of parental care. Young women in Fielding Community College, unlike those of Grange Park High School and Fraser Preparatory School, were positioned as the 'at-risk' girls described in Harris' (2004) *Future Girl* who are held responsible for the 'failing' conditions in which they live. However, ironically, because their school did not centre attention on issues related to obesity, the girls in this institution perceived its commitment to 'health' as inadequate and piecemeal, and as confirmation that they were in a 'failing school'. Thus some of the girls and young women interviewed made reference to their sense of themselves and their future potential generated within school life as not only limiting their capacity to learn but also shaping their future health. While they were no less aware than young people elsewhere of what was required of them to be successful either academically or in public health terms, they believed that the inadequacies and limitations of their school, communities and families, which they interpolated as their own, meant that they were not likely to achieve these things

> Rules need to be strict, people are getting away with a lot. (Joanne)

> We're not learning as much as we should be. (Joanne)

> Your decision whether you want to do well or not ... there's not a pressure to do well. (Becky)

In the voices of Becky and Joanne we hear a disjunction between the familiar storyline of disaffected troubled teenage girls who are uninterested in education or who do have the proclivities to even care about their bodies (who typically are perceived to not care and harm their bodies through substance abuse, alcohol, sexual risk). We hear not the disaffection of inner-city pupils in 'troubled' areas, but of two young women with aspirations to achieve some form of social distinction and difference, e.g. where 'others' do not take school seriously, misbehave, do not stay healthy or work hard. In many ways they reflect the 'can-do' girls who take up a new kind of 'self-made subjectivity' (Harris 2004, 6) but, unlike the girls and young women in schools like Grange Park High School and Fraser Preparatory School, they remain positioned by others as 'at risk'.

These young women were no less aware of the discourses, pedagogies and practices of health and its ubiquitous visions of regulation, of how the body should be. However, its associated body makers were perhaps not as significant in terms of the classed and institutional habitus as for those in the independent schools. Equally, they were attuned to the class-based inequalities preventing them from achieving these ubiquitous futures, particularly in terms of socio-economic position. They knew how they should act/exercise and what they should eat 'ideally' but costs, tastes and perceived risks, overrode all other concerns. Decisions about what to eat and engagement with exercise were thus shaped by having to find inexpensive and 'safe' opportunities:

Weekends stay in, 'mum and dad go out but do something for them'. (Jenna)

Not allowed to go out so don't get to walk around – main road, don't trust people in the streets. (Becky)

Lack of money, perceived risk, parental concern, and the failings of school and wider social systems all underpinned their decisions to eat 'unhealthy' food and exercise little, or indeed the limited means to make particular choices:

Healthier food is more expensive, people don't tend to get a lot of it. (Amy)

Don't manage my 5-a-day. (Becky)

5-a-day ... That's what I try to do with my peaches ... have about five tins ... Brown bread can be 'quite expensive'. (Amy)

The risks, especially for girls, were seen as severely prohibitive but rationalised as either their own or the schools' inadequacy and failing. While girls 'elsewhere' were considered to be enabled by their school to know what to do about such 'risk', in their view, theirs 'don't teach us enough about health' (participant).

> I think we need to learn a lot more than we're learning now, because we're not learning as much as we should be ... they don't teach us enough about health ... we get some information but it doesn't really go very far. (Joanne)

Joanne reported that she couldn't take cooking as an optional subject of study:

> I really wanted to do cooking so I was quite disappointed. (Joanne)

> So we know what we have to do when we're older. (Becky)

Far from having 'deficient knowledge' about health, these girls and young women were both aware of the ostensible risks of weight constructed through public pedagogies of health and of the social stigma's of weight. However, as the comments above allude to, they also felt that the school neither taught them 'enough' nor gave them the 'right' health knowledge. Such practices may therefore inhibit the already disadvantaged, providing a differentiated sense of themselves as abject, and restricted their 'imagined futures' (McLeod and Yates 2009) in terms of future health, deemed by some to be a deviation from the privileged and sanctioned health agendas in the wider public domain. Their occupation in different social-cultural, economic and physical-cultural spaces means they also inhabit different opportunities to engage with pedagogies of health positioned within these discourses. Whilst their bodies may be made abject, in need of correction and read as markers of the social ills of working-class culture, the girls and young women's imagined futures described little possibility of escaping such contingencies.

Conclusion

This paper has reported on data from a range of school sites in the UK and points towards the importance of understandings of health in relation to how young women imagine their 'futures'. Such data reveal the close relationship between 'subjectivity and pathways' (McLeod and Yates 2006) in the construction of possibilities and opportunities for particular forms of embodiment and citizenship. Pedagogies of health coalesce strongly with visions of girlhood which draw upon risk society and future achievement as central to the new kinds of subjectivity. Whilst these may be offered as 'new choices' for all, our data suggest that these visions of the future are received and read by young women within life contexts which are mediated by school culture, public pedagogies, gender, class, ethnicity, etc. For all the girls and young women in this research, understandings of health play a significant role not only in shaping their understanding of their bodies, health or medical status, but also the narrative they construct in relation to their 'future lives'. However, classed-based differences are clearly revealed in these imagined futures. For the middle-class girls in the independent schools described above, these instructional charges of investment in the body to demonstrate the successfully healthy future girl may suggest particular gains in physical capital, health benefits and social mobility. However, for many such 'charges' are embodied through intense forms of surveillance, scrutiny and individualism, reinscribing traditional gender inequalities through ostensible 'new choice'. Conversely, for the working-class young women in Fielding Community College, school-based pedagogies relating poor future health with working-class location significantly shape their imagined trajectories and position them as the 'at-risk' (failed or failing) girls described by Harris (2004). These mediations allude to the 'the delusionary character of self-determining, individualistic and autonomous ideas of subjectivity' (Gonick 2004, 204) which are so central to the contemporary visions of girlhood which position young women as benefiting from new forms of citizenship and choice.

Notes

1. This paper arises from the UK Economic and Social Research Council-funded seminar series 'Young Women in Movement: Sexualities, Vulnerabilities, Needs and Norms' (ESRC RES-451-26-0715), based at Goldsmiths, University of London, 2009–2011.
2. Stanley Cohen, in his work *Folk Devils and Moral Panics*, refers to a moral panic as 'a condition, episode, person or group of persons which emerge to become defined as a threat to societal values and interests' (1972, 9). Cohen makes specific reference to the role of the media in intensifying and shaping these moral panics.

References

Armstrong, D. 1995. The rise of surveillance medicine. *Sociology of Health and Illness* 17: 393–404.

Atencio, M., and J. Wright. 2009. 'Ballet it's too whitey': Discursive hierarchies of high school dance spaces and the constitution of embodied feminine subjectivities. *Gender and Education* 21: 31–46.

Burrows, L., and J. Wright. 2007. Prescribing practices: Shaping healthy children in schools. *The International Journal of Children's Rights* 15, no. 1: 83–98.

Cohen, S. 1972. *Folk devils and moral panics: The creation of the Mods and Rockers*. Oxford: Martin Robertson.

Cole, C.L. 1998. Addition, exercise, and cyborgs: Technologies of deviant bodies. In *Sport in postmodern times*, ed. Genevieve Rail, 261–76. Albany: State University of New York Press.

Crawford, R. 1980. Healthism and the medicalisation of everyday life. *International Journal of Health Services* 10: 365–88.

Department of Health. 2010. *Healthy lives, healthy people our strategy for public health in England*. London: Department of Health.
Department of Health. 2011. *UK Physical activity guidelines*. London: Department of Health.
Davies, Bronwyn. 1989. *Frogs and snails and feminist tails: Preschool children and gender*. Sydney: Allen and Unwin.
Davies, B., and R. Harré. 1990. Positioning: The discursive production of selves. *Journal for the Theory of Social Behaviour* 20, no. 1: 44–63.
Dinan Thompson, M., ed. 2009. *Health and physical education: Contemporary issues for curriculum in Australia and New Zealand*. Melbourne: Oxford University Press.
Evans, John, Emma Rich, Brian Davies, and R. Rachel Allwood. 2008. *Education, disordered eating and obesity discourse: Fat fabrications*. Abingdon, UK: Routledge.
Fisette, J. 2006. Exploring how girls navigate their embodied identities in physical education. *Physical Education and Sport Pedagogy* 16, no. 2: 109–24.
Foucault, M. 1972. *The archaeology of knowledge*. London: Tavistock Publications.
Francis, B., and L. Archer. 2005. Negotiating the dichotomy of boffin and triad: British Chinese pupils' constructions of laddism. *The Sociological Review* 53: 495–520.
Giroux, H. 2004. Cultural studies, public pedagogy, and the responsibility of intellectuals, communication and critical. *Cultural studies* 1, no. 1: 59–79.
Gonick, M. 2004. Old plots and new identities: Ambivalent femininities in late modernity. *Discourse: Studies in the Cultural Politics of Education* 25: 189–209.
Halse, C., A. Honey, and D. Boughtwood. 2008. *Inside anorexia: The experiences of girls and their families*. London: Jessica Kingsley Publishers.
Harris, Anita. 2004. *Future girl. Young women in the twenty-first century*. London: Routledge.
Hauge, M.-I. 2009. Bodily practices and discourses of hetero-femininity: Girls' constitution of subjectivities in their social transition between childhood and adolescence. *Gender and Education* 21: 293–307.
Heywood, L. 2007. Producing girls: Empire, sport, and the neoliberal body. In *Physical culture, power, and the body*, ed. J. Hargreaves and P. Vertinsky, 101–20. London: Routledge.
Ise, C. 2009. Bio-Citizenship: Virtue discourses and the birth of the bio-citizen. In *Biopolitics and the "obesity epidemic": Governing bodies*, ed. J. Wright and V. Harwood. London: Routledge.
Jette, S. 2006. Fit for two? A critical discourse analysis of Oxygen Fitness Magazine. *Sociology of Sport Journal* 23: 331–51.
King, S.J. 2003. Doing good by running well. In *Foucault, cultural studies and governmentality*, ed. J.Z. Bratich, J. Packer, and C. McCarthy, 295–316. Albany: State University of New York Press.
Lucey, H., and D. Reay. 2002. Carrying the beacon of excellence. Social class differentiation and anxiety at a time of transition. *Journal of Education Policy* 17: 321–36.
Markula, P. 2001. Beyond the perfect body: Women's body image distortion in fitness magazine discourse. *Journal of Sport and Social Issues* 25: 134–55.
Markula, P. 2008. Affect[ing] bodies: Performative pedagogy of pilates. *International Review of Qualitative Research* 1: 381–408.
McLeod, J., and J. Yates. 2006. *Making modern lives: Subjectivity, schooling and social change*. Albany: State University of New York Press.

McRobbie, A. 2000. *Feminism and youth culture*. New York: Routledge.
Miah, A., and E. Rich. 2010. The bioethics of cybermedicalization. In *The new media and cybercultures anthology*, ed. P.K. Nayar, 209–20. Oxford: Wiley-Blackwell.
Petersen, A. 1996. Risk and the regulated self: The discourse of health promotion as politics of uncertainty. *The Australian and New Zealand Journal of Sociology* 32: 44–57.
Probyn, E. 2004. Teaching bodies: Affects in the classroom. *Body & Society* 10, no. 4: 21–43.
Rail, G. 2009. Canadian youth's discursive construction of health in the context of obesity discourse. In *Biopolitics and the 'obesity epidemic': Governing bodies*, ed. J. Wright and V. Harwood, 141–56. London: Routledge.
Rich, E. 2011. 'I see her being obesed!': Public pedagogy, reality media and the obesity crisis. *'Health': An Interdisciplinary Journal for the Social Study of Health, Illness and Medicine* 15, no. 1: 3–121.
Rich, E., and J. Evans. 2005. 'Fat ethics' – the obesity discourse and body politics. *Social Theory and Health* 3, no. 4: 341–58.
Rich, E., and J. Evans. 2009. *The impact of new health imperatives on schools: Full research report*. ESRC end of award report, RES-000-22-2003. Swindon, UK: Economic and Social Research Council.
Rich, E., J. Evans and L. De-Pian. 2011. Childrens' bodies, surveillance and the obesity crisis. In *Debating Obesity: Critical Perspectives*, ed. E. Rich, L.F. Monaghan and L. Aphramor. Palgrave.
Rose, N. 1999. *Powers of freedom: Reframing political thought*. Cambridge: Cambridge University Press.
Savage, G.C. 2010. Problematizing 'public pedagogy' in educational research. In *Public pedagogy: Education and learning beyond schooling*, ed. J.A. Sandlin, B.D. Schultz, and J. Burdick, 103–15. New York: Routledge.
Skeggs, B. 1997. *Formations of class and gender*. London: Sage.
Skelton, C., and B. Francis. 2009. *Feminism and the schooling scandal*. London: Routledge.
Susinos, T., A. Calvo, and S. Rojas. 2009. Becoming a woman: The construction of female subjectivities and its relationship with school. *Gender and Education* 21, no. 1: 97–110.
Walby, S. 1997. *Gender transformations*. London: Routledge.
Warin, M., K. Turner, V. Moore, and M. Davies. 2008. Bodies, mothers and identities. Rethinking obesity and the BMI. *Sociology of Health and Illness* 30: 97–111.
Wright, J. 2009. Bio-power, biopedagogies and the obesity epidemic. In *Biopolitics and the "obesity epidemic": Governing bodies*, ed. J. Wright and V. Harwood. London: Routledge.
Wright, J., and R. Dean. 2007. A balancing act: Problematising prescriptions about food and weight in school health texts. *Education and Democracy: Journal of Didactics & Educational Policy* 16, no. 2: 75–94.
Wright, J., and V. Harwood. 2009. *Biopolitics and the obesity epidemic: Governing bodies*. New York: Routledge.
Youdell, D. 2005. Sex–gender–sexuality: How sex, gender and sexuality constellations are constituted in secondary schools. *Gender and Education* 17: 249–70.
Zannettino, L. 2008. Imagining womanhood: Psychodynamic processes in the 'textual' and discursive formation of girls' subjectivities and desires for the future. *Gender and Education* 20: 465–79.

From DIY to teen pregnancy: new pathologies, melancholia and feminist practice in contemporary English youth work[1]

Fin Cullen

Centre for Youth Work Studies, Brunel University, London, UK

> In this article I consider past and current forms of feminist practice and 'girls work' and debates within contemporary English youth work. Drawing on previous scholarly work in Girlhood studies, youth work and youth policy, I explore the range of dominant discourses that have come to shape youth work practice within the current economic and policy climate. Taking two examples of present-day 'girls work', Feministwebs and Girlguiding UK, I map the similarities and differences between these distinctive forms of practice, before considering the potential of feminist and queer pedagogies in reclaiming the potential for a liberatory praxis within twenty-first-century girls work.

Introduction

This article reflects on the future of feminist 'girls work' within English youth work, in relation to scholarly feminist debates about policy and practice initiatives relating to young women. The article originates in my professional and personal experiences as a feminist youth work educator, and youth worker, and my interactions with feminist practitioners and 'girls work' groups as a young woman in the 1980s. There is a bittersweet challenge in writing this paper at this particular juncture. Recent years have seen a renewed interest in feminist youth work with new practice events, conferences and resources – these include recent conferences on a 'girls work' theme by UK Youth (2009), *Youth & Policy* (March 2010), and events and resources from Feministwebs (established in 2008). Yet simultaneously, state-funded English youth work in its current context faces massive cuts in services at this time of austerity. This paper argues that there is a continued need for a contemporary feminist praxis that is responsive to the challenges of austerity and turmoil in the youth and education sectors.

My interest is in the kinds of pedagogic responses offered by contemporary feminist youth work, especially in responding to the changing position of young women. I draw out the developments in contemporary feminist youth work to reflect on the current state of play in theory, policy and practice terms in relation to the figure of the 'girl'. My key question here is: *what future is there for feminist youth work practice, and in particular 'girls work', in relation to a new policy and theoretical landscape?*

Here, I explore youth work's specific capacity to draw on feminist pedagogic approaches in striving for gender equity. While much writing on feminist pedagogy has explored its role in formal education environments such as school and higher education settings, I argue that its use within informal education settings such as youth work provides a space which is ripe for analysis and exploration.

Emerging in the mid-nineteenth century, English youth work throughout its history has been delivered by a variety of providers and practitioners. Providers include local churches, housing groups, community associations, charities, schools and local authorities. Practitioners range from part-time volunteers to experienced professionals with postgraduate qualifications, and youth work settings can include dedicated youth centres, youth clubs based in community centres and church halls, schools-based 'youth wings', mobile provision on 'youth buses' and detached 'street'-based work. This multiplicity of practice contexts has meant a range of practice agendas and ways of working have arisen from the emergence of youth work. However, despite this variety in provision, the National Occupational Standards for Youth Work emphasise its educational aspects including voluntary engagement, empowerment and enabling young people to become 'critical and creative' as central features of the practice (Lifelong Learning UK 2008).

In the contemporary climate, there are tensions in the direction and purpose of modern English youth work. As Bradford (2011a, 2011b) notes, the relative liminality of English youth work, in relation to its status as a profession and practice amongst a variety of other education and welfare services, has meant a plurality of traditions have emerged. For Bradford, youth work's liminality positions it as poorly insulated in relation to its capacity to make knowledge claims in contrast to other similar but more established and esteemed professions, such as school teachers or social workers. He states:

> Historically, youth work has been positioned on the margins of other practices and institutions, somewhere between schooling and social work. (Bradford 2011a, 102)

Historically, English youth work has been framed as part of a wider social education, or more recently, informal education initiative with groups of young people (Smith 1988; Jeffs and Smith 1999b). It has been seen as a site to ready young people for adulthood, as well as from the 1970s onwards to arguably more 'radical' forms of practice for political education influenced by the dialogic critical pedagogy of Freire (Batsleer 2011b).

Critical tensions have emerged as much state-funded work has specifically focused on easing transitions into adulthood, crime prevention and 'keeping young people off the streets'. Thus, multiple forms of youth work practice, shaped by relatively conservative, paternalist as well as radical traditions, have co-existed in many local authority and voluntary-sector contexts. These forms have changed across time. Bradford argues that from the mid-twentieth century onwards, English youth work practice has seen an 'influential expressive discourse held in tension with growing demands for an instrumental practice' (2011a, 103). From the mid-1990s, the growing demands for accountability and cost-effectiveness in UK public services have led to a resulting decline in the expressive (and liberatory) approaches within youth work that had briefly flourished in earlier decades.

The widespread public-sector reforms under the New Labour administration reshaped contemporary integrated youth services, via prescriptive commissioning models and specific outputs, away from the former 'peculiarly English youth work' (Bradford 2011b, 1) of earlier years. Youth work moved from a position of a relatively high degree of autonomy for individual youth workers, and an emphasis on expression, to an instrumentalist, individualising youth development model of an increasingly prescriptive and audited practice. This is demonstrated in the current thrust of much contemporary youth policy. For example, the recent Coalition policy, *Positive for Youth* (Department for Education 2011) is resolutely about developing an individual's capacities and aspirations within these new youth development frameworks – in contrast to the group focus of much traditional 'youth work' practice. As scholars note, this individualistic turn differs substantially from the collective and group focus of many earlier English 'youth work' traditions (Bradford 2011b; Davies 2011).

This reflects the continued decline in issue-based groupwork in much contemporary youth work. In the 1970s and 1980s an explicit feminist youth work practice, in the form of a new single-sex 'girls work', was influenced by the Women's Liberation Movement. It included the creation by feminist youth workers of resources and services aimed at work with groups of young women in challenging sexism, and raising consciousness including the establishment of manual trade workshops, self-defence training, sports and outward bound residentials, and issue-based groupwork (Batsleer 2006; Spence 2006, 2010; Oliver 2008).

The rest of the paper considers recent debates within theory, policy and practice, and reflects on the continued salience of current and future girls work to reflect on the enduring possibilities for feminist-influenced pedagogy within modern youth work.

Failing boys and problem girls

In recent years, within schooling the perceived educational 'failure' of boys has been a central concern of education policy makers in many Western national contexts, including the UK. In earlier decades the focus was on girls' underachievement, yet more recently, this concern had become replaced by an emphasis on the underperformance of young men (Epstein et al. 1998; Francis 2000; Gordon et al. 2008). This policy and practice focus on boys positions girl pupils as dutiful, passive and conforming in contrast to their male peers (Gordon et al. 2008, 181). The boys' underachievement debate has thus resulted in a relative lack of focus and funds on the needs of young women in both formal *and* informal education settings including youth services.

Parallel to this public concern with boys' (under)achievement in school, the focus within youth work settings has also remained centred on the behaviour and attainment of boys. Within a UK youth policy context, Jeffs and Smith note that funding and practices have increasingly been targeted around viewing young people, and young men in particular, as *thugs, users* or *victims*:

> As *thugs* they steal cars, vandalise estates, attack older (and sometimes, younger) people and disrupt classrooms. As *users* they take drugs, drink and smoke to excess, get pregnant in order to jump the housing queue and, hedonistically, care only for themselves. As *victims* they can't find work, receive poor schooling and are brought up in dysfunctional families. Yet so many of the troublesome behaviours associated in this way with young people are not uniquely theirs. (Jeffs and Smith 1999a, 45)

This trio of youth policy discourses of *thugs, users* and *victims* echoes the various discourses of deficiency, disaffection and sexual deviance in Griffin's earlier exploration of 'troubled' and 'troubling' youth (Griffin 1993, 1997). Young people's unsupervised leisure time has long been seen as a source of social problems, and related to the series of moral panics around anti-social behaviour, drug use, drinking and sexual activity.

Many scholars concur that much youth work remains a male preserve (Baines and Alder 1996; Griffin 1997; Oliver 2008; Batsleer 2006), with the directing of contemporary English youth services towards crime prevention and employment targets aimed predominantly at young men. Indeed the youth workers in Hills' study (2005) also identified that it was the visibility of 'boys' as a problem category that made them a key focus for government targets and practice interventions:

> I don't think (anti-sexist) work is strategically planned because a lot of the work now is about government targets and outcomes and is focused on ... community safety ... so what we are looking at is the behaviour of young men... (Nina, youth worker, quoted in Hills 2005, 71)

Despite the enduring 'malestream' (Griffin 1997) dominance of much youth work, increasingly 'moral panics' concerning new perilous youthful femininities have emerged, especially around young women's perceived hyper- and precocious sexuality (Griffin 1993, 1997; Kehily 2001, 2005; Hudson 2002; O'Neill 2005), drinking and drug taking (Jackson and Tinkler 2007; Cullen 2010b), eating disorders and violence (Brown 2005). The growing media and public interest in troublesome young women – in the forms of gymslip mums, girl gang members and ladettes (Jackson and Tinkler 2007), highlights the simultaneous notion that the modern girl is similarly out of control. The troublesome, hedonistic girl is increasingly visible within media and policy discourse, perceived as probably drunk, and precociously sexually active. The public concerns around girls' sexual precocity and childhood innocence shape political discourse about young women, as clearly evidenced in a number of recent government-sponsored policy reviews (see Papadopoulos 2010; Bailey 2011). These 'girl-anxieties' have also translated into limited specific funding streams aimed at young women, e.g sexual health and teenage pregnancy projects. However, the funding for such programmes has further diminished since the end of the Teenage Pregnancy strategy in 2010.

Under New Labour, and more recently, under the Coalition in the UK, a 'new authoritarianism' (Jeffs and Smith 1999a; St Croix 2011) has increasingly marked youth policy. Within the media and political realms, the bodies, minds and practices of British young people are placed the hopes of the future national 'good' in order to tackle the notion of a 'Broken Britain'. Wider anxieties about national decline are reimagined as a 'youth problem' in youth policy interventions, with a resulting increased criminalisation of youthful transgression via a range of punitive criminal justice interventions under New Labour (e.g. Anti-Social Behaviour Orders; Youth Dispersal Zones; Acceptable Behaviour Contracts), and a proliferation of services in managing such risky, and potentially criminal, youth (Youth Inclusion Programme; Youth Offending Teams; Youth Inclusion and Support Panels). Such approaches aimed at 'criminal' (male) youth – in the wake of the summer riots across England – are unlikely to face major reform in the near future. These civil disturbances across a number of large English town and cities in August 2011 followed record rises in youth unemployment, rising distrust of the police amongst some sections of young people, cuts to youth services, the withdrawal of educational maintenance allowance (EMA) for students aged 16–19 to attend college, and hikes in higher education tuition fees.

Thus, English youth work becomes aimed in policy terms at controlling 'at risk' populations. In such a gendered formulation much of youth work's role becomes about socialising working-class young people into a 'successful' adult citizenship. A renewed strengthening of this focus is apparent in the current UK Coalition Government's National Citizenship service aimed at all Year 11 pupils[2] in socialising young people via 'positive community activities', and plans for increased involvement of business interests in the shaping of modern youth services (St Croix 2011; Davies 2011). This has significant potential consequences for the liberationist aspects of work such as feminist traditions within informal education. Indeed, as Bradford notes:

> Youth work may have to become a significantly more subversive activity if it's to preserve its optimistic educational stance and sustain its modest but important contribution to young people's well being. (2011b, 8)

The challenge is thus in considering what this '*subversion*' might resemble, and how a subversive engagement might work between the cracks of this wider neoliberal audit culture in contemporary, targeted youth services.

Feminist traditions and 'girls work'

While the origins of much single-sex work with girls in youth work originates in the pre-war Girls' Club Movement (Spence 2006, 2010), the Women's Liberation movement and second-wave feminism strongly shaped UK-based 'girls work' from the mid-1970s onwards. From the mid- to late 1980s, feminist youth work – although already a marginal practice in many youth services – became increasingly peripheral, and less 'feminist' in focus, framed around girls-in-crisis in funding and policy streams (Spence 2006, 2010). As Spence notes:

> On the central questions of essentialism, and the political meanings and implications of youth work, feminist workers of the 1970s and 1980s singularly failed to influence generic practice. What they did achieve was an extension of the scope of youth work to acknowledge there was some specialist work needed to work with girls. (2006, 258)

Such a move hollowed out 'girls work' from its earlier feminist roots. Indeed, as Batsleer (2006) argues, the resulting single-sex work with young women seemed to be mainly predicated on maintaining enduring appropriate norms of heterofemininity, and attending to 'moral panics' around young femininities in public discourse, rather than engaging in critical debates on gender equity or feminism, more broadly. Indeed, although increasingly scarce in the face of public service cuts, the remaining fragments of traditional 'drop-in' open-access youth work, in the form of the pool table, football and ping pong, perhaps has changed little from the kinds of 1970s Mill Lane youth club described by McRobbie (2000), with young men monopolising both space and resources.

Where contemporary forms of 'girls work' continue to exist, they can also be seen to reproduce a refashioned older form of traditional models of heterofemininity (Batsleer 2006), for instance, via the beauty, childcare and babysitting accreditation and careers advice offered by some services (including schemes such as apprenticeships and the previous Entry to Employment (E2E) programme). These are often highly gendered and aimed at working-class young women in developing job capabilities and readiness for work in the lowly paid, care and beauty sectors (Francis 2002; Cullen 2011). The continuation of third-sector organisations originating in the earliest wave of girls work in the UK, such as the YWCA (now Platform 51) and Girls Friendly Society remain active, yet due to targeted funding constraints these can be shaped by neo-liberal policy priorities, and thus often target specifically 'at-risk' groups of young women in increasingly clear outcome-driven work. This resulting new post-feminist girls work is thus regulated around the neo-managerialist and neo-authoritarian intent for youth work as a form of social education, in order to 'fix' the perceived lack of 'at-risk' girls:

> ...the rationale for separate (girls) work seems to have changed post feminist. More often than not, separate work seems to exist because of a perceived 'lack' in girls. Lack of confidence, lack of self esteem is mention a lot. Or else it is justified because of some 'risk' against which girls need special protection, particularly the 'risk' of unplanned pregnancy. (Batsleer 2006, 60)

The remit of much contemporary youth work for these often working-class young women is thus primarily to rectify and 'fix' excessive behaviour, rather any explicit feminist agenda of 'empowerment'. The 'at-risk' young women who are targeted by new youth services echo the discursive formation of the 'phallic girls' (McRobbie 2009) who drink, smoke, have sex and swear. Indeed, it is the 'at-risk' girls perceived 'phallicism' that is both pathologised and judged by policy agendas and the gamut of welfare services created under New Labour, to channel such young women into narrow appropriate notions of (feminine) success.

These new discourses of 'success' (Bradford and Hey 2007) persist to marginalise working-class girls, who continue to be 'measured against the white bourgeois ideal they can never have the "right" femininity' (Reay 2001, 157). It is into this space of presumed feminine deficit that post-feminist girls work often finds a niche in relation to funding and expected 'educational' outputs. As regards education interventions, whilst the *'can do'* girl may be the focus of teachers' attention, the *'at-risk'* girl now has a host of allied professions from learning mentors, social workers, youth workers and until recently, Connexions[3] advisors, to manage her 'risky' bodily practices.

Whilst excessive alcohol use, smoking and 'risky' sex practice may have health consequences, it also may be argued that the problem with such troublesome girls is their transgression of normative respectable femininities (Jackson and Tinker 2007; Cullen 2010a, 2010b). The language of 'risk' is thus clearly gendered. Yet the focus on the 'riskiness' of some contemporary young women's behaviour masks the issue that historically there are ongoing concerns around the nation's youth, with a kind of constant amnesia that today's youth are somehow much worse behaved than their predecessors

(Jackson and Tinkler 2007). Indeed, Jackson and Tinkler (2007) note that it is the *very* visibility of girls' public bad behaviour within wider media discourses that frame the focus of the concern and the construction of this 'risk'.

The contraction of youth services under the Coalition does little to destabilise the discursive framings of these 'troubled girls'. Although, under austerity, the rolling back of the welfare state does reconfigure the professional landscape, with many of the new services (e.g. Sure Start, Connexions, Children Centres) and professionals created under New Labour now facing redundancy. Within this configuration, neo-liberal youth work with girls becomes predominantly about cost-effectively and demonstratively managing the 'risky' bodies and minds of troublesome girls.

So what about a modern critical girls work?

Within contemporary English youth work policy and practice, Batsleer has suggested that feminist youth workers as informal educators have an 'illuminating' aspect to their role (2010, 225). More recently, Batsleer (2011b) also argues for the potential for a Freirian critical pedagogy (Freire 1972) in creating and sustaining new ways of engaging with feminist approaches in youth work, and 'girls work' in particular. Earlier work on a Freirian-influenced 'feminist pedagogy' imagines it as a dialogic classroom practice in order to explore collective gendered experience within formal education settings (Shrewsbury 1987). However, beyond the classroom, Freirian critical pedagogy has been highly influential on models of liberatory youth work and community development (Ledwith 2005); particularly in the focus on a 'community of learners' and 'empowerment', as arising through 'mutuality' of shared experience and dialogue (Shrewsbury 1987, 10).

Although some contemporary youth work practice shares aspects of formal education such as the use of curriculum and accreditation, much still draws on dialogic approaches to group learning, and the place of the youth worker as educator that arguably destabilises traditions of 'expertise' and authority within much traditional schooling. Coburn (2011), drawing on Giroux (2005), has suggested that youth work might be imagined as a 'border pedagogy'. By this, she means that youth workers – in common with teacher-educators – 'may be defined as cultural workers who take a problem-posing approach to education and who, in some settings, adopt the value base and methods of critical pedagogy' (Coburn 2011, 480). Such youth work provides an educational and cultural practice that can support young people in thinking across boundaries in order to shape new identities and transform social relations, emphasising dialogic learning and empowerment for consciousness raising – although I note the critical differences in relation to possibilities and potentialities in relation to context, curriculum and compulsion that highlight the differences in history and potential for feminist endeavours in a classroom in comparison to youth work settings.

However, there remain limitations to critical pedagogy on a theoretical and practice level across educational contexts. As Weiler (1991) notes, there are some tensions in drawing on Freirian critical pedagogy when developing a feminist pedagogical approach. She questions the singular oppression indicated in Freire's work, and instead argues that a feminist approach could develop a Freirian analysis that can validate personal experience and question traditional notions of expertise and authority. Ellesworth (1992) also questions the limits of critical pedagogy, and the challenges of privileging certain knowledges and experiences over others. Similarly, she notes the role of the educator as critical pedagogue is often under-realised in theoretical texts, creating often-tricky situations within the complexity of real-life learning environments. Many of the central concepts within critical pedagogic educational texts, such as 'freedom' and 'empowerment', are slippery and contested, and as such, may not be so easily realised in a straightforward manner within education interventions (Ellesworth 1992) – whether that be in the school classroom, or I would also argue, in the youth club or street-based detached youth work setting. Indeed, the very 'oppressed' subjects of critical pedagogy may be resistant and reluctant to be 'liberated' and 'empowered' by well-meaning educators, whether they be teachers or youth workers.

Another tension remains. Critical pedagogic approaches, as utilised in earlier feminist work, often reproduce or are based on essentialist gender binaries, and/or arguably mobilise a zero-sum approach to the conceptions of power, and are thus potentially incompatible with other poststructuralist and/or queer pedagogies' conceptualisations of sex–gender mutability (Butler 1990, 1993). Such theoretical work from the 1990s onwards began to question the unitary and enduring categories of gender and notions of 'girlhood'. From this perspective, the creation of single-sex approaches working specifically with 'girls' can uphold problematic normative gendered categories around 'girls'' experience, identity work and aspects of what it is perceived 'to be' or 'to do' a normative 'femininity' (West and Zimmerman 1987), and how this is linked or not, indeed to a 'sexed' body (Butler 1993).

This has consequences beyond the theoretical realm, in that conceptual models shape policy and practice. I would argue that both critical *and* poststructuralist-influenced pedagogic approaches in educational settings may look very similar (in being conversation/dialogue based, and critically exploring power dynamics in play). Yet the interpretation and theorisations based on such practices may differ substantially – particularly around the analysis of power, the constitution and endurance of the subject 'girl', and what and how 'femininity' and other genders are constituted. However, other scholars have previously appropriated the notion of 'strategic essentialism' (Spivak 1988) to navigate out of this tricky bind when wishing to make claims for the enduring need for an identity politics within a new theoretical territory that disavows 'fixed' identity claims. I note the use of the concept of 'strategic essentialism', in both highlighting the theoretical tensions and coherence of drawing on an essentialised subject within a wider identity politics. However, it is also important to maintain the continued tactical need for a feminist youth work that interrogates essentialist/non-essentialist debates around gender binaries, and, in addition, highlights the role of 'girls work' with *all* 'girls', as an important strategic political act within a wider historical palette of feminist and critical praxis. Following Youdell's (2009) use of Butler (2004), I would concur with the present need to forge 'new collectivities in mobile ways' (Youdell 2009, 49), in order to re-engage with social movements, and consider the possibilities of socially just practice in schools and youth services for all genders.

The youth work scholars, Jeffs and Smith (1999b), have long described the informal education process, as contained within youth work, as an 'art of conversation'. Such conversations create micro-moments for work beyond and between any specified curriculum, where spaces may be questioned and even, momentarily 'queered', and gender debated and deconstructed. The very marginality of youth work as a practice creates exciting spaces of potential and challenge, beyond what may be possible for teachers in schools. The potential arises from the legacy of operating in the margins, where there has historically been a freedom, and until recently, a relative professional autonomy for youth workers, to create and negotiate expressive and dialogic approaches in their practice. Feminist youth work scholars note the potential in critical pedagogy in democratic practice for young women, Lesbian, Gay Bisexual, Trans and Queer young people and other marginalised groups (Batsleer 2010, 2011a, 2011b). However, the very marginality of youth work also produces challenges, often in the vulnerability of non-statutory services to deeper cuts, the move from universal to targeted work, and the focus of youth work on perceived 'problem' populations (Jeffs and Smith 1999a; Davies 2005). Following feminist poststructuralist scholars in education, such as Bronwyn Davies (1989, 1993), the notion of using groupwork and a critical dialogic engagement via conversation and re-readings and re-writings of sex–gender discourse provides an accessible intervention for youth workers, arguably perhaps even more so than is possible in the school classroom due to the negotiated nature of the youth work 'curriculum' and dialogic relationship.

While the 'empowerment' aspect of much youth work has long been used by practitioners to defend the democratic aspects of their work, trying to replicate earlier historical legacies without due care may be perceived to deny contemporary young women's agency, or decry their experiences as not suitably 'conscious' enough. This is exactly what Hey acknowledges in calling for educators (including youth workers) to 'construct a pedagogical discourse capable of respecting the autonomy of girls' and young women's social relations whilst providing them with a resource to think with and against their limits?' (2010, 219). The second tension that arises is, if feminist youth work concentrates only on young women, then it risks further marginalization as such an essentialised focus would potentially render it unable to adopt a critical engagement on gender regimes with young people of all genders.

Some moments of resistance

I want to reflect on how a feminist praxis may continue to flourish in the cracks between in a now sadly, ravaged, post-recessionary local authority and voluntary-sector English youth service, and what this particularly means for sustaining feminist youth work. The wider decline of feminist activism within and outside youth work has further sidelined feminist and anti-sexist youth work practice, and/or diluted it into a wider equalities and diversity agenda (Batsleer 2010; Spence 2010). Despite this, I seek comfort in the breadth of the limited girls work that continues to flourish in a range of settings. In the contemporary youth work landscape there are multiple versions of girls work happening across the UK, sometimes within the same organisational context, and sometimes at different times, by the same practitioner. Traditional voluntary organisations such as the Girl Guides and the YWCA (now Platform 51), have increasingly become interested in contemporary issue-orientated social education on a range of health education and citizenship agendas – for example, in challenging stigmas against young mothers and mental health (Platform 51) and campaigning for positive role models (Girl Guides). These forms of contemporary girls work have aspects that are both explicitly feminist *and* post-feminist in focus. They thus respond to the traditions of 'social control' and 'empowerment' that youth work interventions historically have continually swung between (Davies 1999). At this crucial time with such deep cuts into youth services, politicised girls work has an important role, especially in the wake of record rises in youth and women's unemployment, and the withdrawal of funds from child care provision, young parents groups, women's shelters and rape crisis centres (Fawcett Society 2011).

I briefly draw on two examples – that of the recent organisation, Feministwebs, and that of the Girlguiding UK. In common with many contemporary youth projects, both have an online presence that is complementary to, and extends, their offline activity by providing downloadable resources for practitioners and networking spaces. This online work requires less funding compared with regular youth provision, and can nurture the development of socially and/or geographically isolated workers and groups. The first example, Feministwebs, remains a small, but growing grassroots practice established in 2008, by feminist practitioners in the North West of England. As previous scholarly work exploring emergence of Feministwebs has noted, it resurrects and celebrates earlier forms of expressive practice within an on- and offline realm (Batsleer 2010). Ever mindful of feminist pasts, the project's endeavours have included archiving earlier feminist youth work resources, materials and artifacts, and facilitating intergenerational dialogue between new and old feminist youth work practices and participants. The focus on chronicling women's history, within this new feminist youth work space, perhaps reflects the melancholic thrust of McRobbie's (2009) argument that there is a need to remember what has been lost in the move to a neoliberal appropriation of a feminist agenda. Indeed, as Batsleer (2010) argues, the 'web' aspect has a dual meaning beyond that of the internet to hark back to the feminist anti-nuclear activism of Greenham Common women[4] of the early 1980s, and the notion of women's knowledge and experience being held and shared in a matrix of the 'personal, political and professional' (Batsleer 2010, 220). This interplay with past and present appears in both the Feministweb rationale and practices. For example, as the Feministwebs' youth worker in McCabe's blog states:

> When OFSTED[5] came into the youth club, the boys were playing on the pool table and the girls were hiding out in the toilets ◇ In the session there were young women who had never worn make-up in their lives, and they had all been given by their youth worker a 'Girl's world' head to practice putting make-up on ... and I thought ... have we stepped back to the 1950s?! (Youth worker, quoted in McCabe 2008)

The standpoint approaches privileged in the second-wave feminist flavour of the contemporary youth work of Feministwebs stands in marked contrast to either the erasure of politics of sex–gender in the remaining youth provision, and/or the specific funding regimes for practice with 'problem' categories of girls around issues such as the prevention of teen pregnancy. The retrospective approach upheld by Feministwebs goes beyond a melancholy for a feminism lost. Indeed, Feministwebs as a new space is also in the business of creating and engaging in dialogue about gender equality and feminism with a new generation of young women. This *'cross-generational'* conversation is facilitated through events for youth workers and young women, production of a film, archiving of historical resources, art projects and an interactive website. This is not to negate space of conflict as well as consensus. After all, dialogue can take many forms, and while an intergenerational aspect is a helpful starting point, I am reminded by other feminist scholars' concerns that critical pedagogic approaches can re-orientate and reinvest new power hierarchies (perhaps between and within generations of feminist practice) whilst dismantling others (Ellesworth 1992; Morley 1998).

On the Feministwebs site,[6] participants are encouraged to share resources and sessions plans on a range of topic areas including: body image, sexuality, feminism, the political case for feminist youth work and politics.

The first Feministweb campaign pack, 'Done Hair and Beauty, Now What?', challenges and refutes the aesthetic ideals and beauty norms of heterofemininity which can be reproduced in providing 'something for the girls' in many youth work settings. Furthermore, this interaction also takes place offline, where youth workers and young people meet in North West England to organise and celebrate their work.

The online space has thus created another realm in which disparate practices can be consolidated and celebrated. While much of the Feministwebs' approach reproduces earlier second-wave feminist pedagogic practices, the move into the virtual and intergenerational takes it across space and time, from the local to the national to the global, as feminist youth workers can access resources that are shared online and enter into dialogue with other practitioners internationally. With such a dearth of opportunities for a liberatory feminist youth work to exist, there has been, for example, minimal apparent dialogue represented between trends within second-wave and third-wave feminist thinking. Feministwebs appears distinctly second wave in approach, content and sensibility, highlighting its generational forbearance, grounding in activism and its indebtedness to the 1970s women's movement, in addition to the inertia of state-sponsored feminist youth work since the late 1980s.

Girlguiding UK, as one of the oldest uniformed girl youth groups, established in 1909, has an extensive presence in local groups across the UK as part of a worldwide Guiding movement, and has also during the past few years expanded its range of practices and online presence. If Feministwebs reproduces an earlier 'standpoint' and activist pedagogic approach in reproducing and developing second-wave feminist practice, then Girlguiding UK as represented by the contemporary new website seems to have engaged with a more explicitly post-feminist agenda celebrating the successful, '*can do*' girls who, via diligence, hard work and accreditation, can '*have it all*'. Whilst Feministwebs' resource pages appear to be largely aimed at practitioners, the Girlguiding UK website has a multi-layer format, appealing to Guiders and young women themselves to engage in Guiding in both the online and offline realms. In common with other youth practice sites, it offers a range of downloadable resources and session ideas.

The move to campaigning, research and an online interactive service builds on the long traditions of local Guiding groups. The Girlguiding UK[7] website is split into age-specific sections, with pages for Guide leaders and young women. The sections aimed at young women echo popular teen girl magazines in style and content including quizzes, polls and activity ideas. The Guides section for young women aged 10–14 has a trio of slim, fashionable, *Manga*[8]-style cartoon-style, girl figures in the opening page, highlighting the aspirational aspects of the site. The senior section for 14–25-year-olds emphasises aspiration, community action, blogging and tips on personal safety, beating bullying and money management. The site also reports on extensive results from an annual survey of girls' attitudes. These results have formed the basis for a range of recent campaigns and media reports, including those on how many young women interviewed in the Guides' survey self-identified as feminist (Cochrane 2007), girls' notions of 'success', and the Guides more recent UK-based campaign and petition against 'airbrushing' of images within media aimed at young women (GirlGuiding UK 2010).

The Girlguiding UK site also provides magazine-style content and quizzes aimed at young women themselves and formulated around an expressive depiction of 'Girl Power'. The Girl Guides is much less explicitly 'feminist' in tone, content or form than the Feministwebs site. Indeed, the 'Girl Power' discursive framing of the site reproduces the imagery of teen girl magazines, and also potentially echoes the sensibilities and 'contradictory discourse' of post-feminism (Griffin 2004, 33). Such contradictions can include an assumption that girls have already achieved equity with boys, and that via their power to consume can achieve their aspirations. Such representations, for Griffin, render feminism in such media as 'self evident and redundant' (2004, 33). Whether the new Girlguiding UK site becomes a space of 'post-feminist' or 'feminist' potential remains to be seen. However, the need to appeal directly to girls in fashionable and media-savvy forms, including a social networking Bebo site, reproduces dominant 'raced' and classed norms of heterosexual aesthetic desirability. Beyond the website imagery, the Girl Guides highlights a new (post) feminist approach to youth services working with young women.

Indeed, on both the Feministweb and Girlguiding UK sites, there are similar preoccupations around girls' perceived problematic relationships with 'body image' and 'bullying', and so even here, the public 'girl-anxieties' runs even through these more girl-friendly sites. The collective action and mutuality of Girl Guide groups, with young women meeting because they *choose* to, rather than being primarily targeted as needing 'protection' or 'intervention' for their perceived troubles, is a powerful and valuable asset in delivering a contemporary and relevant feminist girls work. Perhaps surprisingly, I could argue that in relation to the neo-managerialist and highly targeted thrust of much state-sponsored youth work practice, the universal and group orientation of the Guides enables it to even become one of the potential 'subversive' sites (Bradford 2011b) that might engender a newly reinvigorated feminist youth work practice with girls. Yet I also note the Guiding tradition within England – with local groups often linked to churches – has had a different classed and faith composition than many modern state-funded, local youth clubs, which from the 1960s onwards have often been based in urban sites in areas of deprivation. The need would therefore be for the Guides to reach out to a much wider classed and 'raced' demographic in order to establish themselves as a site of inclusive democratic and feminist practice for *all* girls. Thus, both Feministwebs and the

Girl Guides, despite their very different histories and agendas, offer a critical and creative space beyond the neo-managerialist agenda for new spaces of (older) traditions of youth work practice.

The plurality of youth work traditions within England, and in the UK more broadly, has meant that the seeds of Feministwebs lay in pockets of practice to be reawakened by a new generation of feminist youth workers and young people in the North West of England. The main difference between Feministwebs and Girl Guiding as two forms of single-sex youth work practice is the engagement of Feministwebs with a critical pedagogic-based and explicitly politically feminist focus. However, Feministwebs is an example of a small, emergent and enduring feminist practice; in contrast, Girl Guiding remains resolutely mainstream, and holds the potential, in common with other larger girls youth organisations such as Platform 51, to provide a valid and potentially explicitly feminist site of knowledge and practice in campaigning for gender equity both nationally and internationally. Such approaches have the potential to also build upon aspects of a feminist pedagogy in supporting young women to think differently about sex–gender issues, and to call for wider greater gender equity in practice. Whilst the work of Feministwebs might be more overt in this tradition, other more conservative traditions such as the Girl Guides also provide a space for challenging gender inequality and provide a site for feminist education.

Some concluding thoughts

Following feminist poststructuralist and queer theoretical debates, the endurance of the essential subject 'the girl' also creates a greater challenge for the theoretical base of much feminist youth work practice, in that it fundamentally destabilises and questions essential sex–gender categories. However, there is a need to reinvigorate and reimagine feminist youth work practice in response to recent moves with theory, policy and practice. Despite the challenges that such theoretical movements may hold for some forms of feminist practice, I hold that there is still an enduring need for a contemporary creative and critical feminist youth work (including 'girls work'). This new '*girls*' work could be aimed at engaging with debates within second-wave and third-wave feminism, reflecting upon and negotiating differences between and within groups of 'girls', as well as the interactions of multiple sites of oppression and the endurance of heteronormativity. In addition, it might enable practitioners and young women alike to think critically about the sex–gender discourses that produce the 'girl' as subject of policy and practice interventions. It also requires that, in the challenging youth sector and higher education climate in the UK, the remaining youth work training courses enable practitioners to engage further with such debates in theory, policy and practice, and young people's gendered practices – in order to consider the continued salience of feminism for youth work and youth workers.

In the final chapter of *The Aftermath of Feminism*, McRobbie (2009) states that pedagogy provides 'a vital space of encounter', where it might be argued that a Freirian-orientated view of education as a practice of freedom can provide intellectual and emotional spaces to rekindle a project of feminist hope and mutuality. Poststructuralist feminist and queer theory also offers potential insights for youth practitioners towards building a more socially just (*and subversive*) youth work praxis, in order to create spaces of critical reflection with young people of all genders to interrogate hegemonic sex–gender norms.

In summary, in the contemporary difficult youth work climate there is a need to consider the kinds of feminisms that can be imagined, or viably enacted within and beyond state-sponsored work, and the class and 'raced' dynamics of such shifts. For example, this may include the need to think beyond the heterosexual binary, and whilst reflecting on our practice histories, also take new steps in forging new alliances and practices – 'the new collectivities' (Butler 2007; Youdell 2009) – in promoting social justice.

Second-wave feminist-inspired girls work can and does provide a helpful springboard for a contemporary praxis that engages with third-wave and queer debates – although as I noted earlier the potential contradictions in using 'identity'-based 'girls' work to unpick binary sex–gender and the notion of 'fixed' identity categories. My argument remains that 'girls work' provides a helpful starting point for wider work in the area in thinking critically about sex–gender issues more broadly, within a wider palette of interventions based on pedagogic approaches for sex–gender equalities.

Whilst state-funded, feminist-orientated anti-sexist work has increasingly been diminished and/or incorporated into wider policy-led equality and diversities agendas, there is a need to reflect and consider new of ways of reinvigorating, and drawing on, these earlier politicised, liberatory traditions. Firstly, this may follow from a wider resurgence in feminist activism more generally, that may once again revive anti-sexist (and feminist) practice. Secondly, the present severe economic challenges faced by English youth services can re-politicise and bolster education and youth practitioners into reimagining existing services away from the dominance of neoliberal agendas – see, for example, the anti-managerialist activism of the In Defence of Youth Work[9] campaign. These new 'subversive' practices highlight the rewards of revisiting and creating new youth work practices for social justice, including the capacity for feminist pedagogies in youth work to engage on a policy and practice level with how the intersection and interactions of 'race', gender, generation, class and sexuality play out in the lives of all young people.

Notes
1. This paper arises from the UK Economic and Social Research Council-funded seminar series 'Young Women in Movement: Sexualities, Vulnerabilities, Needs

and Norms', (ESRC RES-451-26-0715), based at Goldsmiths, University of London, 2009–2011.
2. Age 15–16; the final year of compulsory schooling.
3. At the time of writing, many English local authorities have been involved in severely cutting and disbanding youth services such as Connexions. However, in some local contexts the Connexions' role has been retained as part of a targeted integrated youth service focused at the most 'at-risk' young people.
4. Greenham Common was a women's peace camp established in Berkshire, England in 1981 to protest against the basing of US cruise missiles in the UK. For more on Greenham, see http://www.greenhamwpc.org.uk/.
5. Ofsted (Office for Standards in Education, Children's Services and Skills) is the regulatory and inspection agency for schools and youth services in England.
6. See http://www.Feministwebs.com/.
7. See http://www.girlguiding.org.uk/guides/.
8. *Manga* is a highly stylised contemporary graphic art form originally from Japan, and has growing popularity in UK youth culture.
9. For more on the In Defence of Youth Work campaign, see http://www.indefenceofyouthwork.org.uk/wordpress/.

References

Bailey, Reg. 2011. *Letting children be children: Report of an independent review of the commercialisation and sexualisation of childhood*, June. Bailey report, Crown Copyright.
Baines, M., and C. Alder. 1996. Are girls more difficult to work with? Youth workers perspectives in juvenile justice and related areas. *Crime Delinquency* 42: 467.
Batsleer, J. 2006. Every girl matters! Young women matter! A feminist comment. *Youth & Policy* 90, Winter: 59–63.
Batsleer, J. 2010. Feminist Webs: A case study of the personal, professional and political in youth work, in *Critical practice with children and young people*, ed. M. Robb and R. Thomson. London: Sage, Open University: 217–231.
Batsleer, Janet. 2011a. What kind of eyebrow bar should I have? Feminist pedagogy in youth work. Paper presented at the BERA annual conference, September 8, in London.
Batsleer, J. 2011b. Voices from an edge. Unsettling the practices of youth voice and participation: Arts-based practice in The Blue Room, Manchester. *Pedagogy, Culture & Society* 19: 419–34.
Bradford, S. 2011a. Anomalous identities, youth work amidst 'trashy daydreams' and 'monstrous nightmares'. In *Reflecting on the past essays in the history of youth and community work*, ed. R. Gilchrist, T. Hodgson, T, Jeffs, J. Spence, N. Stanton, and J. Walker, 102–18. Lyme Regis: Russell House Publishing.
Bradford, S. 2011b. Current policy and practice imaginations in English youth work. Paper presented at the First International Conference on Youth Development (IC Youth, 2011), November 1, in Putrajaya, Malaysia.
Bradford, S., and V. Hey. 2007. Successful subjectivities? The successification of class, ethnic and gender positions? *Journal of Education Policy* 22 (6): 595–614.
Brown, J. 2005. 'Violent girls': Same or different from 'other' girls? In *Problem girls: Understanding and supporting troubled and troublesome girls and young women*, ed. G. Lloyd, 61–74. London: RoutledgeFalmer.
Butler, Judith. 1990. *Gender trouble: Feminism and the subversion of identity*. London: Routledge.

Butler, Judith. 1993. *Bodies that matter: On the discursive limits of 'sex'*. London: Routledge.
Butler, Judith. 2004. *Undoing gender*. New York: Routledge.
Butler, Judith. 2007. Sexual politics: The limits of secularism, the time of coalition. British Journal of Sociology Public Lecture, October 30, in London.
Coburn, A. 2011. Building social and cultural capital through learning about equality in youth work. *Journal of Youth Studies* 14: 475–91.
Cochrane, Kira. 2007. Sidelines. *The Guardian*, March 2. http://www.guardian.co.uk/world/2007/mar/02/gender.uk
Cullen, F. 2010a. 'Two's up and poncing fags': Young women's smoking practices, reciprocity and friendship. *Gender and Education* 22: 491–504.
Cullen, F. 2010b. 'I was kinda paralytic': Pleasure, peril and teenage girls' drinking stories. In *Girls and education 3–16: Continuing concerns, new agendas*, ed. C. Jackson, C. Paechter, and E. Renold, 183–97. Milton Keynes, UK: Open University Press.
Cullen, Fin. 2011. Hair, beauty and child care: Gender and careers education for girls. http://www.genderandeducation.com/issues/hair-beauty-and-child-care-gender-and-careers-education-for-girls/ (accessed November 19, 2011).
Davies, Bronwyn. 1989. *Frogs and snails and feminist tales*. Allen and Unwin: Preschool children and gender. Sydney.
Davies, Bronwyn. 1993. *Shards of glass: Children reading and writing beyond gendered identities*. Sydney: Allen & Unwin.
Davies, Bernard. 1999. *From voluntaryism to welfare state. A history of the youth service in England*. Vol. 1, *1939–1979*. Leicester, UK: Youth Work Press.
Davies, B. 2005. Threatening youth revisited: Youth policies under New Labour. In *The encyclopaedia of informal education*. www.infed.org/archives/bernard_davies/revisiting_threatening_youth.htm (accessed December 23, 2011).
Davies, B. 2011. Thinking space: What's positive for youth? A critical look at the Government's emerging 'youth policy'. *Youth & Policy* 107. http://youthandpolicy.org/images/stories/journal107/bernard_davies_what_is_positive_for_youth.pdf (accessed December 12, 2011).
Department for Education. 2011. *Positive for youth: The statement*. http://www.education.gov.uk/childrenandyoungpeople/youngpeople/Positive%20for%20Youth/b00200933/positive-for-youth-the-statement (accessed December 20, 2011).
Ellesworth, E. 1992. Why doesn't this feel empowering? In *Feminisms and critical pedgogy*, ed. C. Luke and J. Gore, 90–120. London: Routledge.
Epstein, D., J. Ellwood, V. Hey, and J. Maw. 1998. *Failing boys? Issues in gender & achievement*. Buckingham, UK: Open University Press.
Fawcett Society. 2011. Cutting women out. http://fawcettsociety.org.uk/index.asp?PageID=1208 (accessed December 20, 2011).
Francis, Becky. 2000. *Boys, girls and achievement: Addressing the classroom issues*. London: Routledge Falmer.
Francis, B. 2002. Is the future really female? The impact and implications of gender for 14–16 year olds' career choices. *Journal of Education and Work* 15, no. 1: 75–88.
Freire, Paulo. 1972. *Pedagogy of the oppressed*. Harmondsworth, UK: Penguin.
Girlguiding UK. 2010. Girlguiding UK against airbrushing. http://www.girlguiding.org.uk/system_pages/small_navigation/latest_news/girlguiding_uk_against_airbr-1.aspx (accessed November 5, 2011).
Giroux, Henry. 2005. *Border crossing*. Oxford: Routledge.

Gordon, T., J. Holland, E. Lahelma, and R. Thomson. 2008. Young female citizens in education: emotions, resources and agency. *Pedagogy, Culture & Society* 16: 177–91.
Griffin, Christine. 1993. *Representations of youth*. London: Polity Press.
Griffin, C. 1997. Troubled teens: Managing disorders of transition and consumption. *Feminist Review* 55: 4–21.
Griffin, C. 2004. Good girls, bad girls: Anglocentrism and diversity in the constitution of contemporary girlhood. In *All about the girl: Culture, power and identity*, ed. A. Harris, 29–45. London: Routledge Falmer.
Hey, V. 2010. Framing girls in girlhood studies: Gender class/ifications in contemporary feminist representations. In *Girls and education 3–16: Continuing concerns, new agendas*, ed. C. Jackson, C. Paechter, and E. Renold, 210–23. Milton Keynes, UK: Open University Press.
Hills, R. 2005. Work with girls and young women: An exploration of changes in practice over the past 10 years in the Oxfordshire Youth Service. A case study. UK: Unpublished MA dissertation, Brunel University.
Hudson, A. 2002. 'Troublesome girls': Towards alternative definitions and policies. In *Youth justice. Critical readings*, ed. J. Muncie, G. Hughes, and E. McLaughlin, 296–310. Buckingham, UK: Open University Press.
Jackson, C., and P. Tinkler. 2007. 'Ladettes' and 'modern girls': 'Troublesome' young femininities. *The Sociological Review* 55: 251–72.
Jeffs, T., and M.K. Smith. 1999. The problem of 'youth' for youth work. *Youth & Policy* 62: 45–66.
Jeffs, Tony, and Mark Smith. 1999b. *Informal education. Conversation, learning and democracy*. Ticknall, UK: Education.
Kehily, M.J. 2001. Issues of gender and sexuality in schools. In *Investigating gender: Contemporary perspectives in education*, ed. B. Francis and C. Skelton, 116–125. Buckingham, UK: Open University Press.
Kehily, M.J. 2005. The trouble with sex: Sexuality and subjectivity in the lives of teenage girls. In *Problem girls: Understanding and supporting troubled and troublesome girls and young women*, ed. G. Lloyd, 87–100. London: RoutledgeFalmer.
Ledwith, Margaret. 2005. *Community development: A critical approach*. Bristol, UK: Policy Press.
Lifelong Learning UK. 2008. National Occupational standards for youth work. http://www.ncvys.org.uk/UserFiles/File/Workforce%20Development/whole%20suite%20of%20Professional%20and%20National%20Occupational%20Standards%20for%20Youth%20Work.pdf
McCabe, Jess. 2008. Feminist youth work in the North West. *The F Word Blog*. http://www.thefword.org.uk/blog/2008/12/feminist_youth (accessed December 12, 2011).
McRobbie, A. 2000. The culture of working class girls. In *Feminism & youth culture*, 44–66. London: Routledge.
McRobbie, Angela. 2009. *The aftermath of feminism*. London: Sage.
Morley, L. 1998. All you need is love: Feminist pedagogy for empowerment and emotional labour in the academy. *International Journal of Inclusive Education* 2, no. 1: 15–27.
Ofsted. 2011. *Girls' career aspirations report*. Ofsted. http://www.ofsted.gov.uk/resources/girls-career-aspirations (accessed November 10, 2011).
Oliver, B. 2008. In from the margins and back again – 25 years of policy: Young people, sexuality and gender. *Youth & Policy* 100: 153–65.

O'Neill, T. 2005. Girls in trouble in the child welfare and criminal justice system. In *Problem girls: Understanding and supporting troubled and troublesome girls and young women*, ed. G. Lloyd, 111–26. London: Routledge Falmer.

Papadopoulos, Linda. 2010. *Sexualisation of young people review*. London: Home Office. http://www.homeoffice.gov.uk/documents/Sexualisation-young-people (accessed November 12, 2011).

Reay, D. 2001. The paradox of contemporary femininities in education: Combining fluidity with fixity. In *Investigating gender: Contemporary perspectives in education*, ed. B. Francis and C. Skelton, 152–163. Buckingham, UK: Open University Press.

Shrewsbury, C.M. 1987. What is feminist pedagogy? *Womens' Studies Quarterly* 15, nos. 3–4: 6–14.

Smith, M. 1988. *Developing youth work. Informal education, mutual aid and popular practice*. Milton Keynes, UK: Open University Press.

Spence, J. 2006. Working with girls and young women: A broken history. In *Drawing on the past: Essays in the history of community and youth work*, ed. R. Gilchrist, T. Jeffs, and J. Spence, 243–61. Leicester, UK: National Youth Agency.

Spence, J. 2010. Collecting women's lives: The challenge of feminism in UK youth work in the 1970s and 80s. *Women's History Review* 19, no. 1: 159–76.

Spivak, G. 1988. Subaltern studies: Deconstructing historiography. In *Selected subaltern studies*, ed. R. Guha and G.C. Spivak, 3–32. Oxford: Oxford University Press.

St Croix, T. 2011. Struggles and silences: Policy, youth work and the National Citizen Service. *Youth & Policy* 106. http://youthandpolicy.org/index.php?option=com_content&view=category&layout=blog&id=37&Itemid=68&limitstart=4 (accessed December 25, 2011).

Weiler, K. 1991. Freire and feminist pedagogy of difference. *Harvard Education Review* 61: 449–72.

West, C., and D.H. Zimmerman. 1987. Doing gender. *Gender & Society* 1, no. 2: 125–51.

Youdell, D. 2009. Lessons in praxis: Thinking about knowledge, subjectivity and politics in education. In *Interrogating heteronormativity in primary schools*, ed. R. DePalma and E. Atkinson, 35–51. Stoke on Trent, UK: Trentham.

A girl is no girl is a girl_: Girls-work after queer theory[1]

Mart Busche

University of Kassel, Department of Sociology, Kassel, Germany

> This contribution gives an overview over 40 years of girls-work in Germany. It highlights certain topics and theoretical implications and emphasises especially the realisation of queer theory and deconstructivism in the last 10 years.

1. Introduction

> So, we find ourselves in a catch-22 situation: On the one hand we want to get rid of girls as deterministic attribution, on the other hand they are so fucking there. (From 'A Girls Work Manifesto', Busche and Wesemüller 2010)

I must admit, I have to start with a sad fact at the beginning: One of the most famous places for extra-curricular girls-work in Germany will by closed when this article is published: it is the 'Alte Molkerei Frille', a former creamery, which is located in the small village of Frille in Northrhine-Westfalia (West Germany) and was rebuilt in a first educational project by unemployed young adults in the 1970s.[2] This house hosted hundreds of school classes in more than 35 years, students who came there voluntarily or most often by a school programme in order to learn something about themselves, about their group behaviour, about gender, sexuality, professional orientation or other topics of interest. Usually the groups were split up into a boys' group and a girls' group and for three to five days they spent up to six hours per day in these groups. These seminars followed a concept of 'learning in processes' which means that the children and youth were encouraged to bring in their own topics of interest, to spend time on interpersonal dynamics which usually do not get any space in school life (dealing with conflicts, personal feedback between the participants, development of a respectful way of treating each other, reflection on swearing terms, etc.). These courses offered the possibility of political education to children, adolescents and young adults, who are usually not targeted for seminars of political education. The roots of such short-term measures lie in the concept of 'learning democracy', which was started after the Second World War under American leadership in order to introduce and improve democratic thinking in the process of German nation building. Therefore political education is mainly thought of as formal education on democracy and political participation. The target groups of youth seminars in Frille were usually not perceived as being able to deal with such information, since most of them came from special needs schools (*Förderschulen*), lower education schools (*Hauptschulen*) and state measures for students who did not finish school or who are not in professional training. Therefore this concept of process orientation was developed: informal learning which shifts between facts, personality building and concrete processes of participation.

What is also special about this place is its engagement in developing concepts and methods for girls-work and boys-work in alliance and reflecting experiences of more than 30 years. Five books and hundreds of articles have been produced by a team of many freelancers and a few employed staff, mainly on the topics of feminist girls-work, anti-sexist boys-work, reflexive co-education and cross work, since these are the four columns of gender pedagogy. The concept of 'anti-sexist boys-work' caused especial controversy since it implies a stigmatisation of boys as perpetrators of sexism. However, the term 'anti-sexist' was originally based on an analysis and critique of gender inequalities and narrow constructions of gender as well as the pedagogical orientation to encourage the individual's behaviour and attitudes to change. One concept that was coined by boys-workers from Frille, which is still in use at different places and has not lost its meaning at all, is the idea of boys-work as 'attitude' ('*Haltung*'), which combines a critical analysis of gender relations with a subject-oriented practice with the concrete boys. 'Reflexive co-education' is a concept of working in a gender-mixed setting in a gender-sensitive way, e.g. in school settings (Faulstich-Wieland 1996). 'Cross work' is a rather new approach: it uses gender differences of participants and pedagogical staff explicitly, e.g. when non-male persons work with boys (cf. Busche 2010).

In Frille, many adults from other organisations have been trained in continuing education courses in gender-sensitive pedagogy and other topics there, since it was also a certified institute for continuing education. This period is over now. I have spent almost 10 years in the team of freelancers, six years in the team of girls-workers, and in the last years was one of the rare persons in boys' work who work from a non-male transgender perspective (cf. Busche 2010). Since the discourse on boys-work has been quite strong in Germany for some years now, some colleagues and I edited a book on feminist girls-work, reflecting on our work in Frille, taking into account the influences of queer theory and deconstructivism, including boys-work as an indispensable part of girls work and treating intersectionality as a mainstream issue. As we now know, it is the last book generated from experiences made in that educational institution. Therefore I am especially happy and grateful to share it with a non-German audience. In order to transmit a little bit of the 'Frille-Spirit', each chapter of this article starts with a quote from 'A Girls Work Manifesto' (Busche and Wesemüller 2010), which concludes the book.

In this article I will give a short overview of the development of girls-work in Germany in the last 40 years and highlight the impact of deconstructivist and queer theory. In the concepts of girls-work, theory and practice have always informed each other. Nevertheless, some topics were lost during that period of time, other topics emerged, and some perspectives have changed completely, e.g. the view on gender itself. The political windows of opportunity for (not only) financial support have also changed many times, but for some time the emergence of cut backs has been a sad reality in the life of institutions of informal learning. So in the end I draw some conclusions on 'girls-work after queer theory' in such a non-supportive political environment.

2. Forty years of feminist girls-work in Germany

> We want a world with freely accessible genders as variable possibilities of expression. A world without societal conceptualised and incorporated gender roles, which divides us and our friends into groups of men and women, our children and seminar participants into groups of girls and boys. And then they get certain characteristics applied – girls don't hit, boys don't cry. If we want a world without all that, why for heaven's sake do we do girls work then? (From 'A Girls Work Manifesto', Busche and Wesemüller 2010)

Feminist girls-work seems to be a western German concept, which seems to make sense since in the German Democratic Republic the aim of gender equality was said to already have been reached – at least by law – and therefore the need for emancipation of girls was somewhat non-existent. I, at least, do not know any source or concept of feminist girls-work from Eastern Germany. The beginnings of girls-work in the Federal Republic of Germany lie in the 1970s and are closely linked to the second women's movement(s). Girls-work set new standards for the practice of youth work in that time, since girls were not at all a target group of youth work concepts in the 1950s: youth work was work with boys. Historically, the education of girls was elitist and debated controversially in central Europe from antiquity until the nineteenth century; it either took place in homogenous girls' groups in monasteries or in private. In the nineteenth century the German bourgeois women's movement demanded higher education for girls and raised the question of co-education (gender-mixed groups). First, the development of education for girls was oriented on the role of the bourgeois mother. It was the proletarian women's movement that demanded an education preparing girls also for participating in the labour sphere and their tasks as citizens of a state (Lange 1983). So before, girls were either not taken into account because they were located solely in the family or they were integrated into co-educative groups as deficit beings. In cases where girls appeared in public youth work they were seen as 'fallen girls' ('*gefallene Mädchen*') or as 'sexually in danger' (Schmidt 2002).

In the 1960s, diverse institutions dealt with the proper preparation for the fulfilment of the female role in marriage and (social) labour, which were in gender-specific offerings, such as make-up courses and courses on child rearing. The aim of this kind of education was to compensate for female deficits in the understanding of the female role, in which girls and women should first of all become good wives and mothers (Klees, Marburger, and Schuhmacher 2000, 13ff).

Analysing class relations in the 1970s, girls become a pedagogical focus as a disadvantaged target group. The emancipation movement of women fought for places only for girls, where they could get education apart from patriarchal cultures of dominance. This was the beginning of a new gender-related pedagogy beyond traditional concepts of femininity and masculinity (Möhlke & Reiter 1985, 20; Schmidt 2002; BAG Mädchenpolitik 2006). Nevertheless it was the time of what is defined as a 'deficit approach' today: girls were always addressed as disadvantaged and perhaps it was necessary to do so in order to scandalise patriarchal power relations and reveal inequalities between men and women and girls and boys. The visibility of such inequalities and girls and women as (political) subjects was one main aim of this deficit approach (BAG Mädchenpolitik 2006). Therefore one important concept was the concept of 'partiality', in which the adult girls-worker takes the side of the girls, raising her voice on behalf of the girls in public and supporting them in critical solidarity. 'Partiality' was also meant to create 'spaces for developing a female culture' (Heimvolkshochschule Alte Molkerei Frille 1988, 27) as well as contributing to a 'feminisation of normality' (1988, 28). One of the first gender-specific projects in feminist girls-work had the aim of 'extending the concepts of gender roles by characteristics and skills of the respective opposite sex' (1988, 8). This means that the approaches of that time were focused on dealing with the girls' deficits. The girls were seen as victims of patriarchy and structurally disadvantaged.

The 1970s were also the starting point for the influential debate on gender-specific socialisation (Bilden 1991). Since that time the category 'girl' has been seen as socially produced and not deriving from anatomic or biological facts.[3] The necessity of taking a gender-differentiating perspective was integrated into what we call today 'gender-related pedagogy': Currently, no other theory and especially no other realisation of a theory has had more influence on concepts of girls-work (Voigt-Kehlenbeck 2001, 240ff). The approaches of girls-work of that time are discussed as approaches of difference, because boys and girls are *made* different in their socialisation. The dualism of femininity and masculinity is acknowledged, and it was the aim of gender-related pedagogical approaches to let the dualism of men/women exist as open categories of the same value next to each other (BAG Mädchenpolitik 2006). One can speak of a parallel existence of deficit approaches and difference approaches in girls-work in the 1980s and 1990s. Continuously taking into account a gender hierarchy in society, Glücks and Ottemeier-Glücks argue that there might be 'role deviances' of normalities but that it is still not possible to develop as a man or a woman in freedom. In 1994, Glücks and Ottemeier-Glücks developed the approach of gender-related pedagogy, which always begins by taking into account gender, and a critique on gender-related hierarchies in gender homogeneous and gender heterogeneous settings.

When in the 1980s the first educational projects for lesbians (and gays) came into being, scientists and pedagogues realised the necessity of special educational concepts for lesbian girls as well as gay boys (Hofsäss 1999). Education of lesbian girls occupies a comparatively small space in the field of feminist girls-work. But lesbian topics emerge with issues of sexualities and ways of life (*Lebensweisen*) in seminars of feminist girls-work and gender-related pedagogy. In this frame of difference-orientation, girls with handicaps and migrant girls appear as target groups for the first time (BAG Mädchenpolitik 2006).

In 2001, in the educational institution mentioned above, a concept for feminist girls-work was developed named 'What I want' (Rauw 2001). The girls' participation and interests, as well as the 'ideal-authority' ('*Vorbild-Autorität*') of the female pedagogue, was placed at the centre of the concept. The conceptualisation of 'the girl' tried to get rid of its essentialist content under the headline of 'girls-work without images of girls'. In this concept, deconstructivist pedagogy was combined with a feminist interest. As in former approaches, the female pedagogue can show advocacy according to her gender, because of which she has a congruence of experience with the girls.

3. Girls work after queer theory and deconstructivism

> We don't understand the girls. Where did they get the idea that they are treated equally? And still, we shouldn't convince them that they are not. How can they think that their future partners will care for their children the same way as they themselves? Current figures speak a different language. In this respect, girls have a bad memory, as the society has a bad memory as well. But still we have to avoid the temptation to talk them out of their future plan in a self-righteous and paternalist manner. We don't want to be precocious and spread bad vibes, even though we do it often enough. (From 'A Girls Work Manifesto', Busche and Wesemüller 2010)

It can be stated that feminist girls-work based on difference approaches is partly institutionalised today. It has found its way into girls' centres, counselling offers, educational institutions, partly into school curricula as well as into action plans, conferences and publications. Nevertheless, only a few feminist girls-work projects are financially independent. Gender pedagogy is not in the mainstream of education, even though since the discovery of the gender of boys and men some years ago, it is experiencing greater attention and undergoing a process of professionalisation.

Feminist girls-work tries to take into account not only the changed social frameworks but also the changed perception of girls: today, since the rise of the 'Alpha Girl' – the girl who can do everything, who is sexy and autonomous and surpasses all the boys – it is first of all the strengths of girls that are focused on both in public discourse and pedagogy. This puts a lot of pressure on girls, because their weaknesses and insecurities are no longer part of the debate. A girl who does not succeed might be seen as individually responsible for her failure, since the 'Alpha Girl' is the ruling image and there is no social movement emphasising gender-related structural disadvantages. Nevertheless, social inequalities still put women and girls in a disadvantaged position compared to men and boys, e.g. regarding pay gaps, sexist violence and other expressions of female inferiorities. The language current figures speak says, for example, that women spend significantly more time with child care than men. In three-quarters of all (heterosexual) families the mother undertakes 75% of care work in the first year of the child, in every second family it is even more than 95%. The average part of care done by men who receive parental subsidies is about 22% in the first year of the child, in families without such subsidies it lies at 8% (BMFSFJ 2009, 23). Of course, girls do not want to be seen as victims: they have to do the split of dealing with formal gender equality, on the one side, and actual discrimination, on the other. They learn that they are allowed to do everything but nevertheless they are confronted with persistent blockades in their process of self-fulfilment.

Such social realities are one side of the coin of current concepts of feminist girls-work. On this side topics like empowerment, sexual education and life planning are placed, but it is also necessary to create spaces for chilling out and finding relief from everyday pressure. The other side are the debates about gender and deconstruction first introduced by Judith Butler in 1991. These debates changed the view on girls as subjects once more and introduced the topic of queer.

Here, the following idea takes the place of girls' identity attributions assumed to be rooted in socialisation: by continuous repetitions of gendered bodies a kind of 'naturality' of the binary gender order is generated. Because of this naturalisation, a hegemonic idea of stability and the unchanging nature of gender dichotomy is realised. Gendered performances depend on power relations and actors. Ways of acquiring an identity are flexible, without being arbitrary. Butler points to gender as a performatively produced meaning which can evoke parodistic multiplications and a subversive playing of the culturally produced gendered meanings (1991, 61). Performativity carries the idea of change of gender identities and gender representations. Today, identities describe construction processes of affiliations or processes of identification rather than 'forms of being' ('*Seinsformen*'). Identities are effects of disciplinary, normalising and regulative techniques of power. Therefore identities are not only descriptive but excluding. Butler pleads for leaving positions of identity fixation in order to avoid the reproduction of such exclusions. She demands an open approach concerning the category gender. Even though gendered identities are subject to normative, normalising and regulating power techniques of hegemonic societies, they have to be reproduced performatively all the time and this indicates their instability.

For some years, the discussion has centred on the reflection of one's own contributions to such dominant power relations as well as the possibility to re-think one's own identity-based placement – this is also the case for pedagogues in feminist girls-work. How can feminist girls-work be a place of de-stabilising the gender order and shifting the narrow borders of dualism?

In practical concepts of current approaches of feminist girls-work, girls are seen as independent subjects, they are neither deficit beings (deficit approach) nor subjects incorporating basic and essential differences (difference approach). Therefore current feminist girls-work wants to support the realisation of interests and needs and to help stretch the scopes of action for girls. Consequently, it is necessary to understand each single girl within her particular situation of life, with all social entanglements. Ways of acquiring an identity do not only function by the category of gender. The life spheres of girls can be very diverse and categories other than gender can be much more important (cf. BAG Mädchenpolitik 2006). A complex view is needed, which captures family situations, class affiliations, skin colours, ethnic affiliations, (dis)abilities, etc., in connection with the current gender performances. Here, gender performance stands for a presentation of gender that becomes increasingly diverse and fluid as well as contradictory: beyond and between the princesses and the tomboys[4] there are so many versions of 'being a girl' that it becomes difficult to define what a girl 'really' is. Of course, in the end it is still the bodily attributes in most cases that determine the kind of social and gendered expectations a girl is confronted with in her socialisation. Usually one is used to a way of thinking that infers biological facts from seeing physical appearance and behaviour; however, these biological facts are then said to be the original reason for such physical appearances and behaviours ('She looks like a girl, therefore she might have/has a vagina, therefore she behaves like a girl'). Girls have to learn to deal with such social demands. Consequently, most of them learn to adapt themselves to a certain gender conformity, so as to behave 'somehow female'.

In western culture, gender and the body are engaged in a quite symbiotic relationship with each other. Therefore girls are somewhat forced to transmit their gender in a credible way to their social surroundings by using gestures, movements, clothes, language, figure, etc. In fact, this limits the possibilities of acting and the scopes of action that could be accessible for all genders should we get rid of the hierarchical order of boys/men and girls/women.

Girls-work that is influenced by deconstructivist thinking criticises such essentialist and biologist thinking. Because girlhood and femininity are social practices that happen in processes, one task of current feminist girls-work is to make such historical and personal processes visible and to disturb commonplace images (*Bildstörungen*). This means enriching mainstream images girls have of gender, family constellations, sexual orientations, cultures, etc., with 'deviant pictures' (see example below). It means questioning norms and everyday practices, being sensitive about heteronormativity, racism and other forms of normative regulations, and being able to intervene in a reasonable way.

4. New topics

> When girls become reality – individuals with independent actions and plans and the ability to see through the fuss, which is the ruling idea of masculinity as well their own contributions to it – then they might get problems. Then they become inconvenient, excluded, feel inappropriate. But then there is something right: They are inappropriate, because nothing is appropriate. They look through the carnivalistic making of gender. They see their own entanglements. Even though they are bound they are able to assess their scope of action, searching for appropriate means to undo their shackles and the shackles of others. At this, we stand at their sides. (From 'A Girls Work Manifesto', Busche and Wesemüller 2010)

It is not only changing theoretical frameworks but also changing perceptions of reality that leads to new concepts. In 2006, the Bundesregierung officially defined Germany as an 'Immigration society'. But concepts dealing with different ethno-natio-cultural perspectives and its effects have existed long before, e.g. intercultural pedagogy or anti-racist girls-work (Eggers 2000; Bremer Jungenbüro 2004; Arapi and Lück 2005). At the centre of anti-racist girls-work are not only categories of inequality like gender and migration, but also heterosexist and racist structures and interactions are placed at the centre of this educational work. Such categories and structures are not perceived as additive but as mutually dependent. This is where intersectionality comes in: intersectionality as a concept was coined by Black feminists in the USA, criticising white, bourgeois feminism (cf. among others Combahee River Collective 1982; Crenshaw 1997; McCall 2005). It first entered the academic sphere of German Gender Studies and Social Sciences as a new research and analysis paradigm and takes up what has been reality in feminist girls-work for a long time. Nevertheless, these practical realities are put into focus under new and even more complex premises: multiple affiliations and social positions of girls, which girls-workers have to deal with, their differences and interdependencies. The intersections of social categories and characteristics – understood as combinations, overlappings and mutual infiltrations – influence the experiences of girls_ and in a complex way structure their life conditions as well as the girls-workers working with them. The way people are affected by structural and individual disadvantages is generated by gender, ethnic and (sub)cultural affiliations, class backgrounds, physical, psychic and mental (dis)abilities, multi-language skills, skin colour, experiences with migration and settlement, generativity, mobility and other social characteristics. The majority of girls who came to Frille was disadvantaged in multiple ways. In contrast, most of the girls-workers are privileged in multiple ways, especially in the fields of education, class and background. It is very important that the girls experience honest encounters with adults who appreciate their multiple experiences even though they might not share them, adults who talk with them about their estimations and scopes of action and who appreciate them as the only actors of their lives. An intersectional analysis helps to capture complexity and to work on the deconstruction of the multiple forms of discrimination. An intersectional perspective in pedagogy stands for a practical critique concerning dichotomies, e.g. German – not German, white – not white or masculinity – femininity, hetero- and homosexuality, by revealing historical processes of construction. Hereby, girls-work has the great opportunity to treat gender as an interdependent category. To treat migration and class as interdependent categories means not to trust black-and-white-patterns anymore; instead the starting points now are complexity and diversity. In doing so, experiences with antiracist education or approaches of social justice are extremely valuable. Intersectionality does not mean inventing the wheel again. It rather means upgrading existing approaches.

For pedagogical staff this could mean being even more sensitive to multiple discriminations and able to intervene. In Frille, it was also the background for a change in the line-up of the pedagogical team. Where once mainly pedagogues from the well-educated German, white majority were working with youths who usually did not belong to those majority groups, in the end the professional staff became increasingly diverse – in sexual orientation, religion, skin colour, background, gender, etc.

5. How does it work? Queer spaces in feminist girls-work

In so far as girls work started from the existence of just this one category 'girl', it is now time to say goodbye to it conceptually. [In German language] the term 'girl' [Mädchen] is singular and plural at the same time – this is different from the term 'boy'. In order to refer to 'girls' and to make at the same time visible the non-speakable, non-definable, the contradictory and all that which points beyond the gender dichotomy, we suggest the introduction of the category 'girl_' ['Mädchen_']. With the underscore we want to express a visible plural, not in the grammatical sense of 'some things of the same kind', but in the sense of diversity, heterogeneity and incompleteness of the category. Understanding heterogeneity in this way includes connections between femininity and other societal differentiations like class, sexuality, 'race', etc. In this way we want to take into account the open category of 'girlhood' as well as showing the relationalities and interdependencies of this category in interaction with other categories that are incomplete as well. We want to push forward irritations and un-naturalisations ('Entselbstverständlichungen') and let sentences like 'Girls need...', 'Girls are...' appear less logical and natural. We want to practise and establish the thinking about girls_ as an open and multi-level category, which in the end is hard to capture and which resists its restricting categorisation in practice anyway. (From 'A Girls Work Manifesto', Busche and Wesemüller 2010)

Generally, deconstructive thinking is 'thinking against the grain'. Deconstructive pedagogy is not about 'dismissing' or 'dissolving' contexts of meanings. Rather, a multi-perspective view on pedagogical settings, situations and participants making it possible to focus on new combinations of meanings and possibilities of agency is put into the centre. Thinking against the grain involves not being satisfied with a simple understanding of meaning, to question naturalness, starting from ambiguities and contradictions as anchor points. In this sense, deconstruction is interesting for the practice of feminist girls-work and for pedagogy as such. Out of an open, deconstructivist reading of terms new possibilities emerge for reading gender hierarchies in theory and practice 'against the grain', which means destabilising violent attribution systems.

In 2009 there was an extra-curricular girls seminar in the 'Alte Molkerei Frille' with 14 girls_ aged 13 and 14 on the topics 'Future, Profession, Life Planning'. It was a three-day seminar, and the girls wanted to speak about life concepts and relationships on the second day:

> The girls demand to converse about relationships with boys. They want to learn how to flirt with boys, one girl states enthusiastically. We, the girls-workers in charge, nod bravely and think: 'Oh shit. Firstly, this is not our seminar topic, secondly, not our competence, and thirdly: where is the critique on heteronormativity?' We develop an idea: We collect forms of relationships on a big sheet of paper. 'Ok, you know heterosexuals.' Blank faces. We explain. 'What else do you know?' Many answers rain down on us: 'fake' relationships (e.g., where one only pretends to be interested in order to take advantage of the other), platonic relationships, something with animals, love relationships, homosexuals' relationships, SM relationships, kiss relationships ... We moved on. 'And what kind of genders do you know?' They answer: 'Gays.' We nod. And write it down. And: 'Transsexuals.' The board is soon filled with words thanks to the knowledge of the girls. In between we add some genders which are important to us. We explain many terms and different life styles. There are many questions. We share our thoughts, have some good laughs together and talk about different possibilities of relationships. At last

we direct the discussion towards the topic demanded by the girls: relationships with boys. A good, interesting conversation develops, in which some girls present their experiences with boys and exchange many tips for getting to know each other. In the end, seven of the fourteen girls say that they learned many knew things today. And Jessica, one of the participants, emphasizes, it was great: 'I didn't know that there is something like transgender.' Some girls express their agreement by nodding. (Report of Sonja Reimann and Ines Pohlkamp; Pohlkamp 2010, 44)

In this example, the girls_ undergo a pedagogical process enabling them to act as experts in their topic of choice. In the collection of different relationships there is no right or wrong answer, what is said has a meaning in the process. But what happens on the level of performativity? Queer and trans* genders are included in the process on the same level as all the well-known genders and acknowledged as everyday forms of gender. By naming and explaining it became possible to make genders thinkable which are located beyond concepts of men and women, without stigmatising. This is a possibility of shifting some normative borders. For doing so it was necessary for the pedagogues to deal seriously with the topics, irritations and questions of the girls. So besides spaces of normative gender dualism and mainstream ideas of relationships there are other possibilities introduced and it becomes clear in passing: it does not necessarily have to be that way, it can also be different. In such an open atmosphere it is possible to transgress the narrow borders of gender dichotomies. At the same time – and this is of great importance for a subject-oriented concept of learning and education – the wishes and interests of the girls_ to talk about relationships and experiences with boys_ were addressed as well. In conclusion, to open queer and trans* spaces means letting complexity and multiple dimensions happen, or even evoking them, instead of reifying simplicity and normativity.

The educational institution in Frille was a place where theory and practice existed in close relation; mainstreaming the critique on heteronormativity, including queer theory, deconstructivism and intersectionality, in the daily work and placing these topics as well as the experiences tied to them in public debate by publications and at conferences. Nevertheless, the time for informal political education for less-educated and potentially disadvantaged children and youth seems to be coming to an end in Germany, since many places have already closed their doors. It is not that it is no longer needed, since an increasing number of people drop out of formal education and might not enter the first labour market and probably as well not the second. But maybe in times of the internet and early adulthood, houses such as in Frille are too old-fashioned and girls-work has to think about other forms like Ladyfest and Facebook, apart from all the established local initiatives. Whatever form it maintains or will find in the future, girls-work has undergone a process of diversification. The discourses on using the underscore, pluralising genders, and thinking in intersections will last, while for children and adolescents 'girl' will also remain a major category for locating themselves. So girls-work keeps its paradoxes.

Notes

1. This paper arises from the UK Economic and Social Research Council-funded seminar series 'Young Women in Movement: Sexualities, Vulnerabilities, Needs and Norms', (ESRC RES-451-26-0715), based at Goldsmiths, University of London, 2009–2011.
2. If you want to get an impression of the house see http://www.hvhs-frille.de (in German). This article is based on different sources and debates originating in that house, e.g. Busche and Pohlkamp on girls-work (2008). I also thank Robert D. Kim for his contribution.
3. The title of a book published in 1977 and much discussed among girls-workers was *Wir werden nicht als Mädchen geboren, wir werden dazu gemacht* [We are not born as girls, we are made girls] (Scheu 1977).
4. Girls who act and/or dress like boys.

References

Arapi, Güler, and Mitja S. Lück. 2005. *Mädchenarbeit in der Migrationsgesellschaft. Eine Betrachtung aus antirassistischer Perspektive* [Girls-work in the migration society. An insight from an anti-racist perspective]. Mädchentreff Bielefeld. http://www.maedchentreffbielefeld.de/download/girlsactbuchkomplett.pdf.

BAG Mädchenpolitik e.V. 2006. *Feminstische Mädchenarbeit und Mädchenpolitik im Kontext aktueller Theorie- und Politikdiskurse* [Feminist girls work and politics in the context of current theoretical and political discourses]. Bundesarbeitsgemeinschaft Mädchenpolitik. http://www.maedchenpolitik.de/download/info6_bag2006.pdf.

Bilden, H. 1991. Geschlechtsspezifische Sozialisation [Gender-specific socialisation]. In *Neues Handbuch zur Sozialisationsforschung* [New handbook on socialisation research], ed. K. Hurrelmann and D. Ulich, 281–303. Weinheim and Basel: Beltz Verlag.

BMFSFJ [Federal Ministry for Family Affairs, Senior Citizens, Women and Youth]. 2009. *Evaluationsbericht Bundeselterngeld- und Elternzeitgesetz 2009* [Evaluation report on legislation concerning federal parental subsidies and parental leave]. Berlin: Bundesministerium für Familie, Senioren, Frauen und Jugend.

Bremer Jungenbüro. 2004. *Respect – antirassistische Mädchen- und Jungenarbeit* [Respect – anti-racist girls- and boys-work]. http://www.bremerjungenbuero.de/respect.html.

Busche, Mart. 2010. It's a men's world? Jungen_arbeit aus nichtmännlicher Perspektive. [Boys-work from a non-male perspective]. In *Feministische Mädchenarbeit weiterdenken. Zur Aktualität einer bildungspolitischen Praxis* [Thinking ahead feminist girls work: Updating an educational-political practice], ed. M. Busche, L. Maikowsky, E. Wesemüller, and I. Pohlkamp, 201–21. Bielefeld: transcript Verlag.

Busche, Mart, and Ines Pohlkamp. 2008. Mädchenarbeit [Girls-work]. *Fortbildungsmodul im bundesweiten Verbundprojekt 'Lernen für den GanzTag'*. http://www.ganztag-blk.de/ganztags-box/cms/upload/gender/pdf/Anlage-Mdchenarbeit-Gender-Modul.pdf.

Busche, Mart, and Ellen Wesemüller. 2010. Mit Widersprüchen für neue Wirklichkeiten. Ein Manifest für Mädchen_arbeit [With contradictions towards new realities. A manifesto for girls work]. In *Feministische Mädchenarbeit weiterdenken. Zur Aktualität einer bildungspolitischen Praxis* [Thinking ahead feminist girls work: Updating an educational-political practice], ed. M. Busche, L. Maikowsky, E. Wesemüller, and I. Pohlkamp, 323–40. Bielefeld: transcript Verlag.

Butler, Judith. 1991. *Das Unbehagen der Geschlechter* [Gender trouble]. Frankfurt/Main: Suhrkamp.

Collective, Combahee River. 1982. A Black feminist statement. In *All the women are white, all the blacks are men, but some of us are brave: Black women's studies*, ed. G.T. Hull, P.B. Scott, and B. Smith, 13–22. New York: Feminist Press.

Crenshaw, Kimberlé. 1997. *Mapping the margins. Intersectionality and identity politics. Learning from violence against women of color.* Washington Coalition of Sexual Assault Programs. http://www.wcsap.org/Events/Workshop07/mapping-margins.pdf.

Eggers, Maisha M.R. 2000. *Antirassistische Mädchenarbeit – Sensibilisierungsarbeit bezogen auf Rassismus mit Mädchen und jungen Frauen* [Anti-racist girls-work – Awareness raising on racism with girls and young women]. Kiel: Autonomes Mädchenhaus Kiel.

Faulstich-Wieland, Hannelore. 1997. Mädchen und Koedukation [Girls and coeducation]. Paper presented at Fern-Universität, Gesamthochschule in Hagen, February 17. http://www.vings.de/kurse/wissensnetz/frauen/pdf/faulstich.pdf.

Glücks, Elisabeth, and Franz-Gerd Ottemeier-Glücks. 1994. *Geschlechtsbezogene Pädagogik – Ein Bildungskonzept zur Qualifizierung koedukativer Praxis durch parteiliche Mädchenarbeit und antisexistische Jungenarbeit* [Gender-related pedagogy – An educational concept for qualifying coeducative practice by partial girls-work and anti-sexist boys-work]. Münster: Votum Verlag.

Heimvolkshochschule Alte Molkerei Frille. 1988. *Parteiliche Mädchenarbeit und antisexistische Jungenarbeit* [Partial girls-work and anti-sexist boys-work]. Frille: Selbstverlag.

Hofsäss, Thomas. 1999. *Jugendhilfe und gleichgeschlechtliche Orientierung* [Youth welfare and same-sex orientation]. Berlin: VWB-Verlag.

Klees, Renate, Helga Marburger, and Michaela Schuhmacher. 2000. *Mädchenarbeit. Praxishandbuch für die Jugendarbeit* [Girls-work. Practice handbook for youth work]. Teil 1. Weinheim and München: Juventa.

Lange, Helene. 1983. *Die Frauenbewegung in ihren modernen Problemen* [The Womens' movement in its modern problems]. Münster: Tende Verlag.

McCall, Leslie. 2005. The complexity of intersectionality. *Signs* 30: 1771–802.

Möhlke, Gabriele, and Gabi Reiter. 1985. *Feministische Mädchenarbeit – Gegen den Strom* [Feminist girls work – Against the tide]. Münster: Votum.

Pohlkamp, Ines 2010. TransRäume! Mehr Platz für geschlechtliche Nonkonformität [TransSpaces! Make room for gendered non-conformitivity]. In *Feministische Mädchenarbeit weiterdenken. Zur Aktualität einer bildungspolitischen Praxis* [Thinking ahead feminist girls work: Updating an educational-political practice], ed. M. Busche, L. Maikowsky, E. Wesemüller, and I. Pohlkamp, 37–58. Bielefeld: transcript Verlag.

Rauw, Regina. 2001. 'Was ich will!' ['What I want!'] In *Perspektiven der Mädchenarbeit: Partizipation, Vielfalt, Feminismus* [Perspectives of girls-work: Participation, diversity, feminism], ed. R. Regina and I. Reinert, 29–43. Opladen: Leske & Budrich.

Scheu, Ursula. 1977. *Wir werden nicht als Mädchen geboren, wir werden dazu gemacht* [We are not born as girls, we are made girls]. Frankfurt: Fischer.
Schmidt, Andrea. 2002. *Balanceakt Mädchenarbeit. Beiträge zu dekonstruktiver Theorie und Praxis* [Balancing act girls-work. Contributions to a deconstructivist theory and practice]. Frankfurt: IKO Verlag für interkulturelle Kommunikation – edition Hipparchia.
Voigt-Kehlenbeck, Corinna. 2001. ...und was heißt das für die Praxis? Über den Übergang von einer geschlechterdifferenzierenden zu einer geschlechterreflektierenden Pädagogik [...and what does that mean for the practice? About the transition from a gender-differentiating to a gender-reflective pedagogy]. In *Dekonstruktive Pädagogik. Erziehungswissenschaftliche Debatten unter poststrukturalistischen Perspektiven* [Deconstructivist pedagogy: Scientific-pedagogical debates under post-structuralist perspectives], ed. B. Fritzsche, 237–54. Opladen: Leske und Budrich.

'Too pretty to do math!' Young women in movement and pedagogical challenges[1]

Ulrike Graff

Educational Science, University of Bielefeld, Bielefeld, Germany

> The article points out some pedagogical challenges in supporting girls and young women in their emancipatory movements today. It spotlights a specific section in gender pedagogy by focusing on the aim of self-determination (rather than achievement) in the field of social-pedagogy and it refers to the concept of 'girls work' in Germany. A critical discussion of new images of 'top girls' leads to a first challenge: the necessity of acting in a self-reflective and sensitive way with these images in the field of pedagogy. The boys' turn in the current gender debate accuses pedagogy of being too girl-friendly. The challenge in this generalising discussion is to shift the perspective away from the boys and girls as being deficient *qua* sex towards pedagogy in general. Regarding the organisational framework this could mean rethinking single- and mixed-sex settings and their impact on gender transgressions. According to this, the concept of girls work is a special point of consideration in the article. It presents some of the results of research on girls' understandings of their self-determination within feminist youth work. It shows how girls and young women value a 'girls-only' place.

Introduction

When I talk about 'young women in movement', I am taking a snapshot which is necessarily open ended. The debate about the deconstruction of gender has sharpened the awareness of the fact that a list of 'young women are…' is, and must be, infinite and it criticises a general tendency of merely swapping new images for old ones. As Barbara Dribbusch said in the Berlin *die tageszeitung* in October 2007, it is not '…about new role models,[2] but about access to the joy of living, the taste of freedom'.

In this article, I will discuss ways in which pedagogy can open pathways towards this 'taste of freedom' for girls and young women. It will put the spotlight on a specific section in gender pedagogy by focusing on self-determination rather than achievement, by looking at social-pedagogy rather than education in school and by referring to the concept of girls work in Germany. From a pedagogical point of view, self-determination is perceived as a human ability which has to be supported. Furthermore, it is conceptualised inconsistently, considering that it is neither the accomplishment of the autonomous subject nor 'made' by education (Koller 2001). 'Girls work', like 'youth work', is a pedagogical concept, which looks at girls from a perspective that reflects gender (Bitzan and Daigler 2001; Cullen 2009).

First, I will focus on the girls themselves: in particular, on the new image of strong girls, which is ideological and attractive at the same time, so that pedagogy is challenged to deal with this shift of gender critically and sensitively. What gives these images the quality of real empowerment? Where are they only used for creating a cliché of girls being 'alpha-girls' – always tough and successful? Following this, I will present some of the results of my research on girls' understandings of their self-determination within feminist youth work – in the 'Girls' Club Bielefeld'. It will show how girls and young women value a 'girls-only' place.

A third part deals with pedagogy in general by rethinking single- and mixed-sex settings and their impact on gender transgressions.

In her article 'Out of the Ruins: Feminist Pedagogy in Recovery', Gaby Weiner pointed out that it is necessary to 'be explicit about *the form of feminism* we aspire to, ... whether as linked to, or separate from one or more feminist waves' (2009, 90, emphasis in the original). In line with this, my work has been inspired by second-wave feminism. Accordingly, I was co-founder of a youth club for girls in 1985 and carried out research on it after 10 years of practical work. This scientific work has linked me to third-wave deconstructive feminism with its critique on speaking of differences in a naive way and on creating new determinative identity policies when doing so.

Young women today

First, I want to take a look at girls and young women themselves. We can find out more about their lives by looking at the ways in which they act. Last year I saw a girl about 13 years old wearing a t-shirt which read: 'Too pretty to do math!' I am introducing this as a small piece of youth cultural study, because it may sharpen one's attitudes towards girls and young women of today. The slogan irritated me very much and my first thought was: 'What a pity – what a self-restriction!' My second thought said: 'Beware of how you judge this girl – be honest, you would rather read "I am pretty *and* I love math!"' This was interesting only for my self-reflection, but what the slogan meant to the girl I could not really tell. Perhaps it could have simply meant that she liked the style of the shirt and did not bother about the words at all, so such a thing should not be rated too highly. But for a self-reflexive access to girls as actresses in the process of doing gender (West and Zimmerman 1987), it may be interesting to imagine different scenarios behind such a statement:

- Perhaps she wanted to say: 'I know, nowadays maths is a must for girls, but I don't care about this, I'm doing my own thing, I'm strong!'
- Or, on the contrary, she was angry with her maths teacher, who did not take her seriously. Then it could have had the message: 'I am showing you old stereotypes: it's being beautiful that is still more important for girls than being good at maths!'
- It may just as well be that she really hated mathematics and she found this shirt in her sister's closet.
- Or she took part in a girls work project which encouraged her in this self-expression.

All of these and even more meanings could be the reason for the choice of the shirt – we do not know which the exact one was and therefore sensitivity and trying to be aware about one's own gender assumptions are to me the central aspects for a feminist pedagogical attitude.

What does the example show about being a female adolescent today, when it is read as a cultural practice? First: images of girls are changing, they are no longer fixed and have become more complex. Girls experience ambivalent expectations: on the one hand, girls and young women have to present themselves as strong and self-confident in public. On the other hand, they know that being nice and caring is still very important. Pedagogy is challenged to give girls (and boys) support for coping with the multiplicity of gender which is attractive and difficult to manage at the same time. Girls (and boys) need a collective space for reflecting on their societal experiences (Eggers 2010), and they need pedagogical relationships in which they are taken seriously and supported in the process of becoming adults.

As a first resumé of the subject 'girls today' I would say:

- The slogan 'too pretty to do math' reflects the ambivalence of changed gendered images of girls and young women – it is just as open for old-fashioned as for deconstructive interpretations.
- According to youth sociological framing, the t-shirt has become a carrier of advertisements for gender identities of girls and boys. Therefore, it may be interesting to take it into account when studying gender.
- In pedagogical practice, it is an excellent stimulus for discussion.
- To explore this phenomenon further theoretically: it may be seen as an example of Judith Butler's (1990) theory, in which parody and satire are recognised methods of de-constructing gender.

The example shows that gender stereotypes are changing and girls are re/acting very differently – and, most importantly – being confronted with their 'doing girl' we are challenged to reflect on the expectations, judgements and pictures we have in our heads.

Disturbing effects of the 'strong girl' ideology

However, I do not want to stop with the conclusion that 'anything goes' for girls today. I think that among the varieties of girls' images, the one of 'girls are strong' has become the dominant one. In the past, girls first of all had to be good and well-behaved. Today, girls are self-confident, girls can do everything – they are Alpha-Girls or, according to Angela McRobbie, 'Top Girls' (2008). This is both true and false. The thing that is true and attractive is the expansion of the gender image of girls by linking femininity and power. The false and ideological part is that experiences of failing, of not being powerful and of discrimination have to be covered up. In this context, Maria Bitzan speaks of 'concealment' ('*Verdeckungszusammenhang*') (Bitzan and Daigler 2001). In the following passage, I would like to introduce two disturbing examples.

First: a page with jokes in the very popular German youth magazine *BRAVO GIRL* under the headline 'These are jokes boys laugh about'. In November 2007, *BRAVO GIRL* published jokes like this one: A man gives his wife a gas mask when he is going to have sex with her, because then she looks better, and wriggles nicely when she runs out of air. Because of this joke, the women's advice-centre in Düsseldorf filed a complaint to the German Print Media Council (Deutscher Presserat). The Council refused the complaint with the argument that 'The young generation of women and girls is much more emancipated and tough towards gender roles than the generation before'.

Beate Vinke, administrator of the Landesarbeitsgemeinschaft Mädchenarbeit in NRW (a non-governmental organisation in the field of pedagogy, education and social work with girls and young women), commented:

> We are concerned that the good news about the increasing self-confidence of girls and legal successes in Gender Mainstreaming are used to trivialise violence against girls and women. In the name of emancipation girls are pushed into an image of being 'Alpha', always cool and strong. This stereotype neglects the real experience of girls in their great diversity. And real experiences are also offence and harassment. That has the effect that girls often think it's their fault when they suffer violence. Therefore, a public debate is necessary about respect between girls, boys, women and men. (Landesarbeitsgemeinschaft Mädchenarbeit NRW 2008)

Against this background, research on how girls and boys feel about jokes like the one above – behind a facade of being cool and insensitive – would be very interesting.

The second example deals with young women's behaviour in reporting cases of rape to the police. Chief superintendent Heike Lütgert (2010) from the Bielefeld police department recognised that, in the current statistics of girls and young women's behaviour in reporting rape, the number of unknown offenders has increased towards the rate of the 1950s, when being acquainted with the offender meant 'your own fault'. She wanted to understand this phenomenon and thus studied the documents. Lütgert found out that many of the girls actually knew the offender, but they would rather deny this than admit to themselves and to others that they, as strong girls, had not been able to prevent a boy, whom they knew, from offending them.

These two examples are very alarming, especially because the representations of girls work have worked on the image of the power girl. In her article 'What is a Girl?', Regina Rauw (2007) points out that the girls depicted on feminist flyers and websites often look tough, posing with their hands on their hips. Therefore, it is necessary to check the publicity of girls work regarding this tendency. When the mainstream focuses only on fit and brave images, it becomes important to show girls' cautious, delicate or freaky sides. It is difficult to talk about girls without serving old or new stereotypes. As Carol Hagemann-White (1993) says, it is *im*possible *not* to construct. But it is possible to be aware of the dilemma of always being involved in the construction of femininity and to try working with images and clichés in a self-reflective way (Plößer 2005).

The concept of girls work

Feminist pedagogy wants to provide more space for self-determination (Graff 2011) for women and girls. With this fundamental aim it is linked, on the one hand, to the humanistic term 'Bildung' classically represented by Humboldt (1785–1795/2007), which was reformulated by the critical emancipatory pedagogy (Gamm 1979). On the other hand, it differs from these concepts in the organisation regarding sex. Feminist pedagogy argues that self-determination of girls is hindered in co-education and therefore a single-sex setting is an important element in girls work (Donning 1997).

In West Germany, girls work was developed within the 'second-wave feminism' (Weiner 2009), as part of the criticism of proclaimed realisation of gender equality. An important improvement was the 'autonomous' girls work in single-sex groups and projects (McRobbie and Savier 1982). Its goal was to offer girls space for self-determination that could go beyond common gender-stereotypes. It is aimed at girls in their cultural, ethnic, physical, sexual diversity and therefore has developed intersectional concepts: girls work on the topics of migration, antiracism, disability and homosexuality (Busche et al. 2010). It does not originate from a biological difference between boys and girls but from critical pedagogy, which was developed further in the *Pedagogy of the Oppressed* (Freire 1972) with its concept of consciousness raising and learning in groups which are affected by similar discrimination and the *Pedagogy of Diversity* (Prengel 1993), where (gender) difference is conceptualised as egalitarian difference. Prengel points out that in a democratic perspective difference and equality have to be thought of as interdependent, because equality without difference would lead to assimilation and difference without equality would lead to hierarchy.

Girls work has to face the paradox that naming difference has the effect of (re)producing and transforming it at the same time, which Mecheril and Plößer describe in the following way:

> Therefore, referring to the relation of difference and pedagogy is not a question of 'difference: yes or no' but a matter of experience-based reflection on how differences can be named pedagogically so that, in consequence, less power over others is necessary.[3] (2009, 206)

Based on this theory, feminist girls work uses single-sex groups. Emancipating effects can lie in the fact that gender-referred structures of dominance, that rather reproduce the relationship between girls and boys in co-educative settings, are suspended in a single-sex context (Hannover 1997; Brinkmann 2006; Metz-Göckel 2010; for a critical perspective, see, e.g., Paechter 2011). This does not mean that these contexts are free of hierarchies. But they can have the character of 'paradoxical intervention' (Teubner 1997, quoted in Metz-Göckel 1999, 136) if not combined with essentialist and normalising ideas of femininity and masculinity. Sex is the criteria for group formation and then can fade from the spotlight as a direct influencing variable for group processes. The sociologist Stefan Hirschauer speaks of the 'sexual relaxation of the (single-sex) situation itself' (Hirschauer 1994, quoted in Kessels 2002, 228). This has the effect that diversity within groups becomes visible. It can be a field of gender transgressions because all positions and tasks have to be taken over by one sex, even those which are often distributed or chosen gender-specifically in mixed groups. Girls, as well as boys, can develop their preferences and try new things, because here adolescents are more likely to dare to do atypical things (Younger and Warrington 2006) and because there is greater diversity within the sexes than between them (Hagemann-White 2006).

Girls' Club Bielefeld – girls' views on their self-determination

The Girls' Club Bielefeld tries to support girls' self-determination. Therefore, it is interesting to take a closer look at girls' experiences in and feedback on this feminist pedagogical context. In the following section, I will present some results of my qualitative research on this institution, in which I evaluated the pedagogical aim 'support of processes of self-determination for girls' (Graff 2004). Since 1985 the Mädchentreff (Girls' Club) has been a youth centre for girls which offers leisure activities, education and advice. Until 1990 it was visited by girls and young women up to the age of 25. The age might be surprising, but those 'older' young women appreciated the 'Girls' Club' because they did not identify with their own concepts of being a woman. Not feeling 'ready', they appreciated the Girls' Club as a place where they allowed themselves to play, experiment and to question their own femininities. The girls vary in their ethnicity, age, class, sexual orientations and abilities. The rooms at the Girls' Club provide various opportunities: there are plenty of rooms (200 m^2 in a former bakery with a café, kitchen, work out or lounging room, a smaller room that is used for support in school work, an internet café, a wood- and metal workshop, a basement disco for dancing and WenDo, and a bathroom) in which different groups of girls can get together, listen to *their* kind of music, dance together, talk, or play, all on a voluntary basis. The activities are a mixture of open meeting place, regular groups and projects.

The evaluation was designed in the methodological context of qualitative social research as an empirical analysis of the pedagogy in the Girls' Club on two levels: on the level of pedagogical situations and on the level of girls who visited the Girls' Club.

(1) *The level of pedagogical situations* was recorded in 10 short stories written by the five instructors, who belonged to the team. The narrative impulse for writing down a memory concerning their work was: 'What was a really good situation with girls?' And: 'What was a situation that went wrong?' Thus, all five instructors wrote two texts, each in more or less 30 minutes time. This material shows subjective professional views on everyday conditions, dynamics of relationships and practices.

(2) *The level of the girls* was recorded in interviews. I asked 13 girls about their time in the Girls' Club, their first visit, what they were doing there, what they like and what they dislike. The interviews were conducted individually following the concept of 'The problem-focused interview' (*Das problemzentrierte Interview*) (Witzel 2000), which is a guideline for research contexts where the participants know each other.

In a first heuristic procedure, I identified traces and phenomena of self-determination in the entire data. According to the subject of the article, my focus is on the girls' perspectives on the Girls' Club. I will now present some examples from the interviews. The girls talk about the Girls' Club as a 'girls-only' place.

'They accept us as we are!'

A key result of the interviews is the repeated statement from the girls that at the Girls' Club they feel accepted the way they are. This acceptance goes beyond their experience in school or in their leisure time. They feel they are taken seriously with regard to their needs for fun and relaxation as well as with regard to their interests and problems. Sandra and Tanja are friends, both are 15 years old, German, they live in the same neighbourhood and go to a secondary school.

> I was at school, had stress at home. That's actually why I came here all the time, so that I didn't have to see my father. I always felt totally good here. I hardly had arrived home, everything was totally stupid. So then I mostly came here, to at least have some fun, so I could have a good time. (Sandra, 308–13; Graff 2004, 162)

> …I had no other friends. I actually did have others, but they didn't really want to have anything to do with me, because the class, well I always felt pretty left out there. Like here it was very different. I could say anything. Here one was accepted, not like in other places. I felt very empty when I was somewhere else. And here one was taken seriously. Here it was easy, the atmosphere was super, everyone got along super. It was a place where one could always go, except for the weekend. That gave one strength. One knew one could go there and one would probably also be understood, there they knew what was going on, could maybe also give advice, maybe it would then be better and so. (Tanja, 423–36; Graff 2004, 163)

At the same time it is really important for the young women that they are not judged for being a 'proper' girl at the Girls' Club. They do not have to compete with boys in order to receive recognition for their needs. Yasemin, a 17-year-old Kurdish girl, who goes to a secondary school, put it this way:

> …for example, girls who have no one around them who cares. Like Bärbel, she was also like that, she didn't stand up for herself. But she was all there at Girls' Club, she committed herself and was the centre of attention. And for the people around her she was not there … If boys had also come here, then I think she would have come once in a while, but she wouldn't have received the attention she got. And that was important for the girls. (Yasemin, 859–68, Graff 2004, 163)

The girls state they have the feeling that the advisers are really there for them. That means they care for the girls' interests regarding others, in school or at home. The girls feel that they have rights and that the advisers are willing to defend their rights. The girls are empowered to be aware of and to stand up for their rights. In the interviews, many girls talk about help they got from the advisers when they were really in trouble. In this context, they make it very clear that it is not at all natural for girls to have people on their side during a crisis. In a culture in which it is still not acceptable for girls to experiment as much, or make as many mistakes, as boys can, they find it extraordinary to get help in defending their interests, managing their mistakes and realising their plans.

On a class trip Yasemin beat another girl up so badly that she needed to go into hospital. Her punishment was to spend several weekends in prison. Because of the support and guidance of an adviser, she overcame being locked up, she did not despair and even had the opportunity to reflect upon her actions.

> I needed to go into detention on the weekends and she helped me very much at the time. I'll never forget that either ... I think to myself, look, you're such a normal person, and that you, with such a mistake, can fall so far. For me it was a really major experience, how one can, for example, look, I don't know what can happen to me tomorrow, I can also immediately get stuck in such a deep hole, that I end on the street. That was such a deep hole for me. And for me it was a reason, all these thoughts, look, what happens there, and when I then think, I would have, if I hadn't had Rebecca, I wouldn't have been able to go so deep. These threats, suicide attempts and such, how could you do something like that?' (Yasemin, 130–4 and 215–23; Graff 2004, 164)

Nowadays, advocatory and practical help for girls seem to be of increasing importance. The effects of neoliberal policies make it not only necessary for feminist pedagogy to ask:

> How can girls' conflicts/problems or attention needs be recognised, when they are supposed to hide these to reflect the image: I have no problems, I am not disadvantaged, I am competent?[4] (Bitzan and Daigler 2001, 209)

'Yeah, then I knew exactly what I did not want'

Bärbel is an unemployed 23-year-old trained sales person who does not like her profession at all. She still lives with her parents, who try to push her into jobs. She seeks support in the Girls' Club to cope with this situation.

> B.: ...and then they offered me another one of those jobs which I don't want to do.
>
> U.: What was that again?
>
> B.: My father also, and you, once wrote down everything, I remember that [giggling]. They had a chambermaid (job) ... Chambermaid, kitchen help.
>
> U.: I once wrote all that down?
>
> B.: Yes, you wrote it all down then.
>
> U.: Why? Do you still know why?
>
> B.: Yeah, because I always talked about that, always said stuff like that. You said: the jobs that Bärbel doesn't like. Wrote them down on paper. [laughs]
>
> U.: And what did I do with the paper?

B.: I don't know anymore either. Somehow you once hung it up on the pin board. But I don't remember anymore.

U.: How was that for you, when you had a list like that: Jobs that Bärbel doesn't like?

B.: Yeah, then I knew exactly what I didn't want. That was the sort of thing they always found in the newspaper. (Graff 2004, 180)

Remembering the events surrounding the list of 'Jobs that Bärbel doesn't like' describes an interaction between adviser and girl where the problem was not directly solved, but simply acknowledged. Bärbel's comments show how this recognition lightens her burden. She is able to laugh about how they wrote down and publicised (on the notice board in the Girls' Club) the list of insultingly inadequate jobs she was offered. It allows her to distance herself from it. She sees herself and her own views presented specifically and individually. Although her situation seems very bleak and without hope, nowhere do we see an indication that she expects the adviser to solve her problem. She is looking for someone who cares, for attention and acceptance.

It becomes clear that the contact with the adviser gives Bärbel the recognition she needs to stabilise her situation. She wants to stand firm despite the fact that she is being attacked from all sides and is under pressure to take on inadequate jobs. Contacts, working modes and room for reflection at the Girls' Club support Bärbel's existing potential for self-determination without creating a paradox by wanting to establish it. This specific case shows an exemplary experience of a girl in a pedagogical relationship. It shows the high value of not being pushed into solving problems, which goes in accordance with the requests of the girls' understanding of self-determination. The adviser is asked to acknowledge a difficult situation, while at the same time withstanding the impulse to intervene and instead just staying in the background.

Current pedagogical challenges

The results of the research on young women's perspectives on a girls-only youth club provide evidence that a single-sex concept which is grounded in feminist pedagogy can offer girls and young women specific support, empowerment and fun. Thus, it should be the standard to have such institutions as a part of youth work and education. These kinds of girls' clubs are rare in Germany. Here the alpha-girl discourse ironically produces a backlash for establishing such work: not only are these effects not valued as positive and perceived as superfluous and unnecessary, moreover, they are thought to be disadvantageous for boys. This reasoning formulates a pedagogically nonsensical rivalry between girls and boys (Eggers 2010). In 2009, the youth-curatorship of the German Federation clarified abbreviations in the current gender-discourse on the basis of a statement themed 'Clever girls – stupid boys?' It said that the debate is founded on essentialist concepts of girls and boys which reproduce traditional stereotypes. Susann Fegter (2012) researched the public discourse of the 'crisis of the boys' and her analysis shows that here rather hegemonic gender-images are conveyed. The discourse works with the powerful subtext of bad parenthood and the neglect of boys by pedagogy.

Nevertheless, I think there is a positive point in the 'boys' turn' because the rhetoric shows it is somehow acknowledged that a gender-sensitive education can be successful and might be helpful for boys as well. The argumentation can be responded to by pointing out that a gender-related view on girls with a non-essentialist emancipatory concern has indeed influenced them positively. The same would be true for all sexes.

However, the topic of the rivalry between girls and boys about specific pedagogical considerations also hints at the fact that girls work in Germany is often framed as 'girl support' and this has led to an impasse. In youth work as well as in school, the term is very common where single-sex groups, projects and institutions are concerned. Why is the label 'girl support' unhelpful? It constructs girls as the ones who have the problems and need help and it turns away from a pedagogy which should be responsible for deconstructing gender stereotypes. This kind of approach implies that girls are deficient and require special promotion. The quotation from the data at the start of the next section illustrates how this image of girls work affects peer talk.

External opinions make the decision to attend the Girls' Club a harder one to make

In the interviews, several girls mention that they have to repeatedly explain why they join the Girls' Club. Lilly, for example (16 years old, German, who goes to a laboratory school), gives a detailed description of the phenomenon:

> I experienced that, in my sports club, when I was telling about: 'yes in my youth centre', so I always say: youth club or youth centre, because I experienced that several times, that they look at me sideways, when I say: 'Girls' Club, it's girls only'. And then some of them wanted to know where it is and how it is named, the youth club. And then I told a girl: yes, it's called 'Girls' Club', there are only girls, there are no boys and so (like that?). Then they were looking at me and asked: isn't that boring? And another boy, ... then also was staring at me and also asked: if there are only girls, isn't that boring or are they all queer? After that I had to smirk and thought by myself: o.k. then ... Then I repeated: yes there are only girls – girls only. And then he wanted to know: what are you doing there the whole day long? As if he wanted to know, 'what can one do alone as a girl, I mean if the boys are not there? That is totally boring – and anyways'. Don't know, I told him: we

drink tea, we jabber, we chat, now and then we go in for something. I told him such things about that. Yes and then he didn't say any more on that. Just said: 'aha'. I didn't experience that only once but often. (Lilly, 599–627; Graff 2004, 166)

A Girls' Club forces one to make a statement about one's gender because the category 'girl' is explicit. Places for girls only are seen as missing something. The construed deficit being for one the situation itself; apparently boys are missing. There is a kind of *black box*. 'What do girls do without boys?' Sociability, fun, interesting and relevant contacts are thought of as things for mixed genders, i.e. boys need to be present for these things. Boys, however, are not seen as 'alone'. Social situations with boys are seen as interesting, exciting, important and correctly attended. Accordingly, social situations with girls are seen as boring, incomplete, temporary, unimportant and not correct. According to the reference to the Girls' Club as a place for lesbians, the questions of the boy may be seen as an effect of the heterosexual matrix which structures current culture (Butler 1990). It is difficult for girls to make a stand against the predominant image of girls that are only strong and accepted, when they have something to do with boys. Lilly shows her strategy for dealing with that. It depends on the level of interest she takes in her conversation partner whether she explains herself and the Girls' Club or not. Depending on whom she is talking with, she decides whether she will show the absurdity of the question or whether she will talk about the Girls' Club as a youth club immediately because she expects she will have to spend too much pointless effort on explanations.

The Girls' Club as a part of girls work is based on feminist criticism of existing relationships between the sexes. When girls go to a girls' club they must come to terms with the cultural status of girls in society. Why should there be a club for girls in a society that assumes that equality exists and that single-sex facilities are old-fashioned? A girls' club is a facility that criticises culture and aims to grant girls their own culture, in the face of a youth culture dominated by boys. A girls' club maintains that this is the girls' right. It does not say that they are in need of this. Against this background, girls can reflect on their own image and when they go to a girls' club, they are forced to make a statement. This makes the step they have to take in order to go to a girls' club very big. On the other hand, once they have taken this step, they have gained more self-determination in the dominant culture of mixed-sexes.

Within the framework of open youth work, a girls' club provides room for girls without the gender-specific limits and attributions that come with direct interaction with boys. Due to the essential task and concept of youth work, girls can come and go as *they* wish, without *having to* and without *having to have problems*. One could join Michael Walzer (1992) in saying that a girls' club provides a 'sanctum of justice' within a 'pedagogy of diversity' (Prengel 1993), parallel to and within a youth culture dominated by boys. It is not just like the girl's room at home but is a public place/space for girls' culture. Therefore, one might say it represents the symbolical realm (Muraro 1989) as a positive space for girls' socialising, self-determination and self-will, far removed from pedagogical deficit constructions. Girls form and live their own culture (Tillmann 2008). The equal recognition and care of different cultures should be allowed expression in places of their own.

Co- versus single-sex pedagogy?
Single-sex pedagogy can have emancipatory potential for girls and for boys (Kunert-Zier 2005; Cremers 2011; Wentzel 2011). But the single-sex approach is often misunderstood: 'Just for girls or just for boys, that's what we've already had in former times due to conservative sex roles!' And in the German debate, the abolishment of co-education is often feared, when single-sex pedagogy comes into consideration (Faulstich-Wieland and Horstkemper 1995; Donning 1997). Most of the time, the issue is discussed as a matter of 'either–or' and not as a matter of 'as well as'. To understand this, a short glance at the history of education is helpful. Nowadays, 'co-education' is taken for granted and is often equated with pedagogy. Until about a hundred years ago, this term did not exist at all because pedagogy was, as higher education, of course single-sex (Kleinau 2004). The significance of this should be underscored here: there has been immense progress since the century-old conservative-based separation between the sexes. However, the general euphoria regarding this change in educational policy was so great that it took a long time before anyone checked to see whether it had accomplished its aims. Because of the current 'boys' turn' there may be the chance to go a step further and separate the understanding of pedagogy in general from its different possibilities in organisational frameworks, according to the sexes: there is pedagogy and it exists co-educationally and single-sex; and beyond that in diverse groups or (sub) cultures differentiated as has been shown in transgender, gay or lesbian pedagogical projects (Czollek, Perko, and Weinbach 2009).

One may argue that pedagogical practice already works like that. In Germany, we have the term 'Reflexive Co-education'[5] of Hannelore Faulstich-Wieland (1994) who provides separation by sex as an addition. While this is true, it is especially this concept that manifests the problem. Its language updates co-education as the general principle and positions single-sex settings as an exception to the rule. These exist as 'girl support', which, as pointed out before, always sounds as though girls are a problem group. Gender-specific opportunities then rank at best as special opportunities and at worst as less-than-ideal solutions. At the same time, and in contradiction to this, a very problematic phenomenon exists, which promotes single-sex education as a panacea for difficulties between boys and girls at school (Younger 2012; Budde, Scholand, and Faulstich-Wieland 2008). It is a challenge to conceptualise a pedagogy for girls with its implicit dramatisation of difference in order to deconstruct constraints of gender stereotypes. It has to be thought of paradoxically as essential to a strategy to develop perspectives on the production and effects of differences.

> To take up the issue of difference is to recognize that the concept cannot be analyzed unproblematically. In effect, the concept has to be used to resist those aspects of its ideological legacy used in the service of exploitation and subordination as well as to develop a critical reference for engaging the limits and strength of difference as a central aspect of a critical theory of education. (Giroux, 1992, 206, quoted in Tervooren 2001, 204 et seq.)

If feminist girls work is critical towards its own norms (Fegter, Geipel, and Horstbrink 2010), it may have a lot to offer for young women (Rauw and Reinert 2001). Bearing this in mind: What could be the specific potential of mixed- and single-sex groupings? For social pedagogy and youth work, it would also be helpful to note what Diana Leonard suggests for education: '…teachers should be enabled to explore with their pupils, in a mixture of single- and mixed-sex situations, the forms of gender itself…' (2009, 200). Perhaps this would transform the debate in which the approaches are often labelled categorically either as conservative or progressive.

Notes
1. This paper arises from the UK Economic and Social Research Council-funded seminar series 'Young Women in Movement: Sexualities, Vulnerabilities, Needs and Norms', (ESRC RES-451-26-0715), based at Goldsmiths, University of London, 2009–2011.
2. In this quote taken from a newspaper, the term is not accurately based on Parsons – but rather used as a chiffre for the contingency of gender; in the article, I refer to gender as a social construction in accordance with West and Zimmerman (1987).
3. Insofern geht es mit Bezug auf das Verhältnis von Differenz und Pädagogik nicht um die Frage , Differenz: ja oder nein', sondern um eine erfahrungsbezogene Reflexion darauf, wie Differenzen pädagogisch so thematisiert werden, dass als Konsequenz weniger Macht über andere erforderlich ist.
4. Wie also können Konflikte/Probleme, auch Zuwendungsbedarf von Mädchen erkannt werden, wenn ihre Bewältigung für das Erscheinungsbild verschwiegen werden muss: ich habe keine Probleme, ich bin nicht benachteiligt, ich bin kompetent?
5. The concept means that pedagogy in general has to be questioned whether its subjects, methods and group settings would rather stabilise existing gender inequalities or whether it would support pupils' critical consciousness towards the issue. It includes mixed- and single-sex education.

References

Bitzan, Maria, and Claudia Daigler. 2001. *Eigensinn und Einmischung: Einführung in die Grundlagen und Perspektiven parteilicher Mädchenarbeit.* Weinheim: Juventa Verlag.

Brinkmann, Tanja Marita. 2006. *Die Zukunft der Mädchenarbeit, Innovationspotenziale durch neuere Geschlechtertheorien und Ungleichheitsforschung.* Münster: Unrast.

Budde, Jürgen, Barbara Scholand, and Hannelore Faulstich-Wieland. 2008. *Geschlechtergerechtigkeit in der Schule: Eine Studie zu Chancen Blockaden und Perspektiven einer gender-sensiblen Schulkultur.* Weinheim: Juventa Verlag.

Busche, Mart, Laura Maikowski, Ines Pohlkamp, and Ellen Wesemüller, eds. 2010. *Feministische Mädchenarbeit weiterdenken.* Bielefeld: transcript.

Butler, Judith. 1990. *Gender trouble.* New York: Routledge.

Cremers, M. 2011. Jungenarbeit. In *Wörterbuch Soziale Arbeit und Geschlecht*, ed. G. Ehlert, H. Funk, and G. Stecklina, 219–20. Weinheim: Juventa Verlag.

Cullen, Fin 2009. Failing youth: the contemporary gendering of youth work in England. Paper presented at the DCSF Gender Agenda Symposium 25-27 March, Gender and Education Association Conference, London.

Czollek, Leah C., Gudrun Perko, and Heike Weinbach. 2009. *Lehrbuch Gender und Queer: Grundlagen, Methoden und Praxisfelder.* Weinheim: Juventa Verlag.

Donning, I. 1997. Koedukation 20 Jahrhundert. Hintergründe einer Debatte. *Pädagogische Rundschau* 51: 721–47.

Dribbusch, Barbara. 2007. Chinaböller B.: Was haben Frauenfußball, Kracher und windelnde Männer gemeinsam? Den Geruch nach Freiheit. *die tageszeitung*, October 18.

Eggers, M. M. 2010. Diversity als Egalisierungspolitik oder als Gesellschaftskritik? Auf der Suche nach neuen Strukturen, die Mädchenarbeit und Jungenarbeit nicht als Förderungsgegensätze polarisieren *BAG Mädchenpolitik Schriftenreihe*, no. 11: 32–6.

Faulstich-Wieland, H. 1994. Reflexive Koedukation. In *Geschlechterverhältnisse und die Pädagogik: Jahrbuch der Pädagogik*, ed. U. Bracht and D. Keiner, 325–45. Frankfurt: Peter Lang.

Faulstich-Wieland, Hannelore, and Marianne Horstkemper. 1995. *'Trennt uns bitte, bitte nicht!' Koedukation aus Mädchen- und Jungensicht.* Opladen: Leske u. Budrich.

Fegter, Susann. 2012. *Die Krise der Jungen in Bildung und Erziehung: Diskursive Konstruktion von Geschlecht und Männlichkeit in den Medien.* Wiesbaden: VS Verlag.

Fegter, S., K. Geipel, and J. Horstbrink. 2010. Dekonstruktion als Haltung in sozialpädagogischen Zusammenhängen. In *Differenzierung, Normalisierung, Andersheit. Soziale Arbeit als Arbeit mit den Anderen*, ed. F. Kessl and M. Plößer, 233–48. Wiesbaden: VS Verlag.

Freire, Paulo. 1972. *Pedagogy of the oppressed.* London: Penguin.

Gamm, Hans-Jochen. 1979. *Allgemeine Pädagogik: Die Grundlage von Erziehung und Bildung in der bürgerlichen Gesellschaft.* Reinbek: Rowohlt.

Graff, U. 2011. Genderperspektiven in der Offenen Kinder- und Jugendarbeit. In *Empirie der Offenen Kinder- und Jugendarbeit*, ed. H. Schmidt, 179–88. Wiesbaden: VS Verlag.

Graff, Ulrike. 2004. *Selbstbestimmung für Mädchen: Theorie und Praxis feministischer Pädagogik.* Königstein/Taunus: Ulrike Helmer Verlag.

Hagemann-White, C. 1993. Die Konstrukteure des Geschlechts auf frischer Tat ertappen?: Methodische Konsequenzen einer theoretischen Einsicht. *Feministische Studien* 2: 68–78.
Hagemann-White, C. 2006. Sozialisation – zur Wiedergewinnung des Sozialen im Gestrüpp individualisierter Geschlechterbeziehungen. In *Sozialisation und Geschlecht: Theoretische und methodologische Aspekte*, ed. H. Bilden and B. Dausien, 71–88. Opladen: B. Budrich.
Hannover, Bettina. 1997. *Das dynamische Selbst. Die Kontextabhängigkeit selbstbezogenen Wissens*. Bern u.a.: Huber.
Humboldt, W. von. 1785–1795/2007. Die Bildung des Menschen. In *Erziehungs- und Bildungstheorien: Erläuterungen – Texte – Arbeitsaufgaben*, ed. F. Baumgart, 94–6. Bad Heilbrunn: Julius Klinkhardt Verlag.
Kessels, Ursula. 2002. *Undoing Gender in der Schule: Eine empirische Studie über Koedukation und Geschlechtsidentität im Physikunterricht*. Weinheim: Juventa Verlag.
Kleinau, E. 2004. Von der klassischen Sozialgeschichte zur, Sozialgeschichte der Erweiterung'. In *Handbuch Gender und Erziehungswissenschaft*, ed. E. Glaser, D. Klika, and A. Prengel, 287–302. Bad Heilbrunn: Klinkhardt.
Koller, H.-C. 2001. Bildung und die Dezentrierung des Subjekts. In *Dekonstruktive Pädagogik*, ed. B. Fritzsche, J. Hartmann, A. Schmidt, and A. Tervooren, 35–48. Opladen: Leske + Budrich.
Kunert-Zier, Margitta. 2005. *Erziehung der Geschlechter Entwicklungen Konzepte und Genderkompetenz in sozialpädagogischen Feldern*. Wiesbaden: VS: Verlag.
Landesarbeitsgemeinschaft Mädchenarbeit in NRW. 2008. Bravo GIRL – Deine beste Freundin? Alpha-Mädchen-Mythos verharmlost Gewalt! Press release, July 9. http://www.maedchenarbeit-nrw.de.
Leonard, D. 2009. Single-sex schooling. In *Skelton handbook of gender and education*, ed. C. Skelton, B. Francis, and Lisa Smulyan, 190–204. London: Sage.
Lütgert, Heike. 2010. 25 Jahre Gewaltprävention und Persönlichkeitsstärkung für Mädchen in Bielefeld aus polizeilicher Sicht. Paper presented at the expert conference , Ganz schön stark!' 25 Jahre Mädchenarbeit in Bielefeld des Bell-ZETT, January 20, in Bielefeld, Germany.
McRobbie, A. 2008. Top girls? Young women and the new sexual contract. In *The aftermath of feminism: Gender, culture and social change*, 54–93. Los Angeles: Sage.
McRobbie, Angela, and Monika Savier, eds. 1982. *Autonomie aber wie! Mädchen Alltag Abenteuer*. Munich: Frauenoffensive.
Mecheril, P., and M. Plößer. 2009. Differenz. In *Handwörterbuch Erziehungswissenschaft*, ed. S. Andresen, R. Casale, T. Gabriel, R. Horlacher, S. Larcher Klee, and J. Oelkers, 194–208. Basel, Weinheim: Beltz.
Metz-Göckel, S. 1999. Koedukation - nicht um jeden Preis. Eine Kritik aus internationaler Perspektive. In *Das Geschlecht der Bildung. Die Bildung der Geschlechter*, ed. B. L. Behm, G. Heinrichs, and H. Tiedemann, 131–47. Opladen: Leske + Budrich.
Metz-Göckel, S. 2010. Geschlechterdifferenzierung in der Collegeforschung und ihre Bedeutung für die Schulforschung. In *Mädchen in der Schule. Empirische Studien zu Heterogenität in monoedukativen und koedukativen Kontexten*, ed. Leonie Herwartz-Emden, 143–70. Opladen: Budrich.
Muraro, Luisa. 1989. *Weibliche Genealogie und Geschlechterdifferenz: Vorträge*. Ed. Verein Sozialwissenschaftliche Forschung und Bildung für Frauen e.V. Frankfurt: Verein Sozialwiss. Forschung u. Bildung.

Paechter, C. 2011. Polyphonie? Ausblicke auf einen anderen Geschlechterdiskurs in der Pädagogik. In *Jungenpädagogik im Widerstreit*, ed. E.J. Forster, B. Rendtorff, and C. Mahs, 147–63. Stuttgart: Kohlhammer.

Plößer, Melanie. 2005. *Dekonstruktion – Feminismus – Pädagogik: Vermittlungsansätze zwischen Theorie und Praxis*. Königstein: Helmer.

Prengel, Annedore. 1993. *Pädagogik der Vielfalt: Verschiedenheit und Gleichberechtigung in Interkultureller, Feministischer und integrativer Pädagogik*. Opladen: Leske + Budrich.

Rauw, R. 2007. Was ist eigentlich ein Mädchen? Reflexionen von Mädchenbildern und Konsequenzen für die Mädchenarbeit. Landesarbeitsgemeinschaft Mädchenarbeit in NRW e.V. http://www.maedchenarbeit-nrw.de/theorie-praxis-pdf/9_011%20Rauw_Maedchenbilder.pdf.

Rauw, Regina, and Ilka Reinert, eds. 2001. *Perspektiven der Mädchenarbeit*. Opladen: Leske + Budrich.

Tervooren, A. 2001. Pädagogik der Differenz oder differenzierte Pädagogik? In *Dekonstruktive Pädagogik*, ed. B. Fritzsche, J. Hartmann, A. Schmidt, and A. Tervooren, 201–16. Opladen: Leske + Budrich.

Tillmann, Angela. 2008. *Identitätsspielraum Internet. Lernprozesse und Selbstbildungspraktiken von Mädchen und jungen Frauen in der virtuellen Welt*. Weinheim und München: Juventa Verlag.

Walzer, Michael. 1992. *Sphären der Gerechtigkeit: Ein Plädoyer für Pluralität und Gleichheit*. Frankfurt: Campus-Verlag.

Weiner, G. 2009. Out of the ruins: Feminist pedagogy in recovery. In *Handbook of gender and education*, ed. C. Skelton, B. Francis, and Lisa Smulyan, 79–92. London: Sage.

Wentzel, W. 2011. Girls' day – Mädchen-Zukunftstag: Entwicklungen, Diskussionen und Wirkungen. In *Generation girls' day*, ed. W. Wentzel and B. Schwarze, 19–76. Opladen: Budrich.

West, C., and D.H. Zimmerman. 1987. Doing gender. *Gender & Society* 1: 125–51.

Witzel, A. 2000. Das problemzentrierte Interview. *Forum qualitative Sozialforschung* 1, no. 1: Abs. 26.

Younger, Michael. 2012. Single-sex teaching in co-educational schools: A panacea for raising achievement? In *Jungen - Pädagogik. Praxis und Theorie von Genderpädagogik*, ed. D.-T. Chwalek, M. Diaz, S. Fegter, and U. Graff, 77–88. Wiesbaden: Springer.

Younger, M., and M. Warrington. 2006. Would Harry and Hermione have done better in single-sex classes? A review of single-sex teaching in coeducational secondary schools in the United Kingdom. *American Educational Research Journal* 43: 579–620.

Becoming accomplished: concerted cultivation among privately educated young women[1]

Claire Maxwell[a] and Peter Aggleton[b]

[a]Department of Humanities and Social Sciences, Institute of Education, University of London, London, UK; [b]National Centre in HIV Social Research, Faculty of Arts and Social Sciences, University of New South Wales, Sydney, Australia

> This paper takes as its starting point the concept of concerted cultivation as coined by Annette Lareau. It examines whether a focus on concerted cultivation adequately captures the various practices observed in young women's experiences of being privately educated in four schools in one area of England. We suggest that a variety of practices of cultivation are evident in the reasons reported as influencing the choice of private education, the ways schools present themselves and organise the curriculum, the manner in which young women in such schools relate to one another, and the experiences young women have in securing different forms of accomplishment. Regardless of whether this accomplishment is 'effortless' or more worked at, the outcomes of these practices support young women in having a high degree of surety in the self. This surety is facilitated through family and school practices and is grounded, for the most part, in educational and economic security. Together, these processes support the reproduction of various forms of privilege in and through young women's lives.

Introduction

Annette Lareau's (2002, 773) work on middle-class parenting practices and processes of 'concerted cultivation' has been taken up by Crozier, Reay, and James (2011), Irwin and Elley (2011), and Vincent and Ball (2007) among others. Children are viewed by some middle-class parents as investment projects (Vincent and Ball 2007) into which parents commit significant time and resources. This may take the form of time spent together on homework, trips to cultural venues and events (Banks 2012), enrolment in enrichment activities outside of their main school education (music, sport, language school), alongside or leading to forms of 'enriching intimacy' (Stefansen and Aarseth 2011, 389) which connect 'love and focusedness' (2011, 402) (i.e. the joy of learning and persistent engagement in the making of the self) in parenting practices. The focus is on 'making and finding the child' (Vincent and Ball 2007, 1070) through 'developing their children's special talents' and facilitating 'an emerging sense of entitlement' (Lareau 2002, 749). This process results in the 'production of a new generation of middle-class cultural omnivores' (Vincent and Ball 2007, 1074).

Vincent and Ball (2007) have argued that processes of concerted cultivation take place in response to anxieties around securing positions of relative privilege (also argued by Reay 2000; Walkerdine, Lucey, and Melody 2001). Irwin and Elley (2011), however, emphasise that not *all* middle-class parents engage in such an active, resource-intensive process of concerted cultivation, and question the suggestion that anxiety underpins concerted efforts to produce specific kinds of sensibilities within children. In fact, Irwin and Elley argue, many of the parents they interviewed already held a degree of 'assuredness' (2011, 486) whereby a 'continued lifestyle across generations' (2011, 489) was assumed.

Building on this work, the present paper aims to consider the concept of concerted cultivation in an educational space that arguably represents the ultimate facilitation of a sense of entitlement – namely the private school. Such schools are frequently seen to offer a 'total curriculum' (Gaztambide-Fernández 2009a; Khan 2011; Walford 2005) with a focus on high levels of educational attainment, access to sport, as well as opportunities to achieve in drama, arts and music. Beyond this, the paper seeks to make a contribution to literature documenting concerted cultivation practices within the middle classes by drawing on the narratives of young women attending four private schools in one area of England. This focus is necessary as, to date, most writing on this subject has foregrounded the views of parents.

In recent years, a range of studies reporting on different aspects of private education have appeared. Research has examined how three Scottish schools are discursively constructed in Web-based representations (Forbes and Weiner 2008) and has considered the ways in which Australian schools produce specific femininities or masculinities (Gottschall et al. 2010; Proctor 2011). The role sports play in the branding of Scottish independent schools (Horne et al. 2011) has also been focused upon. How young women themselves understand middle-class or elite femininities has been considered in one Australian as well as one British single-sex school (Allan 2009, 2010; Charles 2007, 2010). Recent North American enquiry in the fields of private and elite education has focused on developing ways in which such schools can be categorised (Gaztambide-Fernández 2009b) and how a sense of entitlement and privilege is learned and reproduced within them (Gaztambide-Fernández 2009a; Howard 2008; Khan 2011).

Howard's (2008) conception of privilege as identity and Gaztambide-Fernández's (2009a) five 'E's' of elite identification offer crucial tools for thinking further about the reproduction of privilege and inequality – via school processes and also through internalised discourses of meritocracy and entitlement by young people themselves (see also Khan 2011). Howard views identity as a form of 'ideologically mediated action' (2008, 31), whereby self-understandings are constituted relationally between the personal and the social and in which identities are performed through drawing on resources available within particular social–cultural–historical contexts. Howard (2008) uses Thompson's (1990) work on ideology to consider how spaces of privilege, and being positioned as privileged, can 'establish and sustain relations of domination' (Howard 2008, 27). Gaztambide-Fernández (2009a) presents a related framework for understanding privilege from his work in one elite US boarding school. He outlines the interrelated processes of (1) exclusion (the school and its students believing that not everyone can or deserves to be in this particular elite school), (2) engagement (of students in the broad and rich curriculum offered), (3) excellence (students strive to be the best that they can be, and this work ethic translates into an understanding of their privileged position as therefore being merited), (4) entitlement (that admission to an elite school leads to other opportunities beyond schooling because of the school's reputation of producing excellent students), and (5) envisioning (of an elite future for those students graduating from the school). These processes, Gaztambide-Fernández's argues, have the effect of internalising elite status.

Both Howard's and Gaztambide-Fernández's work encourages a relational understanding of the making of privileged subjects and the re/production of privilege, in the sense that privilege is justified through positioning 'Others' outside this space. As we have argued in our previous work on young privately educated women's conceptualisations of social class (Maxwell and Aggleton 2010b), young women are more likely to position themselves in relation to others within their school rather than outside. Thus while an identity of privilege may become internalised, this may not be achieved through a relational positioning of the self in relation to an external Other. We would therefore like to re-look at the positioning and understanding of what a private education offers young people and how families and students engage with these ideas via an examination of the concept of concerted cultivation. Significantly, unlike most in-depth research to date on private and elite education, which has taken place in only one school, this paper draws on the narratives of young women (aged 15–18 years) in four private schools in one small area of England. The focus here is on recurrent themes and perspectives within the accounts young women provided; in later work it is our intention to focus more fully on between-school differences.

The study

Findings reported derive from a three-year study funded by UK Economic and Social Research Council (grant RES-062-23-2667), examining the experiences of young women attending four different fee-paying schools in one area of England. The research seeks to extend the findings of previous work (Maxwell and Aggleton 2010a, 2010b, 2012a, 2012b) to theorise further the agentic practices of these privileged young women across various aspects of their lives, including their education, in relationships with peers and family. The study also seeks to contribute to debates about school choice, the nature of the middle classes and the reproduction of privilege.

Four schools were approached in one small geographical part of England. Institutions differed in terms of level of academic selection, whether they were co-educational or single-sex schools, and offered boarding or daytime-only facilities. St. Thomas' is a co-educational boarding school, Brownstone is a co-educational day school, Osler is a single-sex (highly selective) day school and Rushby is a single-sex boarding school. The first author (CM) spent at least one day observing and attending lessons in each school before facilitating a number of group discussions. The group discussions offered the opportunity to get to know the school a little better and hear from the young women themselves what they liked about the school, what they wished was different, what kinds of students attended the school, which other schools they and their parents had considered, and how young men and women got on at the school (if it was a co-educational school).

Young women from Years 10–13 (aged 15–18 years) were then invited to take part in an in-depth one-to-one interview. These interviews explored how they viewed themselves, their family background, their schooling history, their friendships, whether or not they were in an intimate or sexual relationship, and positive and negative experiences they had had in the last three to six months. It is intended to conduct a second in-depth interview with as many of the young women as possible one year after their first involvement in the study. The main analysis presented in this paper, however, draws on the 85 first-time interviews conducted with the young women (see Table 1 for details of the quoted participants).

Interviews were audio-recorded with permission and transcribed verbatim including laughter, pauses, changes in intonation and so forth. The focus of this paper emerged during discussions between the two investigators (CM and PA) following initial reflections on the interviews by the first author. In particular, we wanted to better understand the extraordinarily competent impression young women gave – in terms of their articulacy, their capacity to reflect on their experiences, and the many achievements they could recall (some unprompted, others emerging more slowly and less overtly during the course of discussions).

We take as the starting point for this paper the idea of 'accomplishment', the wider literature on middle-class parenting and concerted cultivation, and our interest in understanding processes linked to the reproduction of privilege. We read each of the transcripts with these three issues in mind, to

Table 1. Details of the schools and quoted participants.

School	Description	Quoted participants
St. Thomas'	Co-educational boarding school	Jacy (Year 10)
		Nanette (Year 11)
		Lauren (Year 13)
		Tallulah (Year 13)
Brownstone	Co-educational day school	Becky (Year 11)
		Ethel (Year 12)
		Jenny (Year 12)
		Nicole (Year 12)
		George (Year 13)
Osler	Single-sex (highly selective) day school	Georgina (Year 10)
		Miranda (Year 10)
		Christie (Year 10)
		Francesca (Year 10)
		Louise (Year 12)
		Florence (Year 13)
Rushby	Single-sex boarding school	Alice (Year 12)
		Allie (Year 12)
		Kate (Year 12)
		Lucy (Year 12)
		Maria (Year 12)
		Sophie (Year 12)
		Eliza (Year 13)
		Elizabeth (Year 13)
		Georgia (Year 13)

explore instances of accomplishments, to try to understand the discourses the young women were drawing on in their narratives, and to link these to their reasons for coming to a particular school and their aspirations for the future.

Findings

Going private

For some families, the decision to purchase a private education had been strongly influenced by a practice of concerted cultivation. Young women described the breadth of opportunities offered by their schools as a key reason for parents making this educational choice: '[My mum] kind of knew in the back of her mind I would be capable of so much more if I went to a private school' (Georgina, Osler, Year 10). Georgina also described in some detail how her parents had changed their jobs and moved to a part of the country where there were good enough private schools for her and her two brothers.

Similarly, Kate's mother had decided to find a teaching position at a private school (after years of working in state-funded schools), and to move far from their local neighbourhood so that Kate could finish her education in the independent sector:

> I think it wasn't so much that [the school] was private, I think it was more that [my mum] thought it would benefit me in giving me a wider education. I think if she'd have thought that the state system had more to offer in the sense of you know lectures and stuff like that and clubs, then maybe she wouldn't [have sent me here]. I mean not 'cos it's private necessarily, I think it's because of the extras we can do. (Rushby, Year 12)

The benefit of a private education was seen in both 'the extras' as Kate put it, but also the smaller class sizes and closer attention to the individual's needs. Becky explained:

> And I don't know why the full story, but my parents sort of thought that if I came to this school I would get extra help than maybe I would [not] in the state school, 'cos there's a lot smaller classes, they have a really good LS [learning support] department … and um … they just thought I'd probably be able to cope better in smaller classes. (Brownstone, Year 11)

Those families with no prior history of private education seemed more focused on the range of opportunities and additional support offered within the independent sector than those families who for at least one generation had been privately educated. In fact, for most families with a history of being privately educated, it appeared as if there had been no real decision-making about whether to go private or not, the focus had simply been on deciding *which* school to choose. For these families at least, the education offered by private schools is therefore not so much 'chosen' as presumed.

A small number of the young women suggested that their parents had high expectations for and of them, and demanded certain achievements. At Rushby, while waiting for an interviewee, CM observed how the Head of Music approached a young woman asking why she had not attended choir practice or signed up for her singing lessons yet, as her mother kept telephoning to enquire why her daughter was not doing so. The Head of Music said, 'Do you want to sing? Or is it your mother who wants you to sing?' The young woman responded, 'No, I don't really want to'. While such anecdotes support suggestions of concerted cultivation, on the whole, young women reported that their parents' main interest was that they should be happy, try their hardest and enjoy school. Lauren echoed many other young women when we explored with them the expectations their parents had of them:

> My parents have like always said try your hardest, and that's all … [my parents] know that I'm not the brightest cookie in the box, I'm not going to get the top grades. But they're just happy that I put in the work. (St. Thomas', Year 13)

Thus, 'going private' can be understood as not necessarily the ultimate form of concerted cultivation by middle-class parents, but as something rather less calculated for many: in part the recapitulation of largely unquestioned family educational practices; and for some parents the consequence of a concern that the school should support the development of their child's overall sense of well-being.

'We offer...' choosing between schools

The inspection report for one of the study schools introduced it using the following language: 'very high quality of education', 'achieves its broad aims for their academic, sporting, creative and aesthetic experience and success', takes care to focus on all its students, pupils are 'self assured, ... confident ... and standing up for what they believe'. This focus on the whole child, on academic as well as other areas of attainment, and the commitment to creating independent learners and young people, was prevalent in the promotional materials of all of the schools visited, and figured on their websites, the local and national press.

The Director of Studies at Brownstone, for example, wrote in an advertisement supplement in the local paper that, 'the education we offer is one that will enable [the children] to make the best use of their abilities and interests'. In another piece, the Head of St. Thomas' argued the school offers a 'balanced approach to learning and life', supporting all children to achieve, a focus on rewarding effort not just attainment and a 'vibrant extra-curricular programme' including national sporting squads coming to train some of the pupils and 'first-rate' facilities. An 'independent' guide to the private education sector says that at Rushby those who are 'bright' will be supported as well as those who are less so [but 'outside the classroom'], with the aim of all students becoming confident and 'ambitious'. All the schools also sell the idea of opportunities for students to travel to the southern world to support development projects.

The private education sector caters for just under 7% of the English school-age population (Dearden, Ryan, and Sibieta 2010), so competition is fierce as schools try to distinguish themselves and attract income, yet within their promotional texts they appear to describe themselves in very similar ways. In discussions with young women it was clear that schools had different reputations amongst families and young people: as highly academically selective 'you need to be clever to come here'; as a school for 'dumb rich people'; or somewhere traditionally farmers sent their children; as 'really sporty'; or as the girls' school equivalent to another well-known boys school – so if brothers were sent to the latter school, the daughters were sent to the former.

Additionally, and despite the fact that the schools seem to present themselves similarly – as offering a full curriculum, being able to boast high achievements across a number of areas, promising to be attentive to the needs of each individual, and as ensuring that all students become independent, confident and self-assured – families appeared to make the decision about which school to send their daughter to based on recommendations from friends, a history of previous generations attending the school, having looked round the school and being impressed with the 'friendliness' of the students, or just liking 'the feel' of the place. In some cases, the required entrance exams had limited the ability to make a 'choice'. So at Osler, for instance, the pass grades for the exams were quite high, meaning at least two young women at Brownstone had missed out on a place there.

Importantly, much of the promotional material for these schools draws explicitly on discourses of 'cultivation'. Schools promise to develop academic and other potential (sports and creative) as well as personal attributes and skills (i.e. becoming independent and confident). Crucially, this is committed to no matter what a student's (initial) abilities are when they first arrive. Each student thereby becomes a 'project' for the school to work on. However, there is also an emphasis on what might be described as 'concerned' as well as concerted cultivation. This involves supporting young people to find a 'balanced approach to life and learning' through the nurturing of the individual in ways parents are led to believe they might not find elsewhere (i.e. in the state sector). Buying into a private education is therefore as much informed by the desire to achieve particular outcomes as by promoting the processes of cultivation in and of themselves – both from the parents' and schools' point of view. But how did the young women in our study understand these concerns?

The expectation and desire of accomplishment

Interviews with the young women started with the open question – 'tell me a little about yourself' or 'how would you describe yourself to me?' This question was responded to in many different ways, but the young women tended to (1) list the kinds of subjects and extra-curricular activities they did, (2) describe their family and where they lived, and then (3) explain how they saw themselves – as 'happy', friends and family meaning a lot to them, 'honest', 'loyal and I'm very good at keeping secrets', 'quite funny', as being 'socially around', 'eccentric', and so forth.

Jacy (St. Thomas', Year 10), for example, said of herself, 'I kind of do music, I kind of do sport, I do like art, and I try to do academic ... but like I try to like cover each bit'. When asked what she enjoyed doing, Lucy responded:

> Um ... well I do a lot of M.U.N. – Model United Nations debating ... I play the clarinet and the saxophone ... in bands and various different things at

school. I enjoy my school work I guess as well ... I shoot and do a lot of competitions clay shooting. (Rushby, Year 12)

The young women led very busy lives – going to lessons and completing course work was accomplished in between rehearsing for drama productions, performing in local music competitions, preparing portfolios for art college applications, training for sports fixtures, giving prospective parents and pupils tours of the school, being part of a Young Enterprise team, preparing notes for debates against other schools, raising money to fund a charitable visit to a part of the southern world during the school holidays, undertaking the duties required of a 'scholar' or 'prefect'. To some extent, this level of activity was expected by the schools – it was timetabled in (especially for the younger years) and young women understood that being involved in the school life and taking part in many extra-curricular activities was monitored by the school and would in large part determine whether they would be asked to take on positions of responsibility later on in the school - such as becoming a Prefect. Ethel explained, when we were discussing her wish to become a prefect, how she might maximise her chances, 'If there's anything that needs to be done I'll put myself forward for it in the hope that somebody will notice' (Brownstone, Year 12).

Schools' expectations around a degree of involvement and accomplishment across the academic and non-academic spheres of school life was mirrored in peer relations – which could be competitive, leading some young women to see themselves as unaccomplished or their abilities as less noteworthy. At St. Thomas', five young women in Year 11, who were all part of the same friendship group in one of the boarding houses, took part in a one-to-one interview. Three of them, when asked to describe a positive or negative experience in the last six months, discussed their most recent termly report card and how they had either beaten or narrowly lost their position to a close friend in terms of their ranking. At Rushby, those few young women who were not so heavily committed to extra-curricular activities as some of their peers felt this made them relatively uninteresting or even 'lazy'. Alice (Year 12), for instance, felt that, she was 'not a very interesting person, I'm just kind of standard' because although she was good at sport – 'I do lacrosse, hockey, netball, athletics [and tennis] ... [but] I'm not incredible at Drama, I'm not performing for a local company'.

Expectations of accomplishment – across a number of spheres – were therefore promoted by the school community through teachers and peers. Some young women drew more directly on discourses of concerted cultivation when discussing their futures, their hopes of getting into a good university, and the desire to get a particular degree. Maria (Rushby, Year 12) wanted to study medicine. She explained that some family friends had gone to medical school and had been able to give her 'loads of advice on what to do and kind of what to make you look different to all of the other applicants'. She had already completed four one-week holiday placements in various medical settings. At Osler, a group of five Year 10 girls had the following discussion:

> Georgina: I know a girl who's predicted six A*s at A-Level [highest possible grade for final secondary schooling exams in Year 13] and Cambridge [university] were just like 'No' ... and she's so easy to get on with, like her conversation's really intelligent and like she's really quick...
>
> Francesca: But her personality must have been completely flat.
>
> Georgina: No, but they don't like just like academic, 'cos ... actually they want people who do music or art as well.
>
> Christie: Exactly ... my friend ... I do ballet with her, and she went to her interviews at King's ... they ended up talking about ballet the entire interview. The guy was like ... 'tell me something that's not in this [application]' and she was like, 'Oh um, I dance quite a lot ... I did my grade 8 [highest level of ballet exam]...' and he said, 'Oh my gosh, my daughter did this' ... and then they like ended up talking about like...

The degree of accomplishment that young women displayed, however, was not simply the result of a practice of concerted cultivation. Almost without exception, every respondent talked about their creative work and their sporting experiences as offering physical and emotional enjoyment, and the opportunity to invest in self-identity.

George (Brownstone, Year 13) explained that during her photography projects, 'I always get like really like emotional like and into my work'. She went on to say, 'you just come up with your own ideas and it's like really good'. Not only did photography offer George emotional release, but she also seemed to feel that being into photography was what made her, herself: it was intimately bound up in the identity she presented. 'I'm quite deep ... like I do photography', George stated.

Georgina (Osler, Year 10) was a Music Scholar ('I just found out I got two distinctions in my Grade 7 violin and singing'), a member of a number of the school sports teams ('I just got like a hockey prize') and a member of the regional youth orchestra and the National Youth Choir. During her interview, she was asked, 'Isn't it quite exhausting to be Georgina?' She replied, 'Yeah, but I get bored really easily'. This exchange offers some insight into the way Georgina presented herself in this study – both in the group discussion she was part of and also in the one-to-one interview. Throughout the group discussion, four of her Year 10 peers kept re-iterating Georgina's high academic, sporting and musical achievements, although Georgina sought in a way to play this down:

Miranda: And Georgina is clever so she's going to go to X [another local private school with some of the highest academic results in England].

Georgina: Can you stop saying that, makes me feel really awkward.

Despite protesting she felt awkward about the way her peers described her, Georgina continued to debate the merits and disadvantages of Osler, and how best to get into an Ivy League university in the USA. She actively sought to create opportunities for the quietest member of group to be given the chance to share her views. Her overall manner suggested she felt herself to hold clear opinions on many issues relevant to her life and the lives of her school friends, and to be able to manage the flow of discussion. In the one-to-one interview Georgina explained:

> I really enjoy speaking to like people ... [especially if] they're really bright ... I don't know, I don't really know why I'm like how I am ... if [my friends] need something explaining ... and I always like read newspapers and watch the news and stuff, and um ... I just enjoy like knowing what's going on.

The previous summer, Nicole (Brownstone, Year 12) and Georgia (Rushby, Year 13) had raised money so they could travel to spend a week on a local development project in Nepal and Uganda, respectively. This was followed by another week sight-seeing (Georgia) or to climb a well-known mountain (Nicole). Both felt this had been a very significant experience. Georgia felt she had learned a lot from appreciating how others could be happy even if they were poor – something she tried to remember when she got upset over minor issues. For Nicole, there had been a sense of accomplishment at having proved her family, friends and teachers wrong in having first, raised the money; second, having boarded the plane; third, having climbed a high mountain; and fourth, having spent time with other peers who had inspired her to become more serious about academic work. In different ways, this experience had shaped both young women's current and future selves.

Sophie (Rushby, Year 12) sung in local competitions, was in a band, played two musical instruments and had recently taken the lead role in a youth theatre production. Her name could be seen in numerous places across the Music School of Rushby – as the winner of awards, in newspaper clippings about her stage role, and so on. Sophie described herself as 'confident' and able to 'manage myself in kind of situations with different kind of ages of people'. This derived, she believed, in large part from her experiences of doing drama and music, as well as the fact that she was an only child. Sophie intended to apply to Oxford University as well as auditioning for a place at Drama School. In narrative and demeanour she gave the impression of being a young woman who was self-assured, interested, articulate, reflective and experienced. Despite her strong academic record, it was arguably her success in music and on the stage, and its recognition by peers and family, that facilitated her self-presentation as confident, mature and accomplished.

These five young women, together with many of the other participants, relished their accomplishments. Few complained how busy their daily and weekly schedules were – filled with homework, training, rehearsals. Though a certain level of involvement and accomplishment was expected by the school (and in some cases by parents), young women had largely internalised and acted upon these expectations because of the pleasure and sense of achievement they felt these offered.

Effortless accomplishment?

Some young women, like Georgina (above, from Osler) or Nanette (St. Thomas', below) were confident and proud about what they had achieved:

> I really love science, it's my big thing ... I got a prize for Year 9 science which, I think, loads of schools took part in it ... I got put into this thing called the 'Tetra set ...everyone else would do like ... three [languages] but we did four – because 'Tetra' is Greek for 'four' ... [I'm] useless at sport ... I was really good at swimming when I was little [though] ... I think I'm quite academic and like artistic, like I really love art and I've got an art exhibition [scholarship]'. (Nanette, St. Thomas', Year 11)

Others, however, played down their accomplishments, especially in light of the achievements of peers.

> Well when people are like, 'Oh I'm good at this' – I wouldn't actually say I'm good at anything in particular, because ... because there are kind of a few people in my year that strive at everything and you can't really beat them. (Elizabeth, Year 13, Rushby)

Some young women saw their friends and siblings achieving more than themselves, accomplishing things almost effortlessly – doing so 'naturally' after only 'listen[ing] ... once' and without having 'to work for it' (Jacy, St. Thomas', Year 10). At Rushby and Osler, the high academic attainments and accomplishments of so many of the students meant that respondents saw themselves as simply 'average'. Louise (Osler, Year 12) had received an A* (the highest mark) in nine out of 10 of her end of Year 11 exams, but explained that when over 40 other young women in the year got the same result, and the school only celebrated the names of those students who scored A* in all 10 of their subjects in Assembly, this reduced the sense of achievement. Florence added:

You do get the sense [here] that there are some people who are really, really clever, and then if you're not really, really clever, you're just kind of average, whereas in the grand scheme of things you're not average ... but just in this school you are. (Year 13, Osler)

No matter whether the young women in our study understood themselves as accomplished, clever, extra-ordinary or simply average – overall levels of academic and sporting achievement, and being able to play more than one musical instrument to Grade 8 (the highest level), strongly suggests that most young women were highly accomplished. Alongside these more obvious markers of success, however, was the manner in which young women presented themselves in the interviews – the language they used to articulate their views and experiences, and the confidence they showed in speaking about themselves. These are forms of personal accomplishment which schools were keen for students to gain. What impact then do they have on young women's future lives?

Sureties in making the self – the reproduction of privilege

The reflexivity and articulacy of the young women's narratives, together with their achievements and skills, might easily be understood as the outcomes of processes of concerted cultivation. Families have bought a private education, schools have shaped their offer, and young women themselves have turned their energies to ensuring such a product. However, for some parents the decision to 'go private' is not quite so calculated. Furthermore, schools have to balance their focus on concerted cultivation with the promise of supporting individuals to achieve in a secure environment.

The narratives produced by young women also led us to question whether practices of cultivation are largely driven by anxieties to secure positions of privilege, as previous literature has argued (Reay 2000; Vincent and Ball 2007). We have sought therefore to understand more fully how the norm of accomplishment, apparently so strongly embedded within their everyday, facilitates the reproduction of privilege. In the final part of this paper, we suggest three ways in which this 'surety of the self' is supported both by families and the schools: via a set of cultural experiences, through the social relations engendered, and a number of expected educational and economic outcomes.

Jenny (Brownstone, Year 12) was White British but had been brought up abroad due to her father's employment in the Middle East. She felt this had made her 'more aware sort of culturally', so that 'meeting people who are foreign' was not strange for her. This made her 'feel quite different', 'more developed in a way as a person, you know I've seen a lot of the world and I understand it maybe in ways that other people don't'. Similarly, Tallulah's (St. Thomas', Year 13) family situation meant she had developed a set of skills she felt many of her peers had not acquired. Her father held a well-known public position which meant she had met 'a wide diversity of important people' and had had to learn to 'entertain' them. Her family's very public role made her 'feel like my family is just ... is a bit different, and I love that'. Additional support for Tallulah's sense of distinction derived from a family history of attending Cambridge – her father and uncle were both alumni of that university, her brother had just 'gone up' (recently started there), and she herself had recently secured a place to go the subsequent year.

Schools further supported some of the cultural experiences made available by families. The emphasis on art, music, drama and debate was reinforced by external speakers and travel abroad. During the early interviews at Rushby, for example, a famous chef came in for an afternoon (to run a cooking contest) as did a well-known BBC journalist (who talked about her career). The outcome of access to such experiences supported the development of well-rounded, creative, knowledgeable and sociable young woman. It further embedded an assuredness of identity that could be articulated, and which was distinguishable from others – as academic, as artistic, as having experiences which were of note.

Families were also central in positioning the young woman as part of a wider network of social relations. Eliza (Rushby, Year 13) explained she felt very assured of her future trajectory even if she had decided not to go to university, because she was confident that through her family connections she would be able to take up an interesting diplomatic position – 'Nowadays, which is sort of awful, but um ... good for those who have them, there's connections...'. Through her family's extensive networks she had already secured work experience placements at several prestigious magazines, with the royal family, and at a famous jewellery-makers. Schools too played a role in social networking. Older students buddied younger ones, prefects and scholars took responsibility for organising events and dealing with 'issues', teams self-managed enterprise projects or Duke of Edinburgh award challenges, and students were encouraged to approach their teachers whenever they needed additional support.

Long-term connections to the school were fostered via alumni networks with 'old girls' returning to talk about what the future might hold. Furthermore, networking with young people in other private schools through debates, 'socials' and dances, or joint classes for some subjects, mean that long-term social relations extend beyond the school. A number of participants acknowledged that they would likely marry someone who had also been privately educated because of these networks. All these mechanisms offer young women the surety of familiarity, of 'presence' and of belonging, which fostered confidence and poise in the present, and travels with them when they move beyond the safe walls of the school into the wider world.

Allie (Rushby, Year 12) was just one of many young women who presented herself as confident, ambitious, energetic and focused, with a degree of surety that would ensure she remained ahead of the game. Allie began her interview by describing the life-threatening medical condition she had to live with. However, despite missing a whole term of school in Year 9 due to her illness, she returned to sit a Chemistry exam and got 90% 'without even having been to a single Chemistry lesson'. She planned to apply to various Ivy League universities in the USA, but with Oxford or Cambridge and the London School of Economics as her 'back-up's'. Allie explained 'I've always wanted to go to be the best or do the best'. She went on:

> When I was little I always used to think I was going to make myself a millionaire by the time I was 10 [years old] ... and I always had like my ideas book and I always used to like make inventions and stuff. One of them actually worked really well ... it was a solar-powered train, a model of it ... I think [I made it when] I was six [years of age].

Most of the young women in this study planned to go to university and there was no suggestion on their part that they would not succeed in gaining entry to one of their top choices. Those few who opted not to go to university chose Drama or Art School instead, or in one or two cases (at Brownstone only) to begin an apprenticeship in a particular line of work (such as veterinary nursing). The careers young women spoke about, while not always definitively decided upon, were to a large extent planned and many commanded high salaries.

While many of the young women in our study had less grand ambitions than Francesca (Osler, Year 10), they all had ambitions to make a success of their educational and employment careers (at least until they had children):

> I think if you're going to become famous or you're going to become well recognised it better be for something good. And acting was great, you know that's very good, but I think being Prime Minister or being a Member of Parliament is very worthwhile because you get to really understand how the country's run and you can influence important decisions which ... for me like the new train system which is going to go through X [nearest big city], I'm strongly, strongly against ... I'm very open, I'd like to become Prime Minister, but I'd like to be a CEO, I'd like to be a banker, there's all that that's open to me. (Francesca, Osler, Year 10)

Certainly, as Irwin and Elley (2011) argue, the experience of economic privilege within the family offers a kind of surety in respect of future educational and economic position. Thus, the future is understood not as a place of difficulty, but as a destination in which new opportunities will present themselves, which will be navigated with the same ease that young women's experience of becoming 'accomplished' suggests.

Conclusions

Lareau's (2002) concept of concerted cultivation has been widely drawn on by writers theorising the practices of middle-class parents (Clark 2009; Crozier et al. 2011; Irwin and Elley 2011; Stefansen and Aarseth 2011; Vincent and Ball 2007). In recent work, Irwin and Elley (2011) have sought to develop this concept further by distinguishing between concerted cultivation for the present (in terms of a focus on a child's development) and concerted cultivation for the future. The reading of our data offered here also suggests a focus both on the present as well as the future, but we are more hesitant in suggesting these practices are as instrumental and calculated as others might argue. Young women in our study suggested their parents were just as concerned to ensure that they became happy, sociable individuals as success stories in later life.

Looking more closely at young women's perceptions and experiences, our findings suggest new dimensions to cultivatedness beyond those documented to date. Without exception, all young women displayed evidence of a variety of accomplishments, both academic and in spheres such as sport, music, drama, debating. Beyond this, however, they had acquired sensibilities and bodily dispositions which enabled them to come across as able, convincing, confident, articulate, reflective, sociable, mature and poised. In the literature to date, notions of concerted cultivation suggests effort, purpose and an instrumental focus on improvement which we did not necessarily find captured the way our study participants experienced their lives. The desire and pleasure young women displayed in their interactions, as well as the effortless achievement some spoke of, calls for a more grounded and nuanced understanding of what may be taking place, for young women of comparable background at least.

The forms and levels of accomplishment within our sample leads us to consider how these inform the making of the self and what role they play in the reproduction of privilege – the question which led to a focus on middle-class parenting practices in the first place. In this respect, we agree with Irwin and Elley's suggestion 'that anxiety about facilitating a good future for ... children is a *particular*, rather than *general*, account of middle-class parenting experiences' (2011, 492, italics in the original). Here, we encountered many young women for whom there was (like the parents in Irwin and Elley's account) an 'assumption of continued lifestyle across generations' (2011, 489).

Gaztambide-Fernández's (2009a) identification of the five E's of elite schooling and Howard's (2008) conceptualisation of privilege as an identity aim to illustrate how elite status becomes internalised. The argument we have developed here makes a very similar point around the internalisation of accomplishment linked to a surety of the self. However, the more exclusionary practices detailed by Gaztambide-Fernández (and by Howard – in the 'unintentional' (2008, 217) lessons learned by students in the four elite schools he studied) as central to the reproduction of privilege were not so evident in the schools in our research. Though students did distinguish between themselves and peers at other private schools, they did not necessarily see these others as less accomplished, and while some young women accepted that others in their school were more accomplished, they worked hard to find a way of positioning themselves as having achieved in some sphere of the school life (albeit less overtly, perhaps less recognised by others, but through strong friendship skills which were highly valued by all). We have doubts therefore whether Gaztambide-Fernández's five E's framework can necessarily capture the processes at work in schools such as those studied here. In future analyses, we aim to explore these issues in greater depth, especially as second-wave data from the present study become available.

Although the four participating schools arguably present themselves in very similar ways via their promotional materials, our reflections on our experiences of the schools and the research encounters we have had suggest that these schools variously shape their students' perspectives and self-understandings. For instance, the sense of *rounded* accomplishment came across most strongly at Rushby, yet the focus on attainment and on 'getting involved' in sports teams, drama productions and so forth was found in almost equal measure across all four schools. We intend to analyse in greater depth differences between schools in a subsequent paper by considering whether it might be possible to distinguish between the kinds of families who choose particular schools in the local private education market and the various ways the schools (through the staff, the students, the physical and affective spaces within and surrounding the schools, and interactions between students from other local private schools) may create differently privileged subjects. For the present, however, there seems little doubt that both accomplishment and surety in the self have a central role to play in enabling young women to distinguish themselves, laying the foundation for the production and reproduction of later forms of privilege.

Acknowledgements

We would like to thank the Economic and Social Research Council for funding the study (RES-062-23-2667) and the four schools for generously participating in the research.

Note

1. This paper arises from the UK Economic and Social Research Council-funded seminar series 'Young Women in Movement: Sexualities, Vulnerabilities, Needs and Norms' (ESRC RES-451-26-0715), based at Goldsmiths, University of London, 2009–2011.

References

Allan, A. 2009. The importance of being a 'lady': Hyper-femininity and heterosexuality in the private, single-sex primary school. *Gender and Education* 21: 145–58.

Allan, A. 2010. Picturing success: Young femininities and the (im)possibilities of academic achievement in selective, single-sex education. *International Studies in Sociology of Education* 20: 39–54.

Banks, P.A. 2012. Cultural socialization in black middle-class families. *Cultural Sociology* 6: 61–73.

Charles, C. 2007. Digital media and 'girling' at an elite girls' school. *Learning, Media and Technology* 32, no. 2: 135–47.

Charles, C. 2010. Complicating hetero-femininities: Young women, sexualities and 'girl power' at school. *International Journal of Qualitative Studies in Education* 23, no. 1: 33–47.

Clark, S. 2009. A good education: Girls' extracurricular pursuits and school choice. *Gender and Education* 21: 601–15.

Crozier, G., D. Reay, and D. James. 2011. Making it work for their children: White middle-class parents and working-class schools. *International Studies in Sociology of Education* 21: 199–216.

Dearden, L., C. Ryan, and L. Sibieta. 2010. What determines private school choice? A comparison between the UK and Australia. IFS Working Papers. London: Institute of Fiscal Studies.

Forbes, J., and G. Weiner. 2008. Under-stated powerhouses: Scottish independent schools, their characteristics and their capitals. *Discourse: Studies in the Cultural Politics of Education* 29: 509–25.

Gaztambide-Fernández, R. 2009a. *The best of the best: Becoming elite at an American boarding school*. Cambridge, MA: Harvard University Press.

Gaztambide-Fernández, R. 2009b. What is an elite boarding school? *Review of Educational Research* 79: 1090–128.

Gottschall, K., N. Wardman, K. Edgeworth, and R. Hutchesson. 2010. Hard lines and soft scenes: Constituting masculinities in the prospectuses of all-boys elite private schools. *Australian Journal of Education* 5, no. 1: 18–30.

Horne, J., B. Lingard, G. Weiner, and J. Forbes. 2011. 'Capitalizing on sport': Sport, physical education and multiple capitals in Scottish independent schools. *British Journal of Sociology of Education* 32: 861–79.

Howard, A. 2008. *Learning privilege: Lessons of power and identity in affluent schooling*. New York: Routledge.

Irwin, S., and S. Elley. 2011. Concerted cultivation? Parenting values, education and class diversity. *Sociology* 45: 480–95.

Khan, S.R. 2011. *Privilege: The making of an adolescent elite at St. Paul's school*. Princeton, NJ: Princeton University Press.

Lareau, A. 2002. Invisible inequality: Social class and childrearing in black and white families. *American Sociological Review* 67: 747–76.

Maxwell, C., and P. Aggleton. 2010a. Agency in action – Young women and their sexual relationships in a private school. *Gender and Education* 22: 327–43.

Maxwell, C., and P. Aggleton. 2010b. The bubble of privilege. Young, privately educated women talk about social class. *British Journal of Sociology of Education* 31: 3–15.

Maxwell, C., and P. Aggleton. 2012a. Bodies and agentic practice in young women's sexual and intimate relationships. *Sociology* 46: 306–21.

Maxwell, C., and P. Aggleton. 2012b. Middle class young women: Agentic sexual subjects? *International Journal of Qualitative Studies in Education.* Published online 6 August 2012; DOI:10.1080/09518398.2012.705044

Proctor, H. 2011. Masculinity and social class, tradition and change: The production of 'young Christian gentlemen' at an elite Australian boys' school. *Gender and Education* 23: 843–56.

Reay, D. 2000. A useful extension of Bourdieu's conceptual framework? Emotional capital as a way of understanding mothers' involvement in their children's education. *Sociological Review* 48: 568–85.

Stefansen, K., and H. Aarseth. 2011. Enriching intimacy: The role of the emotional in the 'resourcing' of middleclass children. *British Journal of Sociology of Education* 32: 389–405.

Thompson, J.B. 1990. *Ideology and modern culture: Critical social theory in the era of mass communication.* Stanford, CA: Stanford University Press.

Vincent, C., and S.J. Ball. 2007. 'Making up' the middle-class child: Families, activities and class dispositions. *Sociology* 41: 1061–77.

Walford, G. 2005. *Private education. Tradition and diversity.* London: Continuum.

Walkerdine, V., H. Lucey, and J. Melody. 2001. *Growing up girl: Psychosocial explorations of gender and class.* Basingstoke, UK: Palgrave.

Dissident daughters? The psychic life of class inheritance[1]

Valerie Hey[a] and Rosalyn George[b]

[a]Centre for Higher Education and Equity Research, Department of Education, University of Sussex, UK; [b]Educational Studies, Goldsmiths, University of London, London, UK

> This paper arose through a chance meeting between the two authors who are feminist mothers of teenage and 20 years plus daughters. We were attending an Economic and Social Research Council-funded seminar focusing on 'new femininities' in the light of post-feminism and their worth and currency within the new politics of consumption and lifestyle. The seminar contributions resonated for us in two ways. Firstly, we have an interest in femininities, female friendships and how current understandings of these social bonds are being reconceptualised. Secondly, and on a personal note, we were increasingly aware that the seminar discussions framed within the landscape and biographies of risk and hope chimed with the ways our own daughters were currently playing out and negotiating their futures. How do we view the apparent contra-trajectory taken by our daughters who, unlike us, less concerned about seeing education as a ladder to 'getting on', seemed intent on 'down classing' in their various and successive 'choices' of educational pathways and boyfriends? In making sense of shared anxieties, our concerns coalesced around the personal, the familial and, in particular, the maternal relations. It is these inter-generational tensions entangled with the emotional politics of class that are the focus of this paper.

Introduction

This paper arose out of a chance meeting between the two authors who are feminist mothers of teenage and 20 years plus daughters. We were at the time attending an Economic and Social Research Council-funded seminar focusing on 'new femininities' in the light of post-feminism and their worth and currency within the new politics of consumerism, consumption and lifestyle. The seminar contributions resonated for us in two significant ways. Firstly, we have a strong interest in femininities, female friendships and how current understandings of these social bonds are being reconceptualised. Secondly, and on a more personal note, we were increasingly aware that the seminar discussions framed within the landscape and biographies of risk and hope chimed with the ways our own daughters were currently playing out and negotiating their own futures.

As the seminar progressed with speakers commenting on the notions of risk, individualisation and issues of exclusion or empowerment, this created further anxieties for us who as mothers were already feeling a deeply ingrained sense of worry about the futures of those young women closest to us. How do we as upwardly mobile middle-class women academics remain emotionally and intellectually engaged with progressive emancipatory struggles whilst still subject to the same logic of neoliberal self-interest that shapes the political landscape? How do we view the apparent contra-trajectory taken by our daughters who, less concerned about seeing education as a ladder to 'getting on', seemed intent on 'down classing' in their various and successive 'choices' of educational pathways and boyfriends? In making sense of shared anxieties, our concerns coalesced around the personal, the familial and, in particular, the maternal relations that operated across identifications and refusals that traverse the topography and journey our daughters have embarked on from child to adult. In this paper, these inter-generational tensions entangled with the emotional politics of class will be a central concern.

The context

The authors are mothers of daughters, who like them, are making sense of the process of increasing diversity and an accompanying plethora of 'choice' which has, for some, paradoxically induced a paralysing perplexity as they are confronted by too many options. This 'fated individualisation', as theorised by Beck and Beck-Gernsheim (2002), suggests that this is a process of spiralling individualisation which destroys the foundations of co-existence leading to increased fragmentation and atomisation in society. We, like our daughters, are also occupants of contrasting multiple positions, in tension with each other, and live this multiplicity as academics, feminists, mothers and socialists, amongst other positionalities.

As women from a similar, if not identical, working-class location and political position, we set out to reflect on this in light of the different generational, class and gender positions of our daughters. We are using the term 'daughters' literally, as the focus of the piece is partly biographical, and metaphorically, in oblique reference also to political 'daughters', i.e. those younger women who identify with positions in feminisms. What sense do we and our 'offspring' make of the present shifts in political vocabulary – to the vocabularies of choice, success, post-feminisms, post-socialism, post-modernism?

This paper is an attempt to think through a historically specific series of class shifts and gender transformations that we have participated in. This is work in progress, exploratory and speculative. Fragments of auto/biographical reflection are drawn upon from our conversation to re/consider the logics of 'fated' choice in terms of the specific auto/biographical space between particular mothers, daughters and feminism.

One aim of this project is to reconsider social transformations so they are seen as more tied to lived experience. Larger shifts, in turn, play out as more diffuse everyday effects of the social and political processes on young women as social agents. It is in the interstices of society, biography and history that we think it possible to trace the outlines of a bigger picture, multiple resources of hope, compliance and resistance, as well as some tentative suggestions for rethinking the production of feminism(s). In order to do this we will locate our specific reading of the auto/biographical in a number of interlocking debates about the theorisation of identity and power/knowledge. These discussions reference the turn to the affective, to ideas about late modernity and to the significance of notions of subjectivity.

The affective turn

There is a lively debate among those contributing to the 'affective turn' in social and social psychological sciences about what is meant by the 'psychosocial' (see Redman 2009; Wetherell 2012; Skeggs 2002). A review of the range of perspectives is clearly outside the scope and purpose of this paper. Suffice it to say that scholars line up with different conceptual vocabularies even as they all derive significant explanatory power from recognising the valence of affects. The emergent field of the 'psychosocial' is conventionally seen as structured by the promulgation of competing terminology – 'emotions', 'affects' and 'desire'. Our preference is to remain open about the various contributions different positions make available because whilst in the spirit of thinking the psychic and the social as mutually entwined, we do not want to work within a binary formulation, such as biology *or* culture, affects *or* emotions.

Walkerdine's work with Jimenez offers up a more elaborate refusal and seeks to craft a discourse on the matter of the psychosocial encompassing, for example, psychoanalysis *and* neuroscience (Jimenez and Walkerdine 2011). We thus claim a similarly 'agnostic' position in respect to these differences – preferring neither to sign up with those who align with 'emotions' as 'internal' nor that of 'affects' as 'social'. We think rather that the psycho-social could hold bodies, selves, emotions, subjects, the psychic and the social within it. Quite how and in what spaces and places affects, desire and emotions find their force and expression requires much more thinking and work.

In prior work, one of us has tracked an interest in understanding the ways 'affects' freight our investments in identity and social relations (Hey 2004, 2005, 2006a), and more recently considering how emotions impact and effect higher education and how the field of higher education policy analysis might benefit from an infusion of interpretive resources enabling the Academy to be re-theorised as saturated by 'passionate attachments'. The aim of building a cultural sociology of higher education (Hey and Leathwood 2009; Hey and Morley 2011) is in train (David, Hey, and Morley 2011).

George (2007b) has shared a similar concern to illuminate the power of feelings working their way to shape the cultures of girls' friendship groups. Her work describes friendship groups as characterised by a complex web of relations regulating who is included, what can be said and who has permission to speak. These dynamics can result in emotional disruptions within classroom contexts that nevertheless offer a space to challenge traditional pedagogic practices which have marginalised the painful and emotional experiences of the young girls (George and Clay 2012).

What we both agree on is that the affective domain takes intrapersonal, intersubjective and in our respective work in development, manifests its force/s in educational institutions. Feelings are powerful and being able to provoke negative affects in others expresses the relations of subordination and domination (see Jackson 2010 for a similar view focusing on fear in education).

The subject in question

If subjectivity consists of subjectification, it is this that also constitutes agency (Butler 1999). The key motif of poststructuralist work is that subjects never fully occupy or identify with norms (see e.g. Fraser 1997; Skeggs 1997), indeed that there is ambivalence at the very heart of inclination. Ambivalence must, in other words, be understood to be at the very heart of mimesis. Mimesis has multiple meanings but we are referring to the sense of imitation required of people so they become recognisable in social terms. As Butler has put it,

> ...the mimetic acquisition of the norm is at once the condition by which a certain resistance to the norm is also produced; identification will not 'work' to the extent that the norm is not fully ... incorporable. (1999, 118)

Put simply, we are not uniformly 'reproductive effects' let alone what our families may have intended for us – we are both our mothers' daughters and not, and our daughters are also ours and not simultaneously. Where they stand in respect to our ideals of feminism and social class and social justice, is one of the questions we wish to explore.

One conceptual preoccupation is to bring the differences of generation to the conventional complexities of social positioning (race, class, gender), to rethink reproduction. Stephen Ball offers an account of inter-sectionality to reveal 'identity work' as a fragile project, especially so in the case of the newly up-classed – in a 'think piece' he writes of intersectionality as a structure but that it is not simply a structure:

> By definition it is an unstable ensemble of possibilities for identity – constrained, chosen and desired – which are more or less realisable, imposed, opportune or strategically useful according to circumstance. Intersectionality is also an ensemble of signs and impressions, 'given' and 'given off', in terms of gender performance, skin colour, speech, dress, and bodily hexis. (2010, 7)

Tantalisingly, he notes how many of the middle-class black parents he is reporting on offset their 'performances' against a felt 'authenticity', raising interesting questions of the ways that the psychic intersects the social and material in confounding ways. Here temporality and mobility are both implicated as black class 'movers' reflect on the conflict they experience being part of a community bound not only by skin colour but also by class. As one black mother in Ball's research states:

> 'I stand there and I think oh my god, you can't do things like that, you just can't, and you think to yourself why is it that I am feeling a little bit sort of uncomfortable with this issue ... there are some situations where you think oh sugar um yeah I can sit, I can identify with all of these individuals whole heartedly and then on another level I really, really don't.' (2010, 7)

What Ball's data are illustrating is the conflict the mother experiences being part of a community where the levers of power are controlled by the 'well off white middle class parents, whose lifestyle and values are very different to her own'. Yet she is paying for her eldest child to be privately educated. However, at the same time this mother, despite her sense of community affiliation, claims to feel 'at odds with the values and life style of the black working class parents who are the dominant group in the state primary school of her [youngest] child' (Ball 2010, 13) (see George 2007a for a similar discussion on 'race' and school choice).

In a previous paper, Hey (2011) argued the psycho-social was conceived as adding a crucial dynamic understanding to how power/powerlessness arise as activities constituting each other. Accepting cultural readings of power as transactional and positional is not to deny its structuring and material effects. But it is to insist that privilege/power plays out in ways that are not uniform, unidirectional or guaranteed. Even the powerful have to engage in power's subjective maintenance including having a remorseless psychic investment in the attempted othering/subordinating of the powerless. This always entails a double-edged fearing of these same 'serviceable others' (Morrison 1992).

Before we move to the data discussion, we finish our brief synoptic reading of relevant domains of literature by a comment on relevant themes of late modernity literature.

The world in question

We are of the view that there is a need to consider feminist critiques of the theory of late modernity. As we have indicated, there is a need to read late modernity theory through feminist critiques that signal class and gender as multiply cut by each other as well as abiding features of the contemporary social – in this regard we have found the work of Lawler (2005), Skeggs (1997, 2004) and McNay (1999) inspirational. These authors have explored how these concepts circulate by considering the dynamic tension between change and continuity.

Contemporary feminist theorisations have responded critically to the increased emphasis on individualism and individualisation and the increasingly complicated contextual formation of identity within a setting of widening choice, reflexive biographies and discursive multiplicity (Ball, Maguire, and Macrae 2000; Thomson, Henderson, and Holland 2002). The sharpest work has not lost site/sight either of the continuing and enduring influences of the caring work that is manifested in familial relations, love, friendship and passionate attachment, i.e. the 'ties that bind'. This stands in contrast to the theorisation of late modernity as typified by Giddens (1992), who argues that intimate social relations have 'democratised' between partners. This 'transformation of intimacy' claimed as superseding what has gone before, fails to take account of the persistence of patriarchal orders. From a contrasting perspective, empirical work by Evans (2010) examines the enduring commitments and affiliations of working-class young women to their families and communities. These loyalties exist alongside young women's higher education success and show the valuing of 'staying put' as a counter to pathological narratives of such group's 'lack of aspiration' (Francis and Hey 2008). In sum, social change is processual, uneven and complicated – the old (formations, mores, behaviour) can be encased in the new or simply contiguous with it. There is a specifically feminine dimension to how the new order is lived since young women bear the burden of representation both as its emblem (successful Alpha girls) and as its problematic case (teenage mothers) (McRobbie 2000).

Young women (for example) are thus now in positions of having access to increased opportunities. However, this is often accompanied by intensified classed misogyny and increased uncertainty (McRobbie 2005, 2007; Bauman 2001). McRobbie (2007), in particular argues, that there is a 'new sexual contract' which requires that young women invest in a highly sexualised hyperfemininity as their price for entering the workplace, which does not so much yield to their competence as require their self-administered femininity as a mode of discounting it. Moreover, if 'structured individualisation' now characterises the moment, it does not so much as eliminate hierarchies as mobilise differences between those who can accrue capitals and those who cannot.

Our data: talking personally and politically

The data for this paper were generated through a reflective discussion which formed part of an on-going conversation. The conversation was framed by a set of questions that sought to address two concerns: firstly, our own experiences of growing up as young girls, our hopes and dreams and our desires in terms of the choices we have made as adults; and secondly, the choices that our daughters have made and our desires for their futures. Our conversation/dialogue was mediated through our disciplinary background and expertise, 'an academic knowing', and in our discussions regarding the writing of the paper we came to appreciate the difficulty in pulling together the private and public dimensions of our lives. Because of our personal involvement with our daughters, we have felt conflicted about how we should tell ours and our daughters' stories. How can the complex interaction of the subject, the family and its historical location be unravelled and then read through the lens of the contemporary social and political? However, in formatting and structuring the paper for a journal, we have found this exercise to be supportive insofar as we have been better able to struggle with the dilemmas of bringing together the personal and political in such a stark way and render our daughters' stories more as a text telling a story of our selves and thus navigate the ethical issues of appropriation and authorship.

The methodology employed in this paper can be seen as a hybrid form in the space between the use of auto-ethnography alongside that of a more accepted and understood form of ethnography. Ellis and Bochner advocate authoethnography, a form of writing that 'make[s] the researcher's own experience a topic of investigation in its own right ... rather than seeming as if they're written from nowhere by nobody' and 'asking their readers to feel the truth of their stories and to become co-participants, engaging the storyline morally, emotionally, aesthetically, and intellectually' (2000, 745).

The first part of the following analysis is a reflective discussion in which we seek to interpret the significance of choice, auto/biography and its psycho-social complexities. We intend to explore choice partly in terms of: our own backgrounds; the role and type of values exposed between mothers and daughters; and the importance placed on education. Memories are invoked in interviews often called up unprompted, in a stream of consciousness way by questions, but there is also something else going on when academics 'do' interview talk – a specific cultural practice borne of a rationalistic form of reflexivity given that the speakers are situated within an academic as well as an auto/biographical project. The awkwardness of this came home to us as we listened to ourselves. The data as discourse revealed our 'theoretical logic of practice' shown in the transcript, as we slide uneasily around sense making that could implicate us, our own mothers and our families in objectification. The irony that research into subjectivity invariably and always reproduces objectification is not lost on us. We are only too aware that our daughters have not had a voice in this exercise, in the narratives that have been constructed, and we leave unanswered any question about the ethics of doing this so 'close to home'.

The immediate context

In conversation two mothers are talking about their teenage daughters. Both of these mothers are perceived as successful middle-class professionals although both have working-class backgrounds. They grew up in the post-war period, a time of relative austerity with limited opportunities. The themes arising from their discussions featured key preoccupations such as: daughters' reluctance to apply themselves, fears for their future given the hypercompetitive world, tied in with reminiscences of their upbringing and material lack set against their daughters' more affluent lives.

Hey had a classic 'second chance' 'late developer' education. First, because she failed her 11+, an examination determining access to elite secondary education. She subsequently refused to take the second chance 13+ examination when it was offered to her. She might well have found herself the wrong side of the gender 'adjustment'. Fortunately, in staying at her local school, she seemed to benefit from not going to a selective school, being a 'top' girl in many of the arts subjects and being encouraged to go on to a 'technical college' after her four years at secondary modern school. She went to college and then gained enough qualifications to be considered for further education in a nearby city. This enabled her to get sufficient advanced qualifications to go to university. She became a teacher then a feminist – taking an masters degree in Women's Studies – and she was awarded a scholarship from the Economic and Social Research Council to undertake her PhD. George had what would be considered the opportunity to move upwards on the educational ladder in passing the 11+ and attending a voluntary-aided girls' grammar school located in inner London. Coming from a working-class background, she very quickly learnt her place amongst peers and friends whose class location and access to wealth was something she could only dream of. Many of her friends came from 'professional' families where going to university was an unquestioned and accepted part of their lives. Within a year she moved from being a high achiever at primary school to a low achiever in this highly academic middle-class environment. Leaving school to train as a primary teacher was seen as a success in the context of her family even though the need to understand the wider context of how aspiration and opportunity is shaped by patriarchal order and class location drove her to complete a degree in Education, followed by an MA in Sociology and finally a PhD. This in part gave her the deeper insights and wherewithal to lay many ghosts to rest which had created a habitus of not feeling herself as good as her contemporaries.

One can see that both mothers/authors were beneficiaries of chance and contingency as well as free higher education. The welfare state had been a benign presence in their respectable working-class backgrounds and education provided a passport to social mobility – indeed educational expansion sucked in many such working-class women identifying with its more positive effects.

The particular time and place impacted on their sense of self, most notably their desires for 'better things' and their educational biographies. These aspirations were invariably contrasted with how they see their own daughters' position. Here the role of 'natural' maternal anxiety was stoked by knowledge of the current intensified competition for social mobility and success. This suggested a very different emotional material habitus from the one they had to deal with as children in which, for one, the aspiration to 'be happy' was recollected (cf. Thomson, Henderson, and Holland 2002). We explore this aspect of the significance of the material in the following section.

Welfare and wanting; desire, shame and ambivalent success

Money was a major theme of the mothers' talk, there were many references to 'wanting' and 'doing without' recalled in ordinary as well as significant domestic incidents. Such memories were emotionally charged with feelings of shame, guilt and longing: the deferral of the giving of birthday presents 'cos my mum always had to wait for pay day'; of a request for an acoustic guitar that was promised but never materialised because the cheque bounced. The effect was feeling 'mortified' and so as not to put her mother in the position again of 'letting her down', she subsequently avoided such extravagant requests.

More trivial utterances and incidents were recollected; emblematically one of us recalled a friend asking her mother what was for tea; reply – 'a kick up the cat and a run round the table'; of dropping a three-penny bit in long grass, and the scramble to find it; of 'squandering' a whole bottle of Lucozade, breaking it in the hearth at home in pursuit of its golden wrapping in a struggle with a younger sister, provoking intense guilt as it was 'a complete sin because this is very expensive'; of more intense guilt because one was caught in a calculated move to 'embezzle' bread money by buying a cheaper loaf. There were recollections of hunger 'of eating the end of another family's loaf'; of 'stealing' meat from a father's plate as the only one in the family to have this; of a 'brother who always got the ... bigger plate'. This was not a habitus of 'choice' or 'options' but of 'you'll get what you're given'. Wanting, desire and 'doing without' co-existed in a micropolitics of material, rather than Lacanian, lack. This is a discourse not only of social class but of poverty and deprivation – of a culture of not having enough. How did desire persist here and what possibilities of agency and choice feature here?

Yet, the subsequent biographies of the two mothers reveal them as 'shifters in position' (Cohen in Ainley et al. 1999; Lucey, Melody, and Walkerdine 2003), a move that we have argued ties their agency and choice to the existence of public discourses (the Welfare State and feminism) which offered crucial material and emotional resources for enacting personal and social change.[2] Indeed both mothers invested heavily in education, in feminism and in 'fighting back', and in their resistance to class and gender hierarchy were compelled, paradoxically, to conform and perform with education as the only secure route to accruing the capital/credentials to do so.

Given this 'weight of maternal history' (which both mothers had insisted on 'sharing' with their daughters), what did they think of their daughter's current biographies which seemed to be more about risk than choice as manifest in their educational and personal trajectories? Or to put it another way, what sense did they get of how successfully they had transmitted their particular left-bourgeois habitus? Did their daughters invest in what they had so fiercely striven for, and had they also acquired an emancipatory politics of equity? Throughout these questions the mothers were aware of a crucial double aspect of their mobility which entailed a deep ambivalence about the middle class, about the class system and meritocracy. The mothers had apparently 'mastered' the rules of the game but they also constituted it as a political object, theorised it as the source of social injustice. We turn now to discuss this.

Post-welfare; post-politics; the triumph of desire 'Wanting it Now'

We could anticipate that young women benefiting from this inheritance would have some interesting if not tortuous psychic negotiations to deal with in view of: their mothers' ambitious educational expectations for them; the imperative of individualisation; the seductive power of consumption; popular cultural forms of stylised sexualised femininity; and the fears, risks and fantasies that accompany all such growings up (McRobbie 2007).

Where do these twenty-first-century daughters find agency amidst the weight of their personal history? Both mothers were hyper-sensitive to 'risk' though this was not the denatured concept invoked by Beck, Giddens, and Lash (1994), but more serial anxiety, lest their daughters 'downclass' by getting off the education escalator. Class reproduction in such competitive circumstances cannot be imagined as secure (Power and Whitty 2002). One spoke of her daughter's inability to focus despite being passionate about being a vet:

> She lives in a fantasy. She lives in her head in terms of, this is what I want to do and it's going to happen ... she has all these pictures in her head just these pictures of what she wants to do...

But her mother experienced her as 'not working':

> And of course you have to get, really, really brilliant grades ... and she is not going to get them ... the desire again without the effort.

Recently her daughter has 'applied herself' but this is perhaps too late:

> But ... it's come .... to her that she didn't put in any effort, but now she just says 'well I haven't got the brains ... I wish I was clever now'.

The other mother recalls heated confrontations with a 'non-working' daughter also. The daughter would recoil from this 'nagging', by various manoeuvres – talking of someone who was 'driving around in a £40,000 car who didn't go to university'. She later dropped two A levels[3] and, according to her mother, did not work hard or do herself 'justice', ending up at a 'low prestige' university; when she subsequently complained about poor-quality facilities, and teaching, the mother had literally 'to just sit ... on the whole tirade'. There is a recognition that resenting her own daughter's location within a working-class university implicates the mother in demeaning her daughter's situation as well as her own past. This is merely part of the painful paradox induced by reflexive political self-awareness.

This lack of daughterly application especially at high-stakes examination times drove both mothers 'nuts'. They spoke of 'desperation and frustration' as well as reproaching themselves for exerting 'a bit too much pressure'. Both mothers acknowledged that the impact of popular culture and local peer pressure was a more significant influence on the choices their daughters exercised than their own sway as mothers, in figuring the habitus and 'choices' of their daughters.

Interestingly, both daughters had a wide-ranging group of friends with a core of working-class young men as boyfriends, ex-boyfriends or 'boyfriends'. One mother commented on the boyfriend's equivalent 'fantasy' or unrealistic ambition, claiming that he wanted to become a pilot but he was also not working hard at his studies. She thought of this as symptomatic of current times with its stress on desire, 'the instant', with the sheer force of such wishes imaginatively collapsing the gap between wanting and having:

> He was going to be a pilot and what is he doing about it? 'How're you gonna get in there? How you gonna get on to a foundation ... course?' And I thought it's still the same, you know ... and I think it's probably 'I can have it' ... if you don't have to ... ('grind' the other mother interjects) grind, to, to you know to get a new top or whatever. Maybe you don't have to ... work in order to get your GCSE.[4]

Their daughters' dis-investments in education need to be contextualised. It is a cliché but perhaps useful to think of them as defensive moves they had to make. After all, what if they had worked hard and then, comparing themselves to their mothers' success, had not done as well? – an unliveable irony given their material advantage. Given the 'governance of the soul' (Rose 1990), what a terrible burden of responsibilisation to risk being stigmatised as a 'loser'; much better perhaps not to 'really try'.

Maybe there was a paradox in these biographical projects in which, what is imagined as a risk (being disaffected from education) actually seems less risky than investing in it. In refusing the apparently high-risk choice of application they have worked a rift – a space for revoking the orbiting anxiety of their families, especially their mothers' excessive emotional pressure.

In a later part of the discussion, one mother recognises the daughter's own 'shifting' position – turning her from what she had seen as resisting education, feminism and politics into a different sort of person, reflecting on and angered by the poverty of the 'street politics' she experienced in her university location, an institution which was literally in precisely the sort of environment from which she knew her mother had 'escaped' (Lawler 1999). In current analyses of social class, we still feel that the 'emotional' material and convoluted symbolic definition of what is at stake in these processes of choice and distinction is under-theorised and underplayed (though see Walkerdine, Lucey, and Melody 2001; Lucey, Melody, and Walkerdine 2003; Reay 2005; Sayer 2005) even in those analyses influenced by Bourdieu and feminism, not to mention Marxism. For the mothers, they are left wondering what they would have done if their daughters had chosen to 'shift position' into a vulgar self-serving rampant individualism, finding 'posh' boyfriends and inhabiting the cultural habitus of the acquisitional segment of the bourgeoisie.

Was their daughters' ambiguous relation to education not so much a rejection as a 'gift' (Mauss 1925) that the daughters were returning back to their families by 'choosing' to complicate and dilute their privilege? Or is it that 'gifting' could in an ironic sense be our daughters in postmodern times returning the compliment by questioning their mothers' choice of up-classing? Did they prefer working-class locations (boyfriends, institutions?) motivated by affiliations and norms that perhaps they and their mothers simply could not (afford to) see? Did their positive identifications with 'working-class' values call attention to the very contradiction of the mothers' own necessary dis-identification with their origin? Or is this just an archetypal familial rebellion, common to all such struggles in which children seek and exploit the most potent parental weakness to undermine parental power? Or are these positionalities entangled the one within each other?

Some implications

Notwithstanding all this, as has been widely documented, since the 1990s there have been unparalleled levels of success from girls of all classes

(Arnot, David, and Weiner 1999). This gain for girls refocuses attention once again on the changing pattern of adult women's lifestyles and the role of (feminist) mothers in their daughters' academic success. The 'reproduction' of feminism as a cultural, political and educational space was created by collective struggle (Spender and Sarah 1980) but this also occurs more obliquely between mothers and daughters. Part of our concern is to see the contradictions in both old/new femininities and feminisms.

Recent work has begun to consider how feminism has been disarmed: apparently taken as the 'common sense' of our daughters' generation, whilst disappearing from the public agenda (McRobbie 2009; Segal 2000). However, Roof (1997) cautions against this account and remarks on how a previous generation of feminists may have tended to 'locate[s] responsibility and credit for the future in the past; children who do not follow the program become wayward'. She goes on to question feminism's reliance on a generational family motif: 'The family, especially this devoted and Oedipal version of the family, is a particular historical patriarchal formation linked to both ideology and the exigencies of capitalism' (1997, 85). History repeats itself in the form of patterns, but also 'habits of mind'; the familial paradigm imports notions of *'debt, legacy, rivalry, property'* (1997, 84, emphasis added).

Questions of reproduction have been raised in respect to both feminism and social class. Adkins (2004) argues that we should rethink the theoretical purchase of the transmission model in which feminism is rendered ahistorical. Equally, Bourdieu's (1977) notion of habitus has been questioned within feminist debates (Adkins and Skeggs, 2005) for its lack of capacity to fully account for agency. The mothers sought to transmit to their daughters insights into how class worked, not least their own determination through education to overcome their original position by their investment in 'working hard'. They 'failed' to ensure their daughters behaved as they did. The daughters picked up on class in quite another way. We could therefore envisage or imagine the possibility that the daughters might be critically reworking and replaying 'working class' and in the process possibly holding up a mirror to their mothers and their generation in their pursuit of social mobility.

But again maybe we could think that what the daughters were doing was to continue this 'legacy' by bringing class back home as a provocation – as a different sort of politics of resistance. Perhaps the ability to rationalise the ambiguities of our daughters' class relational behaviour *is* precisely the point – that our investment in pedagogising, like that of Walkerdine and Lucey's (1989) mothers, is another modality of oppression – as 'understanding' always takes us away from, rather than into, the emotionally laden histories of mother and child. Yet, we are again caught in another conundrum since 'understanding' them in this instance might be exactly how we have always constituted our daughters and always thus made for their specific form of domesticated feminine subjectification. They had and have no choice but to resist these norms of rationality so as to strive to breathe what they took as their own (chosen) air. As for our 'political' daughters, growing up as feminists in post-feminism, maybe what we need is also to create much more space for listening to their own understandings of the worlds they live and resist imposing on them generational narratives that assumes 'mother' knows best.

Notes

1. This paper arises from the UK Economic and Social Research Council-funded seminar series 'Young Women in Movement: Sexualities, Vulnerabilities, Needs and Norms' (ESRC RES-451-26-0715), based at Goldsmiths, University of London, 2009–2011.
2. For further discussions of the particular features of working-class feminist reconstruction within the possibilities opened up by the combination of the Welfare State, feminism and new social movements in the late twentieth century, see Hey (2006).
3. A levels are a major route to university entrance in England and Wales. Students normally take between two and four subjects at age 18.
4. The GCSE is the main school-leaving examination in England and Wales, taken at age 16.

References

Adkins, L. 2004. Passing on feminism: From consciousness to reflexivity? *European Journal of Women's Studies* 11: 427–44.
Adkins, L., and B. Skeggs, eds. 2005. *Feminism after Bourdieu*. Oxford: Blackwell.
Ainley, P., P. Cohen, V. Hey, and T. Wengraf. 1999. *Studies in learning regeneration*. London: Centre for New Ethnicities Research, University of East London.
Arnot, M., M. David, and G. Weiner. 1999. *Closing the gender gap: Post-war education and social change*. Cambridge: Polity Press.
Ball, S.J. 2010. Intersectionality, Moments, Interactions and Disruptions - Unfinished Thoughts contribution to think pieces for the ESRC Seminar Series on Intersectionality: its relevance to educational research, politics and practice. Half Day Conversational Seminar June 8th 2010, London, IOE.
Ball, S.J., M. Maguire, and S. Macrae. 2000. Choice, pathways and transitions post-16. *New youth, new economies in the global city*. London: Routledge Falmer.
Bauman, Z. 2001. *Community: Seeking safety in an insecure world*. Cambridge: Polity Press.
Beck, U., and E. Beck-Gernsheim. 2002. *Individualization: Institutionalized individualism and its social and political consequences*. London: Sage.
Beck, U., A. Giddens, and S. Lash. 1994. *Reflexive modernization: Politics, tradition and aesthetics in the modern social order*. Cambridge: Polity.
Bourdieu, P. 1977. *Outline of a Theory of Practice*. Cambridge: Cambridge University Press.
Butler, J. 1999. Performativity's social magic. In *Bourdieu: A critical reader*, ed. R. Shusterman 113–129. Oxford: Blackwell.
David, M., V. Hey, and L. Morley, eds. 2011. Challenge, change or crisis in global higher education. Special issue, *Contemporary Social Science* 6, no. 2.

Ellis, C., and A.P. Bochner. 2000. Autoethnography, personal narrative: Researcher as subject. In *The handbook of qualitative research*. 2nd ed., ed. N. Denzin and Y. Lincoln 733–768. Thousand Oaks, CA: Sage.

Evans, M. 2010. A mysterious commodity: Capitalism and femininity. In Gender inequalities in the 21st century: *New barriers and continuing constraints*, ed. J. Scott, R. Crompton, and C. Lyonette 275–290. Cheltenham, UK: Edgard Elgar Publishing.

Francis, B., and V. Hey. 2009. Talking back to power: Snowballs in hell and the imperative of insisting on structural explanations. *Gender and Education* 21: 225–32.

Fraser, N. 1997. *Justice interruptus: Critical reflections on the 'postsocialist' condition*. London: Routledge.

George, R. 2007a. Urban girls' 'race', friendship & school choice. *Race, Ethnicity & Education* 10, no. 2: 115–29.

George, R. 2007b. *Girls in a goldfish bowl: Moral regulation and the use of power amongst inner city girls*. Rotterdam: Sense Publications.

George, R., and J. Clay. 2012. Challenging pedagogy: Emotional disruptions, young girls, parents and schools. Paper presented at the British Educational Research Association Conference, September 6, in Manchester, UK.

Giddens, Anthony. 1992. The transformation of intimacy. *Sexuality, love and eroticism in modern societies*. Cambridge: Polity Press.

Hey, V. 2004. Perverse pleasures: Identity work and the paradoxes of greedy institutions. *Journal of International Women's Studies* 5, no. 3: 33–43. http://www.bridgew.edu/soas/jiws/May04/.pdf/.

Hey, V. 2005. The contrasting social logics of sociality and survival: Cultures of classed be/longing in late modernity. *Sociology* 39: 855–72.

Hey, V. 2006a. 'Getting over it'? Reflections on the melancholia of reclassified identities. *Gender and Education* 18: 295–308.

Hey, V. 2006b. The politics of performative resignification: Translating Judith Butler's theoretical discourse and its potential for a sociology of education. *British Journal of Sociology of Education* 27: 439–57.

Hey, V. and L. Morley. 2011. Imagining the university of the future: Eyes wide open? Expanding the imaginary through critical and feminist ruminations in and on the university. *Contemporary Social Science* (Special Issue: Challenge, Change or Crisis in Global Higher Education edited by M.E. David, V. Hey & L. Morley) 6, no. 2: 165–74.

Hey, V. 2011. Affective asymmetries: Academics, austerity and the mis/recognition of emotion. *Contemporary Social Science* 6, no. 2: 207–22.

Hey, V., and C. Leathwood. 2009. Passionate attachments: Higher education, policy, knowledge, emotion and social justice. *Higher Education Policy* 22: 101–18.

Jackson, C. 2010. Fear in education. *Educational Review* 62, no. 1: 39–52.

Jimenez, L., and V. Walkerdine. 2011. A psychosocial approach to shame, embarrassment and melancholia amongst unemployed young men and their fathers. *Gender and Education* 23: 185–99.

Lawler, S. 1999. Children need but mothers only want: the power of 'needs talk' in the constitution of childhood. In *Relating intimacies: Power and resistance*, ed. J. Seymour and P. Bagguley, 64–88. London: Macmillan.

Lawler, S. 2000. Escape and escapism: Representing working-class women. In *Cultural studies and the working class*, ed. S. Munt 113–128. London: Cassell.

Lawler, S. 2005. Introduction: Class, culture and identity. *Sociology* 39: 797–806.

Lucey, H., J. Melody, and V. Walkerdine. 2003. Uneasy hybrids: Psychosocial aspects of becoming educationally successful for working-class young women. *Gender and Education* 15: 285–305.

Mauss, M. 1925. *The Gift; The Form and Reason for Exchange in Archaic Societies.* Routledge, London. Translation by W. D. Halls, 2002.

McNay, L. 1999. Gender, habitus and the field: Pierre Bourdieu and the limits of reflexivity. *Theory, Culture & Society* 16, no. 1: 95–117.

McRobbie, A. 2000. Feminism and the third way. *Feminist Review* 64: 97–113.

McRobbie, A. 2005. Notes on 'What Not to Wear' and post-feminist symbolic violence. *The Sociological Review* suppl. 2: 97–109.

McRobbie, A. 2007. Illegible rage: Reflections on young women's post feminist disorders. Keynote lecture in ESRC New Femininities Series, January 25, in London.

McRobbie, A. 2009. *The aftermath of feminism: Gender, culture and social change.* London: Sage.

Morrison, T. 1992. *Playing in the dark: Whiteness and the literary imagination.* Cambridge, MA: Harvard University Press.

Power, S., and G. Whitty. 2002. Bernstein and the middle class: Basil Bernstein's theory of social class, educational codes and social control. *British Journal of the Sociology of Education* 3: 595–606.

Reay, D. 2005. Beyond consciousness? The psychic landscape of social class. *Sociology* 39: 911–28.

Redman, P. 2009. Affect revisited: Transference-countertransference and the unconscious dimensions of affective, felt and emotional experience. *Subjectivity* 26: 51–68.

Roof, J. 1997. Generational difficulties; or, the fear of a barren history. In *Generations: Academic feminists in dialogue*, ed. D. Looser and E.A. Kaplan, 69–87. Minneapolis and London: University of Minnesota Press.

Rose, N. 1990. *Governing the soul.* London: Routledge.

Sayer, A. 2005. Class, moral worth and recognition. *Sociology* 39: 947–63.

Segal, L. 2000. Only contradictions on offer. *Women: A Cultural Review* 11, nos. 1–2: 19–36.

Skeggs, B. 1997. *Formations of class and gender: Becoming respectable.* London: Sage.

Skeggs, B. 2002. Exchange, value and affect: Against polite sociology. Paper presented at the Feminists Evaluate Bourdieu Conference, October 11, in Manchester, UK.

Skeggs, B. 2004. *Class, self and culture.* London: Routledge.

Spender, D., and E. Sarah. 1980. *Learning to lose: Sexism and education.* London: The Woman's Press.

Thomson, R., S. Henderson, and J. Holland. 2002. Critical moments: Choice chance and opportunity in young people's narratives of transition. *Sociology* 36: 335–54.

Walkerdine, V., and H. Lucey. 1989. *Democracy in the kitchen: Regulating mothers and socialising daughters.* London: Virago.

Walkerdine, V., H. Lucey, and J. Melody. 2001. *Growing up girl: Psychosocial explorations of gender and class.* London: Palgrave.

Wetherell, M. 2012. *Affect and emotion: A new social science understanding.* London: Sage.

Young women online: collaboratively constructing identities[1]

Carrie Paechter

Goldsmiths, University of London, New Cross, London, UK

> In this paper I examine how young women construct their identities with others in online communities. I argue that the proliferation of social networking and its popularity among young people means that performed identities are increasingly collaboratively constructed, with the individual having less control over their public image than was previously the case. This has implications for how young women can understand themselves. In some ways this leads to an increased visibility and a blurring of public and private, frontstage and backstage arenas. It also, however, makes it possible for girls to gain support for alternative, more marginal, identities through interaction with online communities. I investigate the impact of these communities and the possibility that some may not be entirely benign. I also consider issues of authenticity and performance, and the impact of these on young women's understanding of and feelings about their bodies. Finally, I discuss possible pedagogic responses to these phenomena.

Introduction

Identities are not constructed in isolation. Who we think we are changes in response to time, place and circumstances, to the people, systems and artefacts with which we interact, and to the power relations between us. It has been argued, in particular, that new information and communication technologies and related social changes have had crucial effects on identities and how they are formed and understood (Livingstone 2008; Mallan and Giardina 2009). In this paper, I am going to look at how young femininities are constructed in relation to these social technological developments, and, in particular, to participation in online communities through social networking and related activities.

It is important to remember, when considering the relationship young women have with technologies of all kinds, that technologies themselves are not developed in a vacuum, but respond to users. Many new technologies and uses of technology arise out of a perceived need, or are adapted by users to suit their purposes. This means that although identities are indeed partially forged by technology use, those technologies are themselves developing in response to new identities and the demands they bring. In this way, technologies and identities can be seen as being mutually constructed. This is important in the context of social networking sites (SNS) which, as well as being instrumental in the identity construction of their users, have also developed and adapted in relation to the requirements of this online/offline identity work.

In the paper I will consider four main themes. The first relates to the ways in which performed online identities have become a collaborative construction negotiated between the individual and her or his 'friends'. This will lead to a discussion of the ways in which young people's use of SNS and other online confessional technologies is affecting ideas about privacy and how it is negotiated. I will then look at some specific identity communities and their relationship to members' online and offline lives. Finally, I will consider authenticity, and, in particular, the relationship between online and offline identity performance and the effects of this on body technologies.

Collaborative identity construction in SNS and other online contexts

Young women are prolific participants in SNSs, using them to remain in frequent contact with each other during the day, and as an online extension of offline friendships (Davies 2013; Livingstone 2008). The popularity of sites varies over time, geography and with the age of the group (some are considered to be mainly for younger children; Livingstone 2008), but all have the same basic features: the ability to customise one's 'home page' to reflect one's personality or preferences; the ability to list and stay in touch with 'friends' through the site; and the possibility of posting messages on other people's profiles, so that a person's profile is made up of a combination of things put there by the 'owner' and comments or links from others. These others may or may not be people known in the offline context. While several authors argue that most teenagers only give people 'friend' status if they are already known (Ahn 2011; Clarke 2009; Cohen and Shade 2008; Mallan and Giardina 2009; Ringrose 2011), there is evidence that being a friend of an online friend will in some cases confer sufficient bona fides to be accepted (Robards 2010; Walther et al. 2008). It is also the case that specific online communities, some of which will be discussed below, are explicitly designed to bring together people who do not have sufficient like-minded contacts in the offline world.

Through the choice of background, the information given about the self, the individual profile picture, links to other profiles and sites, and ongoing comments about one's life and activities, a SNS profile allows an individual to perform their identity through their homepage. However, because the 'owner' is not the only person who contributes to this page, this projected identity is, in many ways, collaboratively constructed with others, in particular the individual's friends on the site. Mallan and Giardina (2009) refer to such identities as 'wikidentities', arguing that

> the 'performed expressions' of the users' identities are both individually and collectively constructed, and this collaborative design phenomenon makes a particular statement about the user's identity, which can be expressed as: 'This is who we understand "me" to be.'

This collaboratively constructed identity work takes place through a number of features of SNS, depending on what is available. For example, the 'friends list' is a public display of connections which reflects both 'popularity' (indicated by having lots of friends, though not so many that it appears that one befriends just anyone) and the variety of one's social groups and interests. These lists can both demonstrate someone's membership of a particular social group and at the same time mark their status in that group. They also, by giving access to friends of friends, act as a means through which friendship networks can be extended and developed (Mallan and Giardina 2009; Walther et al. 2008).

Livingstone (2008) argues that in some ways the profile is more reflective of the peer group than the individual, as social networking reveals the self as embedded within the group, both through the comments of others to the owner's profile page and through the use of group photographs as the main image on some profiles (Mallan and Giardina 2009). Livingstone also notes that some young people put together joke profiles or make spoof postings on each other's profiles, with the understanding that anyone reading them will recognise the nature of the relationship rather than take comments at face value as revealing of self:

> For several of the interviewees, it seemed that the position in the peer network is more significant than the personal information provided, rendering the profile a place-marker more than a self portrait. Initially I misunderstood this – for example on Leo's site there was a comment from his friend 'Blondie' saying that she's pregnant: when I ask, he observes that, of course, 'she's joking' – the point being to share (and display) their humorous relationship not a personal self-disclosure. (2008, 399)

Thus, Livingstone suggests, it is not so much the content of the profile page but the way that it is interacted with and used by the social group within which it is embedded that reflects the identity of the person officially behind it.

That online identities are collaboratively constructed by and reflective of the peer group is also supported by evidence about how online profiles are judged by viewers. Ahn (2011) reports previous experimental studies showing that people rate Facebook users not already known to them as more attractive if their profiles show attractive friends, and also if they have positive comments on their wall (the space on a Facebook profile where others can contribute publicly). She also argues that feedback from the social network affects what young people place on their profiles and what friends they display, again supporting the suggestion that online identity performances are collaboratively constructed with the peer group.

This collaborative construction has implications for privacy which will be discussed below. It also makes it harder to control one's identity displays: what is shown on a personal SNS profile is not always chosen by the 'owner'. Walther et al. (2008), for example, found in an experimental study that posts from other people on someone's Facebook wall can affect judgements made by strangers about the owner of the profile. They suggest that, because these comments are seen as unsanctioned by the owner, their value as identity 'evidence' is likely to be high. Although it is possible to remove comments from one's Facebook wall, Walther et al. argue that this 'implicitly challenges the rules of friendship' (2008, 30) and therefore rarely happens. Consequently, the owner of a SNS profile is open to having their public identity constructed by others in multifarious ways, not all of which are entirely benevolent (Walther et al. 2008). Similarly, the facility on SNS to 'tag' photographs with the names of individuals in them makes it much harder to control what aspects of one's life are seen by others and thereby become part of one's performed identity (Cohen and Shade 2008). These affordances have the potential to take what were considered by an individual to be backstage events (Goffman 1959) and bring them into the spaces of frontstage performance (Pearson 2009), leading to possible unwitting and even humiliating exposure. This suggests that media education needs to involve the development of a critical awareness of these effects and their implications for online identity construction.

Online privacy and identity construction

Related to these issues are questions of privacy online and how notions of privacy are changing in relation to the ways in which young people construct their identities in this context. Pearson (2009) argues that identities in SNS are 'deliberately constructed performances that straddle the frontstage and the backstage, the public and the private', blurring the boundaries between these. What feels to the users like intimate space is open to the watchful eyes of others, while deliberate frontstage performances might end up being seen by no-one. She argues that this is not necessarily problematic: the amount of disclosure remains managed by the performer, and many performances can work on more than one level, so that certain aspects will only be understood by close friends. She also suggests that the blurring of public and private allows people to try out emotional engagement or intimacy with others in a relatively safe space, before devoting significant resources to this.

Such a view is supported by Kapidzik and Herring (2011), who report previous research suggesting that young women are more sexually assertive in teenage chat rooms than face to face. It also reflects, to some extent, Ringrose's (2011) research, which suggests that girls in particular experiment with sexual self-commodification online despite expressing concerns about 'slutty' behaviour in offline contexts.

While privacy is an important concern for young people with respect to their online activities and identities, it is not always understood in the same way as it is by adults. Livingstone (2008) notes that many things that previous generations would consider deeply personal, such as religion or politics, are treated as non-private by teenagers. She argues that, for young people, privacy is concerned with having control over who knows what about you, and that visibility to one's parents is generally of much greater concern than having one's posts read by strangers. Cohen and Shade (2008) similarly argue that the 14–24-year-olds they studied were primarily concerned about teachers, parents, the government and future employers viewing their profiles, and actively used privacy strategies to prevent this from happening. While Davies' (2013) and Livingstone's (2008) respondents found manipulating SNS privacy settings difficult, research elsewhere (boyd and Hargittai 2010; Hodkinson and Lincoln 2008; Robards 2010) suggests that most young people, particularly girls, do feel confident in doing this, although boyd and Hargittai (2010) point out that it is unclear whether their respondents fully understood the changes they were implementing. This may be something that educators should address explicitly.

A major aspect of online (and, indeed, offline) privacy within the smaller friendship group is the expectation among many young people that friends will be always and instantly available. While SNS allow children to maintain friendships in ways that were not possible before, for example when changing schools or meeting people at summer camp (Clarke 2009), mobile technologies can be problematically compelling to users (van Manen 2010). Clarke (2009) argues that adolescents spend more time talking to friends than in any other single activity; the constant availability of SNS and instant messaging facilities in contemporary mobile phones means that a good friend is expected to be constantly available to her peers (Davies 2013). Paradoxically, this constant possibility of contact allows people to feel in touch with others without having to be too close; it provides a 'virtual experience of present absence (van Manen 2010, 1027).

This requirement of continuous contact and at least an illusion of openness online has other implications for how privacy is understood. van Manen (2010) argues, for example, that the increasing use of SNS, personal websites and confessional blogspaces represents a proliferation of 'Momus technologies',[2] which reveal a user's innermost thoughts for all to see. He suggests that

> Privacy, secrecy, and innerness in young people's lives play a critical role in the development of self-identity, autonomy, intimacy, and the ability of learning to negotiate closeness and distance in social relations ... Are Momus technologies profoundly altering the quality and nature of social relations, and especially the possibility of and need for self-identity, solitude, intimacy, and closeness among young people? (van Manen 2010, 1023)

van Manen argues that secrecy is essential to human existence and especially to intimacy, and that online openness is in danger of breaking this down. It seems to me, however, that young people do continue to maintain secrecy with relation both to key figures, such as parents, and within the apparent openness of their SNS presence, using alternative means, such as private chat facilities, face-to-face encounters, or texting, to communicate more intimately. While SNS, as a place for young people to 'hang out' (Ahn 2011) does share some features with the bedroom, previously a key site for young women's friendship cultures (Cullen 2007), that does not mean simply that the bedroom has expanded to accommodate a much larger group. Some of the activities previously taking place there have moved to more private online spaces, or, indeed, continue to take place face-to-face, in the bedroom itself.

Pearson (2009) argues that much online communication takes place within a 'glass bedroom': a place in which intimate conversations and exchanges occur but whose occupants have varying awareness of more distant friends or strangers moving past the walls and looking in. She suggests that such spaces are not truly backstage in the way a real bedroom may be, but bridge the public and private, allowing those outside the bedroom to engage or not with what is going on inside (Robards 2010). On the other hand, writing before the explosion of SNS use, Harris (2003) argues that the internet operates as a liminal space in which girls can actively manipulate public/private boundaries. She suggests that self-authored e-zines operate as a private space from which adults can legitimately be excluded, not dissimilar to a girl's bedroom. Hodkinson and Lincoln (2008), similarly, see online journals as much more closely aligned with real teenage bedrooms, having the same status as personal territory. They argue that:

> Like the bedroom ... the interactive and multidimensional space for the online journal offers a safe, personally owned and controlled space which is used as part of the negotiation of youthful transitions via marking out of territory, the exploration and exhibition of identity and the generation and living out of personal social networks. (Hodkinson and Lincoln 2008, 27)

In similar ways to the bedroom, they argue, online journal spaces offer high levels of ownership and control, with privacy restrictions giving control over entry and 'keep out' signs prominently displayed. As with bedroom spaces, which are arranged so as to display the self to visitors, the 'look' of online journals is customised to reflect the identity of the user, changing in parallel with rites of passage. Within the journal itself, the author can experiment with identities and establish her or his own limits in relative safety. Furthermore, those commenting on journal entries are expected to behave as guests, so that it is considered rude to make critical remarks. Hodkinson and Lincoln (2008) note that users did not just host conversations in their own journal spaces, but visited those of others, commenting on previously posted comments in a way that parallels teenage socialising. Although this frequently meant that more people were involved than could fit into an average physical bedroom, those involved would still be a hand-picked network of friends.

Although real bedrooms remain a crucial forum for social interaction among young people (Cullen 2007; Hodkinson and Lincoln 2008), the physical space of the bedroom does seem to have been partially displaced online, making the division between private and public family space much more fluid. For teenage girls in particular, the bedroom used to be a core social space where groups would meet and talk in relative private. Now, however, while the importance of the bedroom may relate more directly to its position as the location of private computer use (Hodkinson and Lincoln 2008), in households in which teenagers do not have their own computers, the location of 'private teenage space' may have moved to what appear at face value to be more public family areas, such as the living room or kitchen. Within that public space, a private realm is constructed online: while being accessed in public, its interactions take place in (relative) private. Girls' changing relationship to new technologies may mean that they are more physically present in the main family arena, while being more emotionally or socially absent, due to their constant engagement with others online or through texting on mobile phones (Wajcman 2008). What this can mean in practice is that a young woman is more visible in the public spaces of the family, ostensibly taking part in family meals, outings, collective television viewing and other activities, while remaining active within the friendship group throughout, using a variety of technological means.

Another aspect of the proliferation of Momus technologies (van Manen 2010), however, is the increase in mutual surveillance that becomes possible through a constant SNS presence. In this case, issues of privacy operate more in relation to a young woman's closest friends than with regard to more distant contacts or strangers. The mutual disciplinary gaze of pubertal and teenage girls' peer groups is well established (George 2007; Hey 1997; Paechter 2007; Paechter and Clark 2010). However, the spread of intimate and confessional revelation into the online world gives it much greater potential to extend into all aspects of girls' lives. The posting of photographs, in particular, while in many ways a celebration and reification of shared experience (Cullen 2007), also renders the subjects and their follies visible to a much wider and potentially derisive audience. The ability to 'tag' pictures with names in SNS also extends the reach of mutual surveillance while making it much harder for individuals to control what is publicly available about themselves. In addition, the conventions for sexualised display in photographs on SNS that seem to prevail among some groups of young women (Ringrose 2010, 2011) mean that the mutual disciplinary gaze is also strongly sexualised in these cases. Ringrose (2010) argues that there is an ideal visual feminine being performed online, and notes that it is common to manipulate images digitally to make them look 'better'. This construction of a sexualised online identity can involve anything from airbrushing out blemishes such as acne through adding special effects such as sparkling stars on one's breasts (Ringrose 2010), to slimming down the overall body shape. In this sense, the constant surveillance via the online world contributes to a general requirement for constant physical perfection mutually enforced by some girl groups (Paechter and Clark 2010).

Identity communities

The increasing tendency for young people to conduct parts of their lives online gives them access to identities or spaces for identity construction that were previously unavailable. Davies (2005) writes of the connection felt by teenage Wiccans involved in an internet subculture constructed around this identity. Most of the people she studied rarely if ever met offline, but supported each others' practice and identities, reminding newcomers to keep to the Wiccan Law and teaching them how to construct altars or conduct rituals. Through these sites the participants appear to maintain a sense of community and mutually appreciated identity, while gaining support for both their Wiccan and non-Wiccan lives. Davies argues that in this way 'the Internet can open out the social lives of participants, not just in terms of on-line activity, but also in terms of impacting upon off line worlds' (2005, 15).

Similarly, Chittenden (2010) discusses the importance of fashion blogs in identity construction for some young women. Such blogs, she argues, provide girls with a place to display cultural capital in the form of designer clothing and originality in putting together a 'look'. Young women, she suggests, use these blogs as a way of trying out wacky or risqué ways of dressing with others interested in fashion, without compromising their face-to-face social capital or leaving themselves open to bullying. She points out that critical comments made to blogs can be received more easily than those given in person, as there is time to compose one's 'face' before replying, and that there is also the potential for enhanced social capital within the fashion blogging group if another blogger with a high reputation comments on your blog. Within the fashion blogging community, originality of 'look' is encouraged, with members sharing tips about designing outfits and supporting each other in experimenting with 'looks' and therefore providing a more fluid notion of identity display than might be available in the offline world (Chittenden 2010).

While, on Davies' evidence, the online construction of Wiccan identities seems to be more or less entirely benign, other online communities are potentially more problematic. Some researchers have argued, for example, that pro-anorexia (pro-ana) websites induct young women into anorectic practices in a parallel way to those for teenage Wiccans, providing 'rules' to be followed and a place in which to construct an anorexic or bulimic identity (Day and Keyes 2008). Rich argues that

> Such websites are indicative not only of the 'desire' to have anorexia, but are also illustrative of the ways in which for many people, particularly young women, anorexia is central to particular subjectivities around which relationships may be formed with the self and others. They are perhaps also suggestive of the ways in which those people with anorexia may come to 'resist' the pathologising stereotypes that often ensue from their interactions with others. (2006, 285)

Parsell (2008) argues that the accessibility of the internet facilitates the formation of such 'narrowcast' communities, in which interaction with like-minded people polarises attitudes, with extremely restricted membership and the silencing of dissenting voices. Thus, when engaging in such sites, young women are encouraged to do identity work that is focused around very narrow parameters, while the conditions themselves may be presented as lifestyle choices (Day and Keyes 2008), social protest or even counter-discursive practices (Pollack 2003).

Other researchers, however, point to the supportive aspects of pro-ana sites, suggesting that the situation is rather more complex. Rich argues, for example, that many anorexic young women have to cope with their condition alone, and that having contact with a 'virtual community of care' (2006, 295) allows them to feel understood by others (Brotsky and Giles 2007). Fox, Ward, and O'Rourke argue that many users of pro-ana sites see the recovery from anorexia as not an option for most with the condition. They use the sites 'as a means ... to take an active role in living with what society considers a debilitating, dangerous and shameful disease' (2005, 955); part of the ethos is being able safely to manage a dangerous condition. Fox, Ward, and O'Rourke also found that those on the site they studied felt that anorexia was symptomatic of an underlying life disturbance with which it helped them to cope; respondents argued that therefore 'cure' was an inappropriate strategy.

Rich (2006) argues that, even when in treatment, anorexic young women try to hold on to an anorexic identity, associating it with strength of purpose and fortitude in refusing food (Day and Keyes 2008; Schmidt and Treasure 2006). This association of anorexia with inner strength is common on pro-ana sites, supporting the construction of bounded group identities which exclude as inferior those who do not match up to the anorexic ideal, including those with bulimia and people who are simply dieting (Riley, Rodham, and Gavin 2009). Giles (2006), in a study of 20 pro-ana sites, argues that there is an underlying assumption that anorexia is the eating disorder ideal. Anorexics, in this context, are seen as occupying the higher moral ground, with bulimia treated as morally lax in comparison, although participants in bulimia-focused sites argue that cycles of bingeing and purging take more willpower than 'mere' starvation.

This desire on the part of some young women with anorexia to maintain an anorexic identity has implications for our evaluation of the pathological aspects of pro-ana sites. Here the research evidence is equivocal. Rich points out that many of the young women in the anorexic treatment unit she studied maintained anorexic identities through 'anorexic tricks' (2006, 298): ways of appearing to comply with treatment while continuing anorexic practices such as hiding food, chewing gum for its laxative effect, constantly moving so as to burn more calories, or pretending to be allergic to or to dislike certain high-calorie foods. Tips about these practices are passed between anorexics on pro-ana sites and appear to be part of the sites' role in supporting group constructions of anorexic identities (Giles 2006; Riley, Rodham, and Gavin 2009; Rodgers, Skowron, and Chabord 2012). This has led to a situation in which some young women attempt to join pro-ana sites as a 'cool' means to diet (Fox, Ward, and O'Rourke 2005). Consequently, there have been claims by the popular press and some researchers (Rodgers, Skowron, and Chabord 2012) that the availability of such information online is likely to encourage others to become anorexic or bulimic, and there have been numerous attempts to close down pro-ana sites as a result (Giles 2006). The behaviour of pro-ana site members, however, does not generally support this position. While strongly encouraging each other in anorexic practices, they work hard to exclude anyone who does not already have good anorexic or bulimic credentials, partly to preserve the 'elite status' of the anorexic community and partly to guard against accusations that they are helping people to become anorexic (Giles 2006). Brotsky and Giles (2007), who conducted covert research into 12 pro-ana sites, posing as a fellow anorexic, argue that pro-ana sites do not appear to encourage non-eating disordered people to develop eating disorders, or to discourage people from seeking help if recovery seems possible. They note that when their research persona left the sites saying that she was entering into a treatment programme, she was responded to with warmth, encouragement and good wishes, even from people who had rejected that option for themselves.

Authenticity and young women's identities online
Giles argues that a central concern among anorexics online is authenticity, with anorexia being considered the most authentic position:

It is a club with stringent entry criteria, which are not met by [those] who have lapses into the occasional binge, or ... have failed to 'earn' membership through medical diagnosis. (2006, 470)

This reflects a complex set of issues around online authenticity and how it is both represented and tested. While pro-ana site members check authenticity through scrutiny of each others' self-statements for signs of failure to achieve the anorexic aspiration, young women in other SNS settings use alternative approaches. In some cases, such as that quoted by Livingstone (2008) above, there is an explicit embracing of inauthenticity, while in others there is an attempt to approximate or identify the 'real' person behind the online persona.

Larsen argues that in the SNS she studied, used by approximately 80% of Danish teenagers, sincerity and authenticity were of great importance. Young people established this by posting photographs of themselves in everyday situations, such as in their bedrooms, writing detailed profile texts and including testimonials from their best friends on their profiles. In tandem with this, considerable effort was expended in spotting and 'outing' fake profiles, seeing the site as a place to express one's personality in an honest way. At the same time, there was an ethos of 'niceness' throughout the site, with considerable display of affirmative postings from friends on individuals' profiles and very few unsupportive postings.

Other research suggests, however, that authenticity in identity construction online is frequently more complex, with several contradictory self-presentations vying for dominance. In particular, in the context of considerable research about the importance of 'niceness' to some groups of girls and young women (George 2007; Hey 1997; Paechter 2007, 2010) and the continued slag/drag dichotomy to be found in many adolescent social groups (Canaan 1986; Kehily 2002, 2004), there is a question about what it means to be a 'nice' girl within the strongly visual display spaces of most SNSs. While there is clear potential to position oneself publicly as a supportive friend, through comments on other people's status postings, for example, there is also the expectation of sexualised display, both of one's body and of one's life. The line here seems increasingly fine between what nice girls do (or more particularly what they do not do) and what everyone (or everyone within a certain age bracket) is expected to do and display in the online world. Ringrose notes the stark contradictions between girls' simultaneously held positions in this regard:

What I would like to suggest is that the intense visual imperative to represent the self as 'sexy' and sexually confident online creates new contradictions for girls, who appear to still need to navigate not appearing 'too slutty' in peer contexts at school. Contradictions between online representations and what the girls said in interviews in school settings were striking. (2010, 175)

She notes, for example, that girls who spoke of others' 'slutty' profile pictures themselves had online profiles containing sexually revealing photographs and explicitly sexual language. This phenomenon, coupled with the collaboratively constructed aspect of many online personae, suggests that young women's identities are even easier to 'spoil' than they have been in the past.

It is also possible that this striving for a sexualised bodily ideal online is related to the increasing trend for young women to alter their actual, as well as their virtual, bodies in search of perfection. While, on the one hand, this is manifested in the pro-eating disorder websites discussed in the last section, where extreme thinness is presented as an aspirational ideal (Day and Keyes 2008), it is also to be found in the increasing use of surgical procedures to 'enhance' and otherwise alter young women's bodies. In this case, young women are taking advantage of improvements in cosmetic surgery techniques by changing their appearance. Technical advances have led both to a reduction in cost and to a concomitant normalisation of body modification practices in wider society (Tiefer 2008). I suggest that this is another way of doing identity work: if one's identity is framed by particular forms of 'pornification' and the sexualisation of youth society (Ringrose 2010), then alteration of the actual body to render it more 'perfect' is an understandable development of the modification of online images of that body. Certainly, figures for cosmetic surgery uptake in the USA show that the numbers of teenagers undergoing these procedures is increasing, especially with regard to breast augmentation, rhinoplasty and liposuction (American Society of Plastic Surgeons 2011).

While the respondents in Ringrose's research seem to be treading a fine line between authenticity and sexualised display, in other contexts identity construction through SNS participation can be used as a way of maintaining a performed online self that is considered to be more authentic than that performed offline. Zywika and Danowski (2008) argue that some less popular young people use the accumulation of online friends in SNS as a way to bolster self-esteem, and that introverted people reported that they were able to express the 'real me' better in online chat situations than face to face.

In other cases, the collaborative construction of a simultaneously self-presented and other-reflected self allows for some level of disjuncture between the online and an offline 'real' self. In particular, the construction of an online persona that is consciously different from the offline self can be one way in which young people can play with or resist group norms. This could be read as a form of resistance to peer group expectations and power relations, allowing the projection of an idealised or illusory self behind which the 'real' person is able to hide. In addition to the production of spoof profiles and posts, which in themselves resist the wider SNS form (Livingstone 2008; Zywica and Danowski 2008), young people can, almost paradoxically, use the 'always present' aspects of social networking to project a particular socially engaged identity in public while performing another in private. Jackson (2006) reports, for example, that some young people manage their schoolwork and social lives simultaneously by participating in online conversations while doing their homework. This presents a public image of sociability, frivolity and lack of focus on study, while enabling them to work in secret.

Conclusion

The intermingling of frontstage and backstage settings and the phenomenon of the online 'glass bedroom' (Pearson 2009) have the potential fundamentally to alter the ways in which young women construct identities. In particular, the collaborative construction of online personae and the relative lack of control over how one is portrayed by and through the identity displays of others make it possible to think about identity as located as much within the group as in the individual. This has a number of implications and calls up a variety of pedagogic responses.

First, when discussing notions of online privacy and safety with young people, we need to rethink what these concepts mean to them. Most young women seem to be very confident about how to maintain the privacies they want in SNS contexts: they exclude those, such as parents and other adults, whom they have traditionally kept out of bedroom and other teenage spaces, while accepting other young people for whom their friends can implicitly or explicitly vouch. Whether they can in practice accurately manipulate SNS privacy settings to achieve their ends may be another matter, and it may well be worthwhile giving explicit advice and instruction about this. Possibly more important, though, is the need to help young women to understand how their performed identities are being constructed through the comments and photographs of others, as well as through those they put up themselves. It is unclear to what extent young people themselves comprehend how much they are identified with their online friendship groups, or the implications of this.

The question of how young women relate to specialist online communities, such as the Wiccan and pro-ana groups discussed above, is related to this but has different implications. By and large, these groups fulfil a purpose for girls that is not satisfied in other contexts, such as school. Davies' (2005) young Wiccans explicitly sought a community and related identity that they could not find among face-to-face friendship groups, and which is underground, at best, within school. Rich's (2006) respondents welcomed the support and understanding that they got from other young anorexic women in the treatment clinic, something that they did not feel they could find at school; those who are not in treatment may in some ways benefit from the fellow-feeling they find in pro-ana sites. That is not to say that these sites are unproblematically benign; their role in collaboratively constructing anorexic identities should not be underestimated. In a context, however, in which schools can themselves be argued to be promoting anorexic behaviour while failing to support those who develop it (Evans et al. 2008; Rich and Evans 2009), it does not seem to me that the wholesale condemnation of these sites is entirely justified.

Schools do need, however, to work with other agencies to support young women to think more carefully about their self-presentation online, and, in particular, to find ways of resisting the pervasive sexualisation that seems to be the norm for girls in many SNS contexts. It does appear to be the case that the collaborative construction of online identities has made even stronger the pressure to appear sexy and flirtatious on one's home page while continuing to maintain a 'nice girl' image face to face. How girls do this, and the extent to which the online persona bleeds into offline identities requires more research. Ringrose (2010, 2011) suggests a fairly sharp disjuncture between what young women display online and how they think and talk about themselves face to face, at least in the school context.

I said at the start of this paper that identities were not constructed in isolation. With the proliferation of SNSs as a focus for social interaction, this is less the case than ever. Young women can construct multiple personae, in public and in private, and in spaces in between. In learning to be and to become, they can call on commercial and self-made images, widely drawn or narrowcast communities, their own and others' diaries, and responses to these. These collaborative constructions of identities are having a fundamental impact on how young women develop as adults, on how they perceive themselves, and on how they see the world. The long-term effects of this remain to be seen, but it is clear, at least, that conceptions of identity, privacy and authenticity will continue to change, as technologies change, and that those technologies themselves will adapt to provide new ways of thinking about and performing the self.

Notes

1. This paper arises from the UK Economic and Social Research Council-funded seminar series 'Young Women in Movement: Sexualities, Vulnerabilities, Needs and Norms' (ESRC RES-451-26-0715), based at Goldsmiths, University of London, 2009–2011.
2. In Greek mythology, Momus, the god of ridicule and scorn, mocked Hephaestus for not creating man with a window in his breast so that you could see what was going on in his soul. A Momus window is therefore a window into the soul.

References

Ahn, J. 2011. The effect of social network sites on adolescents' social and academic development: Current theories and controversies. *Journal of the American Society for Information Science* 62: 1435–45.

American Society of Plastic Surgeons. 2011. Report of the 2010 plastic surgery statistics. http://www.plasticsurgery.org/Documents/news-resources/statistics/2010-statisticss/Top-Level/2010-US-cosmetic-reconstructive-plastic-surgery-minimally-invasive-statistics2.pdf (accessed February 14, 2012).

boyd, d., and E. Hargittai. 2010. Facebook privacy settings: Who cares? *First Monday* 15, no. 8. http://firstmonday.org/htbin/cgiwrap/bin/ojs/index.php/fm/article/view/3086/2589 (accessed January 31, 2012).

Brotsky, S.R., and D. Giles. 2007. Inside the 'pro-ana' community: A covert online participant observation. *Eating Disorders: The Journal of Treatment and Prevention* 15, no. 2: 93–109.

Canaan, J. 1986. Why a 'slut' is a 'slut': Cautionary tales of middle-class teenage girls' morality. In *Symbolizing America*, ed. H. Varenne, 184–208. Lincoln: University of Nebraska Press.

Chittenden, T. 2010. Digital dressing up: Modelling female teen identity in the discursive spaces of the fashion blogosphere. *Journal of Youth Studies* 13: 505–20.

Clarke, B. 2009. Friends forever: How young adolescents use social-networking sites. *IEEE Intelligent Systems* 24, no. 6: 22–6.

Cohen, N.S., and L.R. Shade. 2008. Gendering Facebook: Privacy and commodification. *Feminist Media Studies* 8: 210–14.

Cullen, F. 2007. Why stop having fun? Drinking and smoking as ways of 'doing' girl. PhD thesis, Goldsmiths, University of London.

Davies, J. 2005. Weaving magic webs: Internet identities and teen Wiccan subcultures. A consideration of a particular on line community and their web based interactions. http://www.shef.ac.uk/content/1/c6/05/05/23/davies_1.pdf (accessed July 12, 2006).

Davies, J. 2013. Trainee hairdressers' uses of Facebook as a community of gendered literacy practice. *Pedagogy, Culture & Society* 21: 00–0.

Day, K., and T. Keyes. 2008. Starving in cyberspace. A discourse analysis of pro-eating disorder websites. *Journal of Gender Studies* 17, no. 1: 1–15.

Evans, J., E. Rich, B. Davies, and R. Allwood. 2008. *Education, disordered eating and obesity discourse: Fat fabrications*. London: Routledge.

Fox, N., K. Ward, and A. O'Rourke. 2005. Pro-anorexia, weight loss drugs and the internet: An anti-recovery explanatory model of anorexia. *Sociology of Health and Illness* 27: 944–71.

George, R. 2007. *Girls in a goldfish bowl: Moral regulation, ritual and the use of power amongst inner city girls*. Rotterdam: Sense Publishers.

Giles, D. 2006. Constructing identities in cyberspace. The case of eating disorders. *British Journal of Social Psychology* 45: 463–77.

Goffman, E. 1959. *The presentation of self in everyday life*. Harmondsworth, UK: Penguin.

Harris, A. 2003. GURL scenes and grrrl zines: The regulation and resistance of girls in late modernity. *Feminist Review* 75: 38–56.

Hey, V. 1997. *The company she keeps: An ethnography of girls' friendship*. Buckingham, UK: Open University Press.

Hodkinson, P., and S. Lincoln. 2008. Online journals as virtual bedrooms? Young people, identity and personal space. *YOUNG* 16, no. 1: 27–46.

Jackson, C. 2006. *Lads and ladettes in school: Gender and a fear of failure*. Maidenhead, UK: Open University Press.

Kapidzik, S., and S.C. Herring. 2011. Gender, communication and self-presentation in teen chatrooms revisited: Have patterns changed? *Journal of Computer-mediated Communication* 17: 39–59.

Kehily, M.J. 2002. *Sexuality, gender and schooling*. London: RoutledgeFalmer.

Kehily, M.J. 2004. Gender and sexuality: Continuities and change for girls in school. In *All about the girl: Culture, power, and identity*, ed. A. Harris, 205–16. London: Routledge.

Larsen, M.C. 2008. Understanding social networking: on young people's construction and co-construction of identity online. In *Online networking - connecting people*, ed. K. Sangeetha. Hyderabad: Icfai University Press.

Livingstone, S. 2008. Taking risky opportunities in youthful content creation: Teenagers' use of social networking sites for intimacy, privacy and self-expression. *New Media and Society* 10: 393–411.

Mallan, K., and N. Giardina. 2009. Wikidentities: Young people collaborating on virtual identities in social network sites. *First Monday* 14, no. 6. http://firstmonday.org/htbin/cgiwrap/bin/ojs/index.php/fm/article/view/2445/2213 (accessed January 24, 2012).

Paechter, C. 2007. *Being boys, being girls: Learning masculinities and femininities*. Maidenhead, UK: Open University Press.

Paechter, C. 2010. Tomboys and girly-girls: Embodied femininities in primary schools. *Discourse* 31: 221–35.

Paechter, C., and S. Clark. 2010. Schoolgirls and power/knowledge economies: Using knowledge to mobilize social power. In *Girls and education 3–16: Continuing concerns, new agendas*, ed. C. Jackson, C. Paechter, and E. Renold, 117–28. Maidenhead, UK: Open University Press.

Parsell, M. 2008. Pernicious virtual communities: Identity, polarisation and the Web 2.0. *Ethics and Information Technology* 10: 41–56.

Pearson, E. 2009. All the world wide web's a stage: The performance of identity in online social networks. *First Monday* 14, no. 3. http://firstmonday.org/htbin/cgiwrap/bin/ojs/index.php/fm/article/view/2162/2127 (accessed May 15, 2012).

Pollack, D. 2003. Pro-eating disorder websites: What should be the feminist response? *Feminism and Psychology* 13: 246–51.

Rich, E. 2006. Anorexic dis(connection): Managing anorexia as an illness and an identity. *Sociology of Health and Illness* 28: 284–305.

Rich, E., and J. Evans. 2009. Now I am NObody, see me for who I am: The paradox of performativity. *Gender and Education* 21: 1–16.

Riley, S., K. Rodham, and J. Gavin. 2009. Doing weight: Pro-ana and recovery identities in cyberspace. *Journal of Community and Applied Social Psychology* 19: 348–59.

Ringrose, J. 2010. Sluts, whores, fat slags and playboy bunnies: Teen girls' negotiations of 'sexy' on social networking sites and at school. In *Girls and education 3–16: Continuing concerns, new agendas*, ed. C. Jackson, C. Paechter, and E. Renold, 170–82. Maidenhead, UK: Open University Press.

Ringrose, J. 2011. Are you sexy, flirty, or a slut? Exploring 'sexualization' and how teen girls perform/negotiate digital sexual identity on social networking sites In *New femininities: Postfeminism, neoliberalism and subjectivity*, ed. R. Gill and C. Scharff, 99–116. Basingstoke, UK: Palgrave Macmillan.

Robards, B. 2010. Randoms in my bedroom: Negotiating privacy and unsolicited contact on social network sites. *PRism* 7, no. 3. http://www.prismjournal.org/fileadmin/Social_media/Robards.pdf (accessed May 15, 2012).

Rodgers, R.F., S. Skowron, and H. Chabord. 2012. Disordered eating and group membership among members of a pro-anorexic online community. *Eating Disorders Review* 20: 9–21.

Schmidt, U., and J. Treasure. 2006. Anorexia nervosa: Valued and visible. A cognitive-interpersonal maintenance model and its implications for research and practice. *British Journal of Clinical Psychology* 45: 343–66.

Tiefer, L. 2008. Female genital cosmetic surgery: Freakish or inevitable? *Feminism and Psychology* 18: 466–79.

van Manen, M. 2010. The pedagogy of momus technologies: Facebook, privacy, and online intimacy. *Qualitative Health Research* 20: 1023–32.

Wajcman, J. 2008. Life in the fast lane? Towards a sociology of technology. *British Journal of Sociology* 59, no. 1: 59–77.

Walther, J.B., B. van der Heide, S.-Y. Kim, D. Westerman, and S.T. Tong. 2008. The role of friends' appearances and behavior on evaluations of individuals on Facebook: Are we known by the company we keep? *Human Communication Research* 34, no. 1: 28–49.

Zywica, J., and J. Danowski. 2008. The faces of Facebookers: Investigating social enhancement and social compensation hypotheses; predicting Facebook™ and offline popularity from sociability and self-esteem, and mapping the meanings of popularity with semantic networks. *Journal of Computer-mediated Communication* 14: 1–34.

Growing-up challenged and challenging: gender and sexuality norms in referential research on 'internet risks' and in children[1]

Renata Šribar

Ljubljana Graduate School of the Humanities, Ljubljana, Slovenia

The paper thematises children's engendering and sexualisation in new media environments, and their ambivalent attitudes toward commercial (porno)sexuality constructions. The inquiry into adaptation to dominant gender identity and sexuality prescriptions in spite of children's ambivalences is contextualised by the critical analysis of grand quantitative survey research in the EU Kids Online II framework. It is argued that gender and sexuality norms introduced by the epistemological, methodological and interpretative input of the research do not transcend the dominant matrices. According to the Slovenian ethnographic research, school children exhibit criticism towards the intrusive and exploitative character of certain new media commercial contents, and this is not included in the analysed referential quantitative survey in any way. As a consequence, childhood remains conceptualised as a state of societal passivity in this context, which brings more disadvantages to girls in new media relations. Besides, the grand quantitative survey research critiqued here supports hypocritical EU sector policies, which have become tolerant of new media-related capital interests, while minors' protection responsibilities are exhibited mainly on a declarative level – as it is the case with the research epistemology under discussion. The same has been established regarding the application of a gender-sensitive approach in the research methodology and interpretation.

Introduction: new media as the privileged relation in growing up
The epistemic contextualisation of topic-related research

New media are constitutive of growing-up in its substantiveness as well as in its conceptualisations in research. As regards the latter, a gender perspective has become obligatory under the EU gender mainstreaming policy which followed feminist thematisations and transformed them. Consequentially some epistemological discrepancies could be observed between dominant EU research policies which accentuate grand quantitative surveys, and the feminist insistence on qualitative or mixed approaches which epistemologically reflect girls as non-homogeneous, yet as a relevant category in analysing social oppressions (for a definition of the contemporary feminist category of women/girls, see Rahman and Jackson 2010). The socio-cultural conditions of unequal power relations in children should not be obscured by the positivistic gender comparative methods of quantitative research. In this epistemological split, post-feminism does not have a very constructive role. The reduction of gender problems to something that has been overcome by emancipation, and to cultural and situational interpretations which suppress the structural relations and systemic conditions, put limits to the reflexivity of gender(s). This argument cannot be denied in spite of cultural micro-spheres or interpersonal situations wherein genders could be conceptualised in their inversed roles as regards power hierarchies. The intersectional approach may have led us to believe that such inversions arise when the dominant accent is on a different source of social divisions and not gender; and in these interrelations socio-economic class very often has the prevailing role (cf. Yuval-Davies 2006). However, even in such cases structural and systemic insight from the hierarchically priviledged gender perspective should not be avoided, because only in this context is the dominant meaning of gender inversions revealed. In relation to this, Slovenian philosopher Mladen Dolar brought to light the inconsistency in Foucault's opposition to thinking structure and his insistence on thinking an event. Dolar (2009) argues that the points of intersections between events and structures were problematisations characteristic of structuralism from Levi-Strauss on.

These introductory words demonstrate my investment in late or third-wave feminist knowledge in the subject of new media and growing-up. It is not an easy research task to analyse how new media (which are based in audio-visual services and products of cyber and digital technology, i.e. new information and communication technology, ICT) are also integrated in growing-up by way of categories, methods and interpretations, used in grand survey quantitative research. In Foucaultian terms: what is known about childhood and new media forms the substantial life – scientific insight is governmentality dependent and one of the mechanisms of reification of the social relations it describes. Governmentality denotes diversified mechanisms of governance, which function at the level of each individual (and not only from the top down). The meaning also implies the form of mind ('mentality') which makes the exercising of power discursively possible. Knowledge production apparatus and the presentation of results articulate the image of certain realities, which in turn form these realities themselves. Knowledge about boys and new media (e.g. 'boys are technically skilled and inclined to computer experimenting') potentially increases opportunities for boys' computer competences if it does not integrate critical reflection of social conditions and the structures of knowledge production – where boys are constituted as a homogenous group in computer competences. An example in the social group of girls might serve our argumentation as well. There is a scarce minority of girls, named *girrls*, who are equipped with high new media skills and are the embodiments of Donna Haraway's (1991) concept of women cyborgs – but because this gender turn in competences has been occurring on societal and cultural margins, it has not been recognised as paradigmatic and *girrls* have not become dominant role models for teenage girls. Neither has this phenomenon introduced new opportunity for equal positioning of girls and boys in relation to new media competences.

Governmentality which is exhibited in power positions in policy making is performed on a micro level, i.e. it is interiorised and incorporated by individuals. Consequently, on an interpersonal level gender hierarchy dominates as the prevailing mode of gender structuring. The power relation between boys and girls corresponds to the gender relations of women and men, which is experienced on an everyday basis in pornographised culture and in the privacy of home. In some porn sub-genres, or in women's ruling the hygienic standards of the family or in partnerships there seems to be a change of power relations, but in fact they are integrated in complex intersections of sources of social power and in a structural complexity of the gender order. The indicated privileges of women/girls are signs of their second-rate status in the domineering gender system. Thus the control over hygiene by women is correlated to their exploitation by domestic labour, and some pornographic cultural artefacts, which put a stress on women's sexual activity, are constructed as an intimate play completely outside the gender order and the related gender roles in all transparent areas of life.[2] This is also true in relation to girls and pornography. All endeavours to reinterpret the (self)pornographisation of girls have not the power to change the traditional economy of looking – which is an integral part of gender structuring in the dominant gender order – and where men's gaze is interiorised and incorporated by women and girls themselves.

Some thematic issues and the hypothesis

New media as a constituent element of globalisation (Nayak and Kehily 2008) often treats childhood and youth as geopolitically uniform in research. We are witnessing a methodological convention which legitimises the usage of examples from one part of the world to support an argument related to another socio-cultural environment. A key concept here is that of the syntagm, which comes from structural linguistics. It refers to a ('synchronic') sequence of linguistic units – signs. Its contemporary extralinguistic meaning is related to the discursive dissemination of certain ideas (cf. Waniek 2005). Thus a pair of words 'bedroom culture' characteristically refers to the change of youth lifestyles via the usage of internet, mobile phones etc., while 'internet risks' indicates the discourse which focuses on the potentially harmful side of new ICT. Bedroom culture, which is one of the characteristic syntagms in defining global new media trends in childhood has been mostly applied to girls' privacy in technologically sustained communication. Mediated interpersonal relations are regarded as being of lesser value compared to eye-to-eye contacts (Lincoln 2001, cited in Nayak and Kehily 2008, 55); but it is the decomposing of the ideologically set boundary-line between private and public space which stimulates expertise. On the other hand, trust in the universally justified formation of privacy and private property strongly supports the regulatory measures in children's usage of new media. Regardless of intensive warnings against risky leaking or spreading of private data and images in cyberspace, the conceptualisation of 'private' is irreversibly changed. The communication contents which transfer privacy to public are important parts of the new media discourse although access to them might be limited. By dissolving the private/public line, bedroom culture became inclusive of boys (cf. Hasebrink, Livingstone, and Haddon 2008: 113). Paradoxically, there is a trend of children's own privatisation of their life by the new media: their privacy which has gone public is often hidden from their parents or guardians. This process depends on the economic status, cultural resources and some other sources of social powers of girls and boys.

The relative autonomy of a re-established world of growing-up was unintentionally supported by parents' or guardians' need to control their minors by restraining them to the home (Wall 2007, 124). Their considerations of safety were immediately challenged by EU policies, if not by the potential disadvantages of new media. The syntagm 'internet risks' was introduced first in relation to computer usage, and was later on proliferated to mobile portals. EU 'internet risks' policy supports grand quantitative survey research, which is an accompanying activity of the loosened regulatory stipulations in the audio-visual media services sector. The last EU grand quantitative survey research, which will be critically analysed below from the discursive formation perspective, does not include data which would confirm that the EU 'risk policy', research included, has a positive impact on parents and guardians as regards their responsibilities and competences in the field of the protection of minors. The results reveal just the opposite: generally parents are not very concerned about the internet risks to their children (Eurobarometer 2008), which corresponds to the low usage of monitoring and filtering technology (Livingstone et al. 2011, 8). This parental attitude directly echoes the EU strategic ambivalences, promoting endeavours against 'internet risks' from the protection of minors' perspective and at the same time supporting the industries' unscrupulousness, exploitation of children's sexual curiosity, their inclination to experiment with violence and cybernetic agency, i.e. 'production' (Strehovec 2007, 53).

Momentarily putting aside the problematic EU new media policies, it should be stated that today new media relations in growing-up could not be consistently reflected in the following dichotomies: home/street, safety/risk, private/public, representation or construction/reality. The intertwining of children's lives with new media is complex, meaning-producing and could be harmful on the psychosomatic level outside the widely thematised risks. Techno-human contact comprises effects on the emotional and sensorial level (Williams 2001, cited in Wall 2007, 129). On the other hand, the notion of external, reality-based events is constantly tested. The latter are constantly provoked to be cyber-transformed or otherwise digitalised. The possibilities of new media in fact produce events in their materiality and interpersonal realities. This inseparability of new media and reality is conceptualised as hyper-reality. With the third millennium and the prosperity of social media, the materiality of life is reflected even to a greater degree in cyberspace and vice versa; there is less anonymity and more spatial, personalised and intimate input (Livingstone et al. 2010). A paradigmatic example of local origin comes from the Slovenian elementary and secondary schools, where recurrent events of sexual harassment related to new media take place. Boys secretly take pictures or make videos of girls undressing and dressing in the changing room before or after gym lessons, and the 'porno-chic' material is then disseminated via mobile phones. This characteristic rite of adolescent boys by which they prove their masculine identities and (hetero)sexual powers has a 'collateral' harm in girls' forced pornographisation, the latter being realised by dissemination of the pictures or videos. This thematisation, however, goes beyond teenage formations of selves in the field of sexuality. The challenge is the hypothesis that the dominant femininity/masculinity norms, transferred via new media, are not simply integrated on the individual level without resistance and ambivalences. In the following discussion, the problem of the integration of dominant norms of engendering and sexualisation of children will be set in the context of a specific scientific attitude implied in the referential EU grand quantitative survey research of 'internet risks' from the minors' perspective.

Gendering of 'internet risks' and the related research attitude

The following part of the study is focused on the critical analysis of the grand survey qualitative research on children in new media relations, which is of core value for European sociological studies. Besides, it really or potentially is the scientific platform for policy making in EU member states, although there is no formal obligation to apply the scientific results. The research study in question is part of the 'thematic network' EU Kids Online, which is structured in working periods (beginnings: 2006–2009, II: 2009–2011, III: 2011–2014), and dedicated to the inquiry into cyber and digital challenges for children and parents. The network is part of the Safer Internet

Programme, initiated in 1999 in the EU framework and co-founded by the European Commission. The present critical analysis of the last grand survey research study (2011) includes a reference to the previous EU Kids Online research (2008). Both of them are gender-sensitive, but the methodological approach to gender-sensitive data gathering and the conclusive interpretations have been changed in the period between the two research projects.

Narrowing the gender perspective in the EU Kids Online referential research

Children's gender-specific internet risks, which are revealed by research results and related interpretations, are part of an 'interpellation' mechanism in the field of gender and sexuality. Interpellation is a philosophical concept used by Louis Althusser to indicate a process by which ideology addresses the individual; only then s/he becomes a proper subject. However, the reality thus represented is co-constituted through the research itself, as has been argued in the introductory section. Findings and interpretations reconfirm the gender-specific behaviour. According to the first EU Kids Online grand quantitative survey research study, gendered internet risks were articulated as follows: boys are more inclined to search for offensive and violent materials than are girls, and they are more curious to be connected to pornographic pages, or they are benevolent receivers of these; they are less hesitant about meeting face to face a person they become acquainted with in cyber space. Besides, they are more spontaneous in revealing their personal data. As regards girls, they are affected more than boys by offensive, violent or pornographic materials; they are more inclined to have conversations with a stranger in a chat-room, and they more often receive unwanted sexual remarks and requests to deliver personal information, which they are not prepared to answer (Hasebrink, Livingstone, and Haddon 2008). Here, gender sensitive data gathering and the interpretations of statistical ratios were clear regarding the 'risky' activities and passive stances from gender positioning perspective.

The latest research study of the kind in the EU Kids Online II framework narrowed the methodological and interpretative gender spectre. The change in approach is indicatively expressed in the articulation of the question on 'sexual messages'. It comprises both the activity of sending and the position of receiving/seeing at the same time. Consequently, we are not supposed to consider gender relations at this point, although data have been gender disaggregated (see Livingstone et al. 2011). It is not evident who is sending and who is receiving the materials in question, and therefore what the gender roles are here. Accordingly, we are not able to check the hypothesis that the specific new media format of sexual communication ('sexting') recycles discriminatory traditional gender roles. Actually, the case is just the opposite: the gender-sensitive problematisation has been concealed on the methodological level in the phase before data gathering by the formulation of the question. Similarly biased is the interpretation of the gender-disaggregated data about children being bothered by overall experiences online. It is claimed that 'social desirability factors might discourage boys – and, arguably, older children – from reporting that they are upset even when they are'. No such interpretation related to gender roles is applied to girls, although according to the same research study they are more inclined 'to be upset by the risks they do experience' (Livingstone et al. 2011, 133). The lack of socio-culturally contextualised observation in relation to girls is found also when inquiring into annoying 'sexual' contents and interpreting the results (Livingstone et al. 2011, 57–8). It is expected that girls are *bothered* by 'sexual images' (and not, for example, angry or furious because of them), which possibly conditioned the number of positive answers they have provided here. There was no option for either girls or boys to register anger at the contents discussed. Another problem is the data-gathering method and the presentation of the result that posits adolescent girls as the stressed target group of bullying (Livingstone et al. 2011). As there are no gender-disaggregated data on ways children cope with bullying online (Livingstone et al. 2011), this makes it impossible to estimate whether the most harmed group, adolescent girls, finds the appropriate way to solve the problem.

Among the failings of the research study under discussion is the terminology used by the authors. Here and there some notion denotes the researchers' inclination to privilege boys. For example, in conclusion it is claimed that boys 'are more exposed to pornography online' (Livingstone et al. 2011, 133). The accentuation on the passive role of boys is in contradiction with the usage of a verb expressing boys' activity as regards porn in the previous research study (Hasebrink, Livingstone, and Haddon 2008). The researchers' gender ambivalences escalate when they refer to pornographic material. Pornography is phenomenologically integrated into the gender hierarchy and its persistence, especially with mainstream formats. In spite of pornography being defined as a commercial genre (Boyle 2008), with specific genre and discursive characteristics, and despite existing legislative definitions (EU normative documents included), the possibility of defining it is problematised in the research study. Apparently this is in line with an anti-regulatory approach. However, at the same time the moral argument is used to assert that children should not be the receivers of the messages on pornography in the framework of the research. Considering that children are every day confronted with porno-chic, and that pornography is the material the researchers explicitly meant when referring to sexual contents (Livingstone et al. 2011), this approach is highly problematic methodologically and from the standpoint of the inherent educational dimension of all research that has children as the target group. Accordingly, it would be useful to imply standards of democratic sexuality education and teach children via formulations of questions to distinguish between pornography and other cultural constructions of sexuality, especially artistic and informational.

Statistically individualised new media harms

The last grand quantitative survey research in the EU Kids Online II framework shows to a certain degree that traditional gender and sexuality norms in boys and girls are reconfirmed by inquiry into new media relations in children as regards the 'risk' dimension of the internet (and mobile portals). Some recycling of discriminatory gender traditionalism is obscured, as argued above, by the methodological approach. Evidently the researchers themselves stuck to the dominant traditional gender norms, which were expressed not only in their methods of data gathering, but also in their formulation of questions and interpretations. On the other hand, there seems to be another side of the growing-up of girls in new media environments which was not transparently tackled in the discussed research study, and which is dominantly considered as transgression of the traditional gender role in sexuality. This transgression is mostly seen in creations of sexualities which appear to be made and disseminated by girls themselves. It has been demonstrated that (self)pornographisation of adolescent girls is often produced or stimulated by the porn agencies and content providers (Šribar 2011). When girls actually pornographise themselves, the interpretation of the phenomenon should consider the omnipresent pornographised images of young women; those have already constituted the sexuality norm in girls. In this interpretative framework the active sexual role of girls is just the proliferation of the traditional mechanism, which constructs women/girls as the solidified metaphors for sexuality and its consumption. Although there might be some perceivably authentic pornographic constructions of girls, they are subjected to dominant ways of looking with unambiguous subject positioning. According to the popularised Lacanian interpretation, women are taking the position of being the phallus – are by default the object of looking, while men are non-transitively supposed to have phallus – they are by the rule the agents of looking. The idea that the 'object' is in power to keep the look of the observer on itself ignores the integrated competitive character of 'objects', whereby each victory is already witnessing the loss: another object is going to gain the sensorial attention. The 'new sexual contract' which binds girls to pay for their opportunities in the field of education and jobs with subjection to the dominant sexuality regime (McRobbie 2007, 730), is related to the problem of sexuality as the most gender-repressive matrix from the women's rights perspective. In the light of the problematisation of sexuality, even legislation in EU member states is insufficient; pornography regulation, constitutional right to abortion and other principles of women's sexual health are the most ambiguous and ideologically marked topics in public and parliamentary discussions. Regarding non-formal indicators of the sexual integrity of women, those are tabooed or discussed in very limited social spaces. Thus girls are not equipped with the rational and emotional tools to confront the pressure of dominant sexuality norms. As Angela McRobbie argued, the adaptation of girls to the dominant modus of sexual attractiveness is possible due to their internal ambivalence, which is demonstrated in self irony and anger (2007; see also Cho 2000). Indeed, our[3] own ethnographic research in the Slovenian public elementary school of mixed urban/suburban pupils in the age groups of 11–12 and 14–15 revealed that a decline from dominant gender and sexuality norms in new media usage could be only of limited character, and relative. This research study is related to inquiry into Slovenian adolescents and their engendered and sexualised attitudes, beliefs and behaviours from the viewpoint of the new media and educational sexuality and gender constructions (Slovenian Institute for Education, 2009–2012). The methodological approach was innovative in integrating two methods, participant observation and focus group discussion. The description of the mixed qualitative method has already been published (Šribar and Vendramin 2012).

The behaviour of one of the girls in the Slovenian research described above was typical. In the research situation, she was dressed in a girlish street-wise style (tight trousers, exposed belly and cleavage, bijouterie and comfortable shoes) and was very self-confident, exhibiting 'masculinity' towards new media – she claimed that she loved to play electronic combat games. She decidedly wanted to share her experience of being groomed, and she told the group that she met an adult groomer in a chat-room. The girl was self-assured when telling peers that she had verbally resisted a groomer by calling him names like 'paedophile'. It was obvious that she considered her confronting the groomer worthy of imitation by her girl-friends. Yet she had not reported the incident to the police or told her parents; indeed she had not even interrupted the online communication immediately. She exhibited no active role which might have consequences for a groomer. Actually, the respondent acted very girlishly in a traditional sense, in spite of her manifested, 'boyish' new media attitude.

From the perspective of girls, the internet appears to be sexually intriguing, but the relations of engendering and sexualisation are not paradigmatically changed by hyper-reality. Their active role in pornographisation, their wish to be autonomous and sexually experimental, and the awareness of traditional gender and sexuality antagonisms (which will be discussed further on) are deeply affected by discriminatory traditional gender and sexuality prescriptions in new configurations. Girls are in hidden or observable confrontation with challenges around sexuality. This problematic interiorisation of different sexuality discourses is of structural character. But what is presumed in the grand quantitative survey research under discussion is the importance of potential individual harms as regards new media sexuality and other contents.

In this quantitative study, the results referring to the percentage of children exposed to the differentiated 'internet risks' are interpreted as the measure of a possibility that an individual girl or a boy becomes a victim of internet-induced offences or crimes. It is indicative that the research study in the EU Kids Online II framework asserts that 'a sizeable minority' of children or 'one in eight' children has been bothered because of something on the internet – or that the 'survey identified 1% of the entire sample', or '241 children, in all', who had not only gone to a meeting offline with a contact made online but also said that they were not bothered or upset by what happened (Livingstone et al. 2010, 50, 98).

The difference in interpretation of statistical data considering individualised or structural relations could be represented by answering the following questions: 'How many…?' and 'Is there a possibility…?' The possibility of offence or crime is indicative of structural relations and should be decisive for sector policies and regulation, just as it is the case with legislative measures in other spheres of society where malfunctioning is a realistic option. Here, on the contrary, we are witnessing ignorance of structural relations in policies and in research. Here, from the protection of minors' perspective, the return to a stress on the individual harms has occurred.

A new epistemological basis for responsible grand quantitative survey research

The conceptualisation of new media-related structurally potential harm in children invites the topic of the technological development, filtering and monitoring software included, and the (un)balanced competences of parents and children. What is of identical importance is the necessity of EU budget-supported rethinking of age, gender, class and other sources of social divisions and discriminations in a new media co-constructed world. It would be unconstructive to argue for the concealing of grand quantitative survey research if there was a chance for an elaborated epistemological basis and researchers' responsibilities in the children's, especially girls', rights domain. The initial steps in rethinking the epistemology, ethics, methodology and interpretation in quantitative or mixed-methods surveys are the reconceptualisation of categories (the disaggregation of gender groups by class; the renaming and defining of 'sexual material'), and the methodologically and interpretatively adequate application of a gender-sensitive approach. This cannot be done relevantly without considering the situatedness of the successive survey research studies in the EU sector policies. Without a clear political aim which would surpass the ambivalent EU policies, the research projects in the EU Kids Online framework will continue to have a vital role in recycling the existent gender hierarchies in children, and the pornographised and violent EU societies.

Gender, sexuality and new media commerciality from the children's perspective

The last part of the present discussion is focused on children in commercial new media environments. Because of the wide dissemination and intrusiveness of the commercial products and services, these are the most persistent of the new media confirmations of the discriminatory constructions of gender and sexualities, violence included. Angela McRobbie articulates the commercial sector as the most transparent and provable in the 'restabilisation' of the dominant gender matrix. In accordance with Foucault's (1986) thought on the nature of modern social ordering, which prefers positive imperatives to prohibitions, McRobbie (2007) claims that norms are prevailingly formed by positive prescriptions. This accentuates wish investments in contemporary normative cultural formats. Willingness to oblige and readiness to invest pleasure in prescribed gender and sexuality matrices have their limitations; restraints are set at home, in schools and in free-time peer communities. Too much 'femininity' or 'masculinity' is supposed to be as socially destructive as too little. A violation is integrated in the formation of a standard, which lays down what gendered characteristics are legitimate or which demonstration of sex-appeal is unacceptably exaggerated. Emma Renold's (2000) research shows that girls decide among themselves what amount of sexual attractiveness is acceptable – just by setting standards for a skirt's length and the modus of sexually attractive behaviour. Similarly, the peer new media community sets hidden codes of behaviour in cyber space, but with reference to new media sexuality constructions. The line between 'vulgar' ('wrong') and 'erotic' ('right') seems to be of moralistic character, yet the values are flexible and trend-set in the new media environment. Ethnographic research with Slovenian school children revealed that the 'normality' and 'suitability' of children's attitudes towards new media sexuality constructions was demonstrated by the avoidance of direct naming of pornographic and porno-chic materials and sexual activities, if the wording should include 'sex'; this was evident especially in the group of early teenagers.

Q: Do you think that some internet pages are harmful?

A1: Yes, they are.

A2: Some of them are.

A3: [muttering]

Q: What did you say?

A3: Some might get it wrong.

Q: About what?

A3: About things, we are discussing now [pornographic and porno-chic contents].

Although children aged 11 and 12 were all aware of pornographic contents and judged them by an aesthetic criterion, they declined instructive conversation about sexuality with the contradictory arguments that they were too young and that they already knew things. In any case, their knowledge about basic 'sexual safety' facts was poor. The syntagmatic expression of their attitude toward pornography was that it was 'ugly' and that 'erotica' (i.e. porno-chic) was nice (a claim of some of the boys), or discriminative (some girls wondered why only women were portrayed). Unease with direct naming and ignorance of basic sexuality facts are not just the consequence of the lack of information in dominant sexuality discourse, but they are produced by the pornographic industry itself. Pornography is explicitly promoted by declaring itself 'immoral', i.e. 'not nice', 'improper', and its genre characteristics do not include sexual health information. One of the girls said: 'Yes, you know things just as they show them.'

Prevailing embarrassment and shame regarding pornographic and porno-chic contents, which were expressed by laughter and avoidance of naming by younger children in our ethnographic research, must have been expressed otherwise in the discussed grand quantitative survey research. The use of a questionnaire and an unfamiliar research situation probably intensified difficulties. It is reasonable to infer from the very low percentage of Slovenian children who claimed that they had seen 'sexual images' (37%, in Livingstone et al. 2010, 55), despite the fact that porno-chic material is widely promoted in Slovenia and is obtainable on mobile portals aimed at children, that some children found a way out of negative feelings through denial. In the Slovenian ethnographic research denial of seeing the object of shame and embarrassment was *performed*, literally, by two of the boys, aged 11 and 12. They covered the discussed porno-chic material with their hands, the gesture which at the same time connoted morality ('I am not seeing it!') and interest, expressed by touching. Touching the advertisement for a mobile portal with a porno-chic photo is a negation and at the same time expresses self-approval as regards pornographic interest ('I am touching the surface – the naked woman's body'). This ambivalence jeopardised the concept of univocal boyish masculine showing off; just as the claims of boys that pornography is 'ugly' did in this peer group of younger respondents. The mechanisms of gender identifying and demonstrative choices of sexual objects are age dependent. The early teenagers might behave differently if they were alone. In this light the declaration that porn or porno-chic is ugly is the exhibition of expected behaviour because early teenagers are not self-confident enough to admit their interest even though it probably exists as an expression of sexual curiosity. The *event* which seems to undermine gender structure on a manifest level confirms it on a narrative level (masculinity confirmed by heterosexual pornographic interest).

Traditional gender prescriptions, new media porno-trend and individualised desires were allocated with reference to dominant gender and sexuality matrices much more transparently in the group of the Slovenian school-girls and school-boys aged 14 and 15. A self-confident boy stated that girls thought pornography was ugly ('for them everything [pornographic] is ugly'). He was dominant sport type and his assertion was understood as a mature heterosexual statement amid girls, most of whom claimed that porn was ugly and interesting just for boys. As a conceptual opposition to the described expression of masculinity through heteronormative utterance, in the younger group (aged 11 and 12) there was a girl with ladette image (McRobbie 2007), but very low status. She was the only one among peers who directly named sexual activity ('masturbation'), but was completely isolated and did not intrigue others by her remark. She was specific in gender self-identification, being the only one with an authentic ladette image devoid of feminised features. On the level of early teens sexualisation she transgressed the silent agreement of (hetero)sexual shyness as regards direct naming. According to Renold (2000), the resistance towards dominant forms of femininity is possible only in cases of active heterosexual performances and competences. The image of the responding girl was inseparable from her silenced behaviour and 'strange' remark on sexuality practice. Although girls in her group were aware of gender inequalities as revealed in gender roles in private life at home (they autonomously began to discuss this topic), they did not question socially determined relations between sex anatomy, and gender roles in sexuality. Their ladette school-mate with operative knowledge about sexuality was obviously unintelligible to them; in their eyes she was queer, which excluded her. Gender identity and intelligible sexualisation are the core of peer pressure – 'we' is constructed by flexible, but agreed borders/norms. They could be challenged but not substantially transgressed. As it was shown by the research in the two Slovenian age groups of children, the peer prescriptions are stricter in middle adolescent years than in early teens. Relative autonomy in gender identity and sexualisation, which was demonstrated by the ladette, exposed her psychophysically among peers. She emanated the image of vulnerability by talking as little as possible and in a low voice, and taking the side positions in sitting arrangements. Her sexuality was not accepted as she was directly referring to the sexual body, which might be not only hers but also their own. Just the opposite was the case when her school-mate, a trend-setting girl (the one who experienced the grooming in a chat-room) tried to show some knowledge about contraceptive pills. As feed-back she got attentiveness, just the same as it was when she suggested the ways to confront a chat-room 'paedophile',[4] a groomer.

The problem of children's knowledge on the nature of new media contents and services

Supposed abstract knowledge about sexuality is one of the indicators of 'proper' sexualisation among peers in their early teens – and it is important what kind of sexuality-related information one possesses. The supposed ignorance of the utterance referring to bodily sexual praxis – the one (masturbation) which is discursively suppressed even in the pornographised cultural environments – was the sign of unsuitability which went beyond shame and embarrassment in the group. While evaluating the event it should be pointed out that this happened with children in a smaller town school. On the other hand, an indirect reference to sexual praxis of pornography consumption, which was performed by the sporty boy with macho attitude, was accepted. That occurred in the group of children aged 14 and 15. As previously argued, the difference in children's ability to be open to mentioning sexual praxis is not related only to age group and the self-assurance of children regarding sexual matters, but also to the image and performance of the pronouncer. The trend-setter was authorised to refer implicitly to sexual praxis by saying that for him porn is not 'ugly', while insulting girls by his tone and the content of his remark. On the other hand, the direct reference to sexual praxis confirmed the strangeness of the 'unfeminine' outlook of the girl in a younger group. She was obviously lacking the competence to properly express the content. As in this group there was a trend-setting girl who was also most talkative when sexuality was discussed (although she was not using direct naming, except 'lay down'), it was not gender as an administratively inscribed category which was decisive in power positioning of both the actors, but the (un)authentic gender identity and (im)proper sexualisation.

What should children (not) know?

Difficulties with children's knowledge about (porno)sexuality in the context of the EU grand quantitative survey research under discussion (Livingstone et al. 2010, 2011) differ from those found out by ethnographic methods. Three levels of troubled relation could be detected and analysed in the criticised quantitative research. First, the assertion that it is not appropriate to use the adequate terminology with reference to pornography (Livingstone et al. 2011, 49) gives the research a tone of hypocrisy, taking into account the expansiveness regarding pornographic discourse: 'For ethical reasons, pornography cannot be defined very explicitly in a closed-ended survey with children, for to do so might introduce new ideas to children who are hitherto unaware of such phenomena.' Second, the problem of pornographisation in children is obscured in the 'sexting' section of the research – the inquiry into who is sending whom what was left off; 'sexting' is by the formulation of the question reduced to rather innocent sexual interplay, although the accompanying text in the study implicitly indicates the possibility of pornographisation of the material by unwanted dissemination (Livingstone et al. 2011). Again, as in the first case, the knowledge implied in the question underestimates the knowledge and experience of teenaged children. And third, by omitting the opportunity to thematise pornography directly, the children's knowledge of the commercial, prescriptive and exploitative nature of the genre is ignored. By that methodological gesture children are denied the ability of critical thinking.

Conclusion: insufficiency of the research norms in the field of new media relations in children

This discussion aims to examine the possibility that referential grand quantitative survey research contributes to the formation of childhood in new media environments in accordance with dominant gender norms, integrating 'proper' sexualisation. Critical analysis of the research study 'Risks and Safety on the Internet: The Perspective of European Children' ('risk' accentuated in the study itself) reveals that the epistemological base, methodology of question formation and data gathering, and the interpretation contribute to the relativity of the problematic new media relations from a gender and sexuality perspective (violence included). The case of pornography thematisation in this research demonstrates that the application of a gender-sensitive approach is in line with dominant matrices of engendering and sexualisation. As such, it is of lesser value for the re-shaping of EU policies in the field of new media from a minors' protection perspective. Similarly, it cannot contribute to the rethinking of the socio-cultural conditions of gender in sexuality as manifested in children's attitudes towards new media. Although children are subjected to the new media-related norms of engendering and sexualisation, they are able to grasp the commercial, exploitative and prescriptive role of pornography (the genre) which has the major impact of recycling discriminatory traditionalism in this domain. The ambivalences, which are shown especially in the group of girls towards traditional discriminatory engendering and sexualisation, cannot be resolved by novel gender and sexuality constructions, if the reference points of the researchers, and thus also policy-makers, do not integrate topics which would empower them. Reluctance and discontent of children with images imposed via new media are not taken into consideration when planning the research and elsewhere. Ignorance in this context is profitable; the seemingly productive gender-sensitive approach is not challenging as regards the existent EU sector policy. It is reasonable to conclude that the conceptualisation of childhood as a state of societal passiveness (cf. Cannella and Lincoln 2009) is not the only thing which is disturbing here. For now, the opportunity for complex dealing with new media relations in children is lost, which is most problematic from a girls' perspective, as they are more challenged and at the same time more challenging in new media environments and hyper-realities.

Notes

1. This paper arises from the UK Economic and Social Research Council-funded seminar series 'Young Women in Movement: Sexualities, Vulnerabilities, Needs and Norms' (ESRC RES-451-26-0715), based at Goldsmiths, University of London, 2009–2011.
2. For analyses of women's porn experiments and their social dimensions, see Schauer (2005); for co-optation of differentiated sexualities in the mainstream sexuality paradigm, the symptom of which is constant questioning 'who is a man, who is a woman', see Butler (2004).
3. This ethnographic research was carried out as a team with Valerija Vendramin and Nina Sirk.
4. The popular usage of 'paedophile' obscures relations of sexual violence against children; according to medical definition paedophilia is an illness while by far not all violators of children's sexual and corporeal integrity are sick persons.

References

Allen, L. 2008. Poles apart? Gender differences in proposals for sexuality education content. *Gender and Education* 5: 435–50.
Boyle, Karen. 2008. Everyday pornographies: Pornification and commercial sex. Paper presented at the international conference Globalization, Media Adult/Sexual Content: Challenges to Media Regulation and Research, September 29–30, in Athens.
Butler, J. 2004. *Undoing Gender.* New York and London: Routledge.
Cannella, S. Gaile, and Ivonna S. Lincoln. 2009. Deploying qualitative methods for critical social purposes. In *Qualitative inquiry and social justice. Toward a politics of hope*, ed. Norman K. Denzin and Michael D. Giardina, 53–72. Walnut Creek, CA: Left Coast Press.
Cho, K.M. 2000. Bodily regulation and vocational schooling. *Gender and Education* 12, no. 2: 149–64.
Dolar, Mladen. 2009. *Kralju odsekati glavo: Foucaultova dediščina* [To cut off the king's head: Foucault's heritage]. Ljubljana: Krtina.
Eurobarometer. 2008. Towards a safer use of the Internet for children in the EU – A parents' perspective. European Commission. http://ec.europa.eu/information_society/activities/sip/docs/eurobarometer/eurobarometer_2008.pdf.
Foucault, Michel. 1986. *Power/knowledge: Selected interviews and other writings*, ed. Colin Gordon. Brighton, UK: The Harvester Press.
Haraway, Donna J. 1991. *Simians, cyborgs and women: The reinvention of nature.* London and New York: Free Association Books.
Hasebrink, U., S. Livingstone, and L. Haddon. 2008. Comparing children's online opportunities and risks across Europe: Cross-national comparisons for EU Kids Online. EU Kids Online. http://www.ifap.ru/library/book363.pdf.
Lincoln, S. 2001. Teenage girls' bedroom cultures: Codes versus zones Unpublished paper. UK: Manchester Metropolitan University.

Livingstone, S., L. Haddon, A. Görzig, and K. Ólafsson. 2010. Risks and safety on the internet: The perspective of European children. Initial findings. EU Kids Online. http://www2.lse.ac.uk/media@lse/research/EUKidsOnline/Initial_findings_report.pdf.

Livingstone, S., L. Haddon, A. Görzig, and K. Ólafsson. 2011. Risks and safety on the internet: The perspective of European children. Full findings. EU Kids Online. http://www2.lse.ac.uk/media@lse/research/EUKidsOnline/EUKidsII (2009-11)/EUKidsOnlineIIReports/D4FullFindings.pdf.

McRobbie, A. 2007. Top girls? Young women and the post-feminist sexual contract. *Cultural Studies* 12, no. 4–5: 718–37.

Nayak, Anoop, and Mary J. Kehily. 2008. *Gender, youth and culture: Young masculinities and femininities*. New York: Palgrave Macmillan.

Rahman, Momin, and Stevi Jackson. 2010. *Gender and sexuality: Sociological approaches*. Cambridge: Polity Press.

Renold, E. 2000. 'Coming out': Gender, (hetero)sexuality and the primary school. *Gender and Education* 12, no. 3: 309–26.

Schauer, T. 2005. Women's porno: The heterosexual female gaze in porn sites 'for women'. *Sexuality & Culture* 9, no. 2: 42–64.

Šribar, Renata. 2011. The other option for sexualisation: Skin as the mother of invention. In *Love and sexuality: Anthropological, cultural and historical crossings*, ed. Alja Adam and Slađana Mitrović, 81–92. Zagreb: Centre for Women's Studies & Red Athena University Press.

Šribar, R., and V. Vendramin. 2012. Constructions du genre et de la sexualité chez des adolescents Slovenes [Constructions of gender and sexuality in a group of Slovenian teenagers]. *Ethnologie Française* 40, no. 2: 325–31.

Strehovec, Janez. 2007. *Besedilo in novi mediji: Od tiskanih besedil k digitalni besedilnosti in digitalnim literaturam* [Text and new media: From printed texts to digital textuality and digital literatures]. Ljubljana: Literarno-umetniško društvo Literatura.

Wall, S. David 2007. *Cybercrime*. Cambridge: Polity Press.

Waniek, E. 2005. Meaning in gender theory: Clarifying a basic problem from a linguistic-philosophical perspective. *Hypatia* 20, no. 2: 48–68.

Williams, M. 2001. Virtually criminal: Deviance, harm, and regulation within an online community. PhD diss., Cardiff University, UK.

Yuval-Davies, N. 2006. Intersectionality and feminist politics. *European Journal of Women's Studies* 13, no. 3: 193–209.

Trainee hairdressers' uses of Facebook as a community of gendered literacy practice[1]

Julia Davies

School of Education, University of Sheffield, Sheffield, UK

> This paper presents research into how four female trainee hairdressers use Facebook. The participants are friends, attending college in the north of England. In this work I was interested in participants' presentations of self as presented through their Facebook activities. This work draws on New Literacy Studies to consider the written texts and photographic representations in Facebook profiles and albums; it also draws on Paechter's concept of communities of gendered practice and combines these theories to examine ways in which the participants' Facebook literacy practices could be considered as gendered – and what this might mean. Through regular online textual representations of their lives, the trainees not only continually reviewed their own lives on a moment-by-moment basis, but kept surveillance of the lives of their online friends. In this process they participated in the maintenance of gendered communities of literacy practice. The data comprise notes and transcriptions of group interviews about the young women's uses of Facebook and from Facebook data itself – the girls' Facebook walls and selected photographs.

Introduction

Through the lens of the New Literacy Studies (Barton and Hamilton 1998; Gee 2004), this paper describes research centred on the Facebook practices of four trainee hairdressers based at a college in northern England. Tracking participants' updates over four months and interviewing them about their usage, I glimpsed participants' lives through their online text making. I used a connected approach (Leander and McKim 2003), tracing meanings and continuities across on- and offline spaces and saw how online literacy practices reflected participants' local lives and concerns. I discerned how meanings from different locations developed through online interaction in the shared space of Facebook pages. I began my investigations with the Facebook texts and used interviews to find out more about the meanings of these online texts and how they represented a kind of anchorage for the group – pulling them together in one space. The trainees' locally situated Facebook practices were located in wider global Discourses[2] of fashion, beauty and gender. Participants' Facebook practices sustained and enriched friendships, allowing peers to co-exist even when physically separated. Facebook practices provided opportunities to constantly review and monitor oneself against the lives of others and this 'always-on' situation seemed sometimes to bind my participants to each other in oppressive ways, having to meet expectations, and group norms.

The concept of communities of gendered practice (Paechter 2003, 2006) highlighted how peer expectations and norms were often learned gendered practices, specific to particular contexts. I drew on Coates' study of the language used between women friends (1996) to identify linguistic expressions of female friendship within the interactions and applied this to written language. I also looked at the displays of Facebook photos and saw their role in reflecting and shaping communities of gendered practice in Facebook. The Facebook texts reflected how my participants managed their behaviour and appearance to fit with what seemed appropriate to be part of the group. In this way Facebook could be seen not just as a reflection of the trainee hairdressers' lives, but as a co-ercive tool.

Social and gendered practices

Barton and Hamilton (1998, 3) argue that, 'Like all human activity, literacy is essentially social, and it is located in the interaction between people'. That literacy is not just a set of skills but a social practice is strongly instantiated on Facebook, where interactants tend to think of themselves as involved not in isolated writing activities, but in social interaction (Lenhart et al. 2008). Vernacular Literacies (Barton and Hamilton 1998) are practices which are voluntary, self-generated and concerned with everyday living, while digital technologies, according to Lankshear and Knobel (2011), enable new literacy practices, sometimes termed 'digital literacies'. This project focuses on vernacular digital literacy practices; literacy practices mediated through digital technologies and which are used as part of everyday life. The approach of the New Literacy Studies explores literacy in context and, for example, identifies social events and practices and the literacy features that comprise those practices. Taking this social approach to literacy, considering the literacy practices of trainee hairdressers on Facebook involves taking account of the contexts in which the texts are produced and consumed, by whom, for whom, and so on. The meanings of Facebook are enmeshed within the contexts from which they are produced.

Facebook interactions often cross virtual and physical spaces, and this allows, in Goffman's terms (1959), for individuals to enact a coherent performance across spaces, demonstrating a certain 'authenticity'. They can develop a particular line or presentation of the self across online and offline spaces, either through images or written comments and updates (see Davies 2012). Facebook enables easy, frequent and sustained monitoring of one's own and others' performances, opening out private spaces into the public sphere in ways unknown before the internet became so easily accessible. Goffman noted how individuals might adjust their behaviour for perceived audiences, and the embedding of Facebook across the many domains of people's lives means that surveillance is often acutely felt. Robards and Bennett (2011, 314) suggest individuals seek to display 'coherent, reflexively constructed performances of self'. Networks of friends can become larger online and thus enable greater numbers of people to witness social acts and performances, with many silent 'marginal' or 'peripheral' members. These are individuals who may read a particular person's Facebook, but not comment. Lave and Wenger's ideas around 'peripheral participation' and 'communities of practice' (1991) have clear relevance here, where they describe how individuals become apprenticed into communities through a gradual process of learning through observation of specific cultural behaviours.

Drawing on Lave and Wenger's work (Lave and Wenger 1991; Wenger 1998), Paechter (2006) describes communities of gendered practice as the process of gender socialisation through apprenticeship. Modelled on how apprentices acclimatise to workplace cultures, joining a community of practice entails learning and adopting group behaviours. Paechter (2006, 14) argues that this 'model of initiation into group practices seems ... to work well for our understanding of how masculinities and femininities are taken up and learned by children as they grow up within local social groups', so that being male or female goes beyond biology, (although embodiment is very important), and performances of gender are required. Gender practices affect language, dress codes, mannerisms, gestures and so on. Paechter emphasises specific gender performances may be contextually bound, arguing it is 'more helpful to focus on localised practices linked together in wider constellations than to discuss genders ... as monolithic entities' (2006, 13). Indicating communities of practice are potentially oppressive she refers to 'Panoptic mechanisms' (2006, 16) and 'coercive conformity' (2006, 15); acknowledging conformity might be pleasurable especially where it gives access to symbolic and material goods. Since Facebook facilitates peer observation alongside opportunities to reflect on one's own behaviour, the panoptic mechanism therefore resonates strongly in Facebook.

Goffman (1959) discusses how individuals develop a particular line under the gaze of others. Similarly, George (2007) describes the tiered friendship structure developed through young girls' complex inclusion and exclusion strategies. Girls in the centre (top) tier, set a moral code which is followed by less influential girls on the margins and periphery (George 2007, 96).

Thus, social research and theory shows how individuals form identities associated with groups in which they wish to participate and how monitoring and modifying norms is essential. I show Facebook as a further tool through which behaviours are monitored, not just on a moment by moment basis but across time, since Facebook interactions and images remain for scrutiny over time and can be viewed by a wider audience than the interactants themselves. My data suggest that setting out online credentials through regular Facebook presence is a requisite friendship ritual. These are often gendered displays and suggest Facebook is a site for gendered communities of literacy practice.

What can you do on Facebook?

Although Facebook seems ubiquitous (Digital Buzz 2011; Facebook 2011; Internet World Stats 2011; Lenhart et al. 2010), not everyone uses it and not all practices are uniform. Thus I provide relevant details about Facebook during the study time of 2011.

boyd and Ellison (2008) provide a frequently cited definition of online social networks as spaces where individuals create public or semi-public profiles within a bounded system. Members display lists of users to whom they are connected, and can reciprocally view and traverse other users' lists of connections or 'friends'. This definition emphasises the centrality of friends and connectivity, something which heavily dominates the content of interactions I have observed within Facebook. The fact that users display lists of friends within their profiles suggests that one's friends and associations contribute to a notional 'online identity'. Kudos through association is clearly not just an online phenomenon (e.g. see George 2007) but, as boyd has suggested, long lists of friends are especially prized online. By friending someone, their updates will appear on one's timeline and so narratives of friends' lives are set side-by-side and become textually combined. This textual arrangement suggests to readers that lives are intertwined and pursued together, connectedness through textual proximity is suggested in new ways within online spaces. One's own Facebook space is as big as one's network of friends, where a busy profile implies popularity, and where one's friends define the boundaries of each site. The more friends one has, the further one can traverse – for the mutual perusal and presentation of oneself and others. The social implications of this feature are immense, because as George's (2007) study of (off-line) school friendships attests, being seen to properly enact the codes of a particular group is crucial for acceptance.

Facebook users can write updates in their own space (or 'wall') and can also write on friends' walls. Interaction occurs with people commenting on other's updates; comments might constitute images, videos, hyperlinks or just text. Members can tag images with names so that these appear on tagged members' walls, but tagged friends can untag themselves from photos thus removing them from their wall. Access to smartphones has made this a very common activity, and multiple images of oneself amongst friends (self-portraits taken from out-stretched arms) and instantly uploaded are highly valued by many users (Davies 2012). Significations of connectedness include numbers of friends, photos and the number of comments on users' walls. All such items are auto-counted by the software and displayed on one's profile. As Gee (2004) has pointed out, being Web-savvy, such as knowing where good content is and bringing it to a particular space via hyperlinks, is often highly valued. Facebookers can 'like' comments by clicking a 'like' button; they can 'poke' someone and this 'poke' will be signalled on that person's wall. Both 'liking' and 'poking' are ways of connecting without necessitating words or pictures, like unobtrusive gestures or smiles. Only positive affirmations are available, although as I discovered, ironic 'liking' is apparent. Thus while the template is fixed, meanings of set functions are sometimes subverted in some groups. Selecting links which attract many 'likes' or comments suggest one is well connected and knowledgeable; good content is a kind of capital within online sites (Gee 2004). Liking and commenting would probably reflect 'legitimate peripheral participation' (Lave and Wenger 1991) where following the links leads to an induction into local values of the group. In terms of gendered communities of practice, such links would be set within the scope of gendered practice in order to gain approval and show credentials for membership.

Smartphones have extended the possibilities for Facebookers, allowing mobile updates, instantaneous sharing of news, location and current companions. Geo-tagging means location can be mapped – although misrepresentation is possible. Such activities assume an avid audience and require dedicated updating, but writing on Facebook is not always a peripheral activity and may constitute an event in itself (Davies 2012). Friends might use SMS text outside Facebook on mobile phones, while also using Facebook on the same phone, often giving different narrative takes within each medium. 'Back-stage' private chat is possible and one can present a 'public face' to many, while giving a different running commentary to others. Social interaction can become complex since a Facebook wall might be used as an ironic commentary or private joke to those who are involved in backstage chat. Thus while Facebook may appear as a 'window' to view other's lives, all may not be represented 'as it happens' and multiple narratives exist.

In sum, Facebook allows individuals to continue conversations online that began off-line and vice versa, creating a sense of continuity, of togetherness and of sharing the same social space despite physical separation (Davies 2012). Facebook allows members to collaboratively and individually reflect on their past, present and future; they can monitor themselves and others, adjust how they are represented and provide multiple narratives of their activities.

Approaches to the research

I now describe how and why I chose and recruited hairdressers as my research participants; my relationship with the participants and ethical considerations; the nature of the data and how these were analysed.

Whilst I have previously explored young people's Facebook practices (Davies 2007, 2012), I worked with young people studying for pre-university examinations who were comfortable and skilled at writing. This study represents the first in a series of studies looking at the vernacular literacy practices of less academically inclined young people since this group seems much less studied in relation to Facebook. As described above, I also wanted to re-position gender more strongly within my work and so drew on Paechter's work (2003, 2006) which outlines a theory of communities of gendered practice. Hairdressers position themselves through their career choice, at the heart of a very female cultural space within the fashion and beauty industry, and so this vocational gendered site presented itself as ideal for the exploration of such ideas. The social spheres which the women inhabited were often purely female and I was interested in gender performances amongst female friends.

I attended a level 3 hairdressing class at the local college and invited interested participants to be involved in the study. I recruited face-to-face rather than virtually since I wanted participants to trust my identity as a legitimate researcher, known to the college. Students quizzed me in a lively and confident way, exploring risks and benefits, then when I left the room privately conferred on their decision whether to participate. Five students volunteered and I revisited the issue of consent regularly; one participant withdrew her consent later. The process of informed consent was crucial, since I was aware that agreeing to be involved would allow me to access myriad personal information, not just from participants, but potentially also from their friends and family.

The four remaining participants were Hannah, Jadie, Josie and Stacey. Rhiannon also later became involved as she was the main interlocutor with Josie on her Facebook wall and was crucial to much of what Josie did on Facebook, so I gained her permission to use some of their interactions. To access participants' sites I sent Facebook friendship invitations from my usual Facebook, so shared similar vulnerabilities as my participants. Our Facebooks became reciprocally visible; mutual friending enabled us to view each other's updates, photos, friend-lists and comments. I sought to achieve a balance between respectful distance and 'lurking'; my occasional comments reminded participants of my research presence without intruding heavily. I interacted occasionally and briefly, such as 'liking' a photo or comment.

As mentioned, friending research participants enabled access to aspects of their friends' information. Although these non-consenting individuals and much of their Facebook content were vulnerable to my research gaze, I did not interact with them or explore their profiles. This helped me define the project within manageable limits although access would have undoubtedly enriched the data and findings. Sometimes I could only draw on a part of an entire event since some parts of the interactions were contained beyond my friends' pages, but this was a price worth paying for the ethical integrity of the work.

Participants did not wish to be known via pseudonyms, arguing they would not post anything 'shameful' so 'anything at all' was open for my use. This was a point of contention for me, especially as they informed me they sporadically indulged in 'mass deleting sessions'. They would 'cull' friends from lists, 'untag' photos they did not like; removed comments or photos they had uploaded; 'hid' friends' content from their walls. Such sessions would be prompted by a new dislike of the deleted content or of the friend. Such temporality in their viewpoints implied they might not later be happy to 'own' data I planned to use in my reports or presentations.

Some of the participants' photos could be read as sexually provocative and these images were often participants' favourites and ones they wanted me to use. These photographs, because of their highly gendered presentations, rendered them highly relevant to the project and, while I wanted to use the data, they required careful consideration. The primary audience for participants' images would have viewed them in the Facebook context, i.e. friends would interpret the images against their wider knowledge of these young women and their intertwined lives. They would not necessarily have regarded the images as sexual but as fashionable. I was cautious about re-presenting images out of context since others might misinterpret them, or treat them disrespectfully; as Mizen describes (2005, 138), photographs are 'of a different order' of data and therefore need to be treated with care. I was therefore cautious about putting sensitive material into the public domain, especially as Facebook has often attracted negative news coverage, but I also wanted to share important data. One option would have been to blur the faces on the images, but I accept Nutbrown's arguments (2011) that the anonymising and unflattering effect of blurring faces in photographs could be considered disrespectful and unethical. Finally, I agreed with participants the manner of presentation of selected images would be discussed individually – photos would either be described verbally, or Photoshopped. Thus I have used a filter so that the images appear like sketches as opposed to photographs, making identification of participants more difficult. We agreed first names only would be used in my writing and that Facebook content would be extracted from screenshots, so that no identifying evidence of friends, etc., could be visible.

Facebook texts are the principal data set. I spent time reading all of the participants' updates, looking at their photos and following links. Close textual analysis of Facebook use over a period of months led me to select examples of 'typical' activities, things that occurred often. I found that behaviours were very repetitive, the social acts tended to be mundane rather than sensational. I focused not just on *what* was being said but *how*; on linguistic features, images, emoticons and on aspects like 'poking' and 'liking'.

In order to make sense of the texts it was important to meet regularly with the young women face-to-face. I had established, along with others (Davies 2012; Leander and McKim 2003; Marsh 2011), an approach that acknowledges the connectedness between online and offline spaces of interaction was essential for understanding how online relationships are set within cultural structures and Discourses from the offline world. Moreover, interactions often pass across multiple spaces and tracing an interaction across spaces opens up further meanings. As mentioned above, I discovered there was much dialogue which was not placed on Facebook walls which participants could describe to indicate contextual meanings. I had four formal meetings with all participants and further individual meetings with three of them. They also commented on my writing and corrected misconceptions.

Over time I identified themes which characterised participants' usage, and considered these in relation to communities of gendered practice. I discuss the data below under the headings of identified themes: Sharing life rhythms; Insiders and outsiders; Intertextuality; Managing girlishness; and Awareness of the panoptican.

Discussion of the data

Sharing life rhythms

Many of the participants' updates were phatic performances of friendship; they could be aligned to smiling at each other, signalling their presence from another place and asking for acknowledgement. Examples of this were where they simply 'liked' someone's post; where they 'poked' someone, or told their friends what they were doing. Frequently exchanges ended with 'Take Care' or 'Be careful'. During one interview I asked about these comments and was told, 'It's like saying bye but more caring. It's like saying 'love you' or giving a hug. We just like to show we care and we only say it to who we really like'.

Typical of this was Hannah's update:

Been for an nice sunday diner now gonna snuggle with a film and hot choc! <3

This comment gained three likes from three people and from one person a row of four lovehearts. Here Facebook was being used to express co-existence, a display of shared life rhythms. Similarly, Hannah updated at the end of Christmas day at 23.11 pm:

> Bet everyones got new jimjams on tonight!! Haha

Implicit within this was an invitation to respond with what friends were wearing and what they were doing. Hannah received 14 likes and 21 comments, where people shared details of presents and what they were wearing. Hannah's comment expresses inclusiveness; an idea of addressing a group of like-minded friends who live similar lives and her friends keenly displayed this. Traditionally a 'family day' in the UK at least, most people will have been apart from friends and so this was a way of showcasing the familial space, opening it out for scrutiny and sharing.

Comments in the 'sharing life rhythms' category conjured cosy domesticity, using childlike vocabulary, as here: 'jimjams'; 'hot choc' and 'snuggle'. Hannah presents as a child in the home and responses echoed this feeling, being supportive, emotional and caring. The presentation of self as child, as vulnerable, wanting protection, fits with one of the stereotypes for women as requiring protection but also as caregivers. The friends display both these characteristics here, as carers and as needing care.

Coates (1996) notes much of the work women do in conversation is polyphonous – where meanings are echoed rather than challenged and where even whole phrases are repeated, thus providing reassurance and emphasising harmony. Polyphonous meanings are evidenced also in participants' photos; with friends often similarly dressed and hugging closely. As shown later, these affectionate displays were directed at each other, but also demonstrated bonds between closest circles to those who lay outside these. Such images, like the written updates, tacitly displayed social cohesion. This particular set of interactions reflect how, as in face-to-face communication, participants align their responses to fit with others, helping group coherence and membership, a linguistic indication of a gendered community of practice. Hannah updated her Facebook only three or four times a day at most, but always gained many comments. She was a quiet member of the group but always gained sympathetic responses. She presented often as fragile and childlike and her friends gave feedback which allowed her to maintain this particular gendered persona.

Moves to elicit interaction and displays of friendship are not always reciprocated and their way of enacting female friendship is much more spirited. Rhiannon posted a series of imperatives on Josie's wall in November at 22.26 pm:

> OoOooooooooohhhhhhh Ring me then xxxxxxxxxxxxx

Rhiannon gives a sense of volume, of shouting and wailing 'OoOoooooooo hhhhhhh' to attempt to catch attention. Gaining no reply she urged five minutes later:

Josie not this game again please hahaha. Ring me I cannot bear the suspense and I've just watched paranormal activity again with mama and I'm scared xxxxxxxxxx

Affection is expressed through rows of kisses and despite her insistent tone presents vulnerability by showing affection – and telling everyone she is frightened of a TV programme. Rhiannon uses Josie's name in the second attempt to grab attention and offers evidence for her 'need' to speak. She tempers her insistence with 'hahaha', a commonly used device between this dyad as a way of softening words that otherwise might seem over dogmatic. The depiction of the domestic scene is clear again here and this seems important in many Facebook exchanges, helping friends to share the sense of space that others inhabit. Underpinning all this is the idea that Josie has read the messages and is ignoring Rhiannon, that she has her phone constantly in her hand to reply. Indeed the women informed me 'We're never without our mobiles. You need them all the time to text, Facebook or take emergency pictures!'

Importantly, Rhiannon posts these messages publically on Josie's wall and so Josie's silent rebuttal is also public. Rhiannon creates a sense of exaggerated exasperation through her spelling of 'OoOoooooooohhhhhhh' and through the hyperbole of her words. Rhiannon repeatedly teased Josie in this way on Facebook while Josie's resistance to answer seemed to be her way of gaining the upper hand. These episodes, while jokey did have a co-ercive edge and despite the softeners (kisses (xxxxx) and 'hahaha') there did seem to be a battle for power here. Rarely did others interject in such exchanges and it was as if the other girls looked on not taking sides with either one. As George (2007) notes, girls are aware of the ramifications of involving themselves in incidents like these and the need to maintain face means sometimes choosing silence to keep the peace.

Here we see how the girls gently pressure each other to be on Facebook all the time and while constant sharing is companionable and desired, there is a sense of being forever 'on call' and to display that they are still part of the group. We see how displays of vulnerability, even alongside cajoling imperatives, are part of female friendship performances, where the women show a constant need for each other.

Insiders and outsiders
Friends and haters
Despite displays of friendship on Facebook, indications of other 'behind the scenes' interaction are apparent. In the example above, Rhiannon wanted to text privately on her phone with Josie but chose a public mode to announce this. Conversations started on walls often moved to other modes or media; participants seemed to judiciously manage when they had an audience. The

choice to display some things but not others signified boundaries between friendship groups or 'insiders' and 'outsiders', 'friends' and 'haters'.

It seemed that not everyone was equal in friendship status; and sometimes that 'liking' was ironic. Participants explained they may 'like' a photo even when they did not and reportedly all their 'proper friends' would know this was 'being sarcastic'. I asked how this could be known, and the women laughed, with one saying,

> because we just know what our real friends think. It does not all go public. There are 'haters' on there and they just hate everyone and are jealous of people. They don't like everyone else and they think they are better. But they are bottom of the pile.

The discussion continued where the women talked about how they had updated sometimes in order to 'piss off haters'; this reflected the complexity of their networks and how these complexities were not just reflected online but that Facebook was a space which enacted them. As will be seen later, offline spaces were crucial in performing the friendship work that identified 'real' allegiances or members of a particular community. The young women's interactions on Facebook were by no means homogeneous. They often indulged in risky talk, swearing, discussions of sex and ventriloquised 'heterosexual male Discourses'. Thus while the women sometimes performed as vulnerable and sometimes as powerful, their femininity was continually defined and re-defined through their interactions.

Risky talk

Updates often comprised provocative comments – often for fun. Initiations of interactions could develop into social events themselves, jokes that might be returned to on or offline. One participant told me, 'I am always trying to think of random ways of starting conversations'. For example, when Josie says she was in the local paper (*The Star*). Her opening remark tacitly invites the question 'why were you in the paper?' but her expectation is denied (see Table 1).

According to conversational pragmatics, Josie's anecdote about being in the paper would attract comment and her illness story would elicit sympathy. Yet Rhiannon repeatedly breaches expected codes. After Josie announces she was in the paper, the less important detail is acknowledged in mock insult ('you look no different then?'); Josie swears at Rhiannon (ironically) and there is silence for over half an hour before Rhiannon introduces a new topic. In fact, the image of Josie in the paper I discovered was extremely flattering and showed her having her hair styled by her prize-winning friend in a competition. It was clear from other conversations that all the women thought Josie was very attractive and in any case the girls all looked similar to each other since they emulated each other's hair and

Table 1. Shame I look vile.

Name	Comment	Likes	Time
Josie	Was in star last night shame I look vile		13.26
Rhi	So you look no different then?		13.54
Josie	Fuq u		13.55
Rhi	Doin owt tonight		14.28
Josie	Nowt apart from dyin. Yesterday I had to leave college early coz I didnt feel well and then I threw up ont tram then when I got home I were throwing up for 12 hours I couldnt even drink water:(so I dont really wanna do owt coz I feel like I might be sick again waaaaaah	1	14.30
Y	You missed my steak and chips. Was epic	1	16.44
Josie	Ah no		16.45
M	Ah yerp		16.47
Rhi	As if you threw up ont tram hahahahahaha	1	17.27
Josie	I know im proper nastaaaaaay		17.28
Rhi	What happened haha?		17.30
Josie	Whaddya mean wha happened?		17.31
Rhi	Did you have to get off?		17.32
Josie	Well I'd just gone past city hall and I knew I were gonna be sick so I thought ill get off at west street so I can get some fresh air, so I went to the doors to get off but before they opened I threw up then just got off the tram and got on the next one, proper smooth move	3	17.33
Rhi	Hahah can I ring ya? Got something to tell you that you won't be interested in but I wanna tell ya		17.35
Rhi	Or you ring me please		17.35
Josie	Orate but I gonna put you on loud speaker coz im gonna vom dont get mad		

fashion style. Images of them on nights out show them similarly dressed standing in similar poses looking like stills from a girl band video. The cohesiveness of the group was often expressed through similarity in style and their Facebook images showed this. The conversation needs to be regarded against this backdrop, situated as it is, amongst images which demonstrate physical and social proximity – of a very feminine nature.

In this story of Josie's woeful bus journey, its comic delivery keeps the exchange upbeat. Rhiannon uses Yorkshire slang, 'owt' meaning 'anything' ('doin owt tonight' = 'are you doing anything tonight?'). Josie's answer is long and detailed, also using Yorkshire slang (nowt = nothing; ont = on the; and adds an onomatopoeic wail like a mock crying sound 'waaaaaah'. The dialect and the attempt at imitating sound are skilfully delivered and another friend intercepts, teasing Josie, jokingly suggesting she would have enjoyed a big meal. It is three hours later that Rhiannon responds with a disbelieving exclamation and the effect of laughter (hahahahahaha). Josie earnestly continues her tale, turning misery into farce. Her long and seemingly breathless but well-constructed sentence ends with a rhyming comment 'proper smooth move' as if she were observing herself in action. Through quite admirable verbal dexterity, she self-satirises, managing the narrative and finally gaining Rhiannon's expression of sympathy. The importance of performance cannot be under-estimated here, with these two powerful girls showing linguistic aptitude and the ability to entertain. The many echoes in this piece, from representing Yorkshire dialect, imitation laughter and comic spellings, accumulate to make light of Josie's experience while indicating social proximity between Josie and Rhiannon. This could have been a friendship in jeopardy here but it was managed by humour and witnessed by many.

The above interaction could be seen as verbal sparring and the young women seemed to mimic male performances. When Josie says 'im proper nastaaaaaaaaay' she apes a more male idiolect, tapping into popular culture male rap style. On other occasions some of the participant's' updates involved taboo vocabulary, and highly sexualised swearing, claims of watching porn, of masturbation and tall tales of extreme sexual acts. The participants sometimes referred to each other using terms such as 'bitch', 'beeeeach', 'slut' and 'whore', terms associated with male usage for the denigration of women in order to subjugate, belittle and regard women's sexuality as obscene. Yet at the same time, the male aspect of the d/Discourse was tempered by the extreme feminine images of the participants which populated their Facebook pages.

In an interview, one participant explained:

> We would not say it if we meant it. It's funny. We all know it's a laugh. You would never say this to someone you didn't know really well. We do it because we are close.

The satirical comments ridiculed men; one series of comments claimed, 'I moulded a penis', 'I have a penis', 'I'm gonna wave my penis', etc. These episodes were playful and seemed to mark out a territory of friendship that dared others to enter at their peril. Here they excluded men from participating in their jokes, claiming power for themselves as women. Yet as other updates show, they value femininity and enjoy moving across the Discourses. A participant explained,

> Other people would not get it. We just lark about. We think its funny. You wouldn't say it in other places. One person says one thing and it kind of builds up.

The sexual satire marks out boundaries and draws individuals into a group; Facebook is a place where dangerous, risky d/Discourses are rehearsed and as Stacey explained, 'People get brave on Facebook. They say things they would not say elsewhere'. Josie's sickness anecdote, seen against a background of sexual banter mixed with softer exchanges, reflects a complex tapestry of Discourses and these alongside all her other updates create a rich online identity – and one where others are drawn in through interactions. Meaning making in this way identifies the group since they lay out a kind of social history of their own collaborative creation.

Intertextuality

As Lemke (2004) explains, intertextuality is a common feature of human discourse; we draw on d/Discourses all the time to make connections between things and to draw on meanings from other places to enhance meanings in the present context. There are d/Discourses we may wish to invoke often in order to present ourselves in particular ways and these may be linguistic or operate through other modes. For example, to appear more fashionable we may wear designer labels with particular significations; meanings from elsewhere become embedded in present d/Discourses.

Whilst local dialect was often expressed through written updates, photographs showed local venues and place notifications referred to their home city, many references to popular culture inflected their worlds with global Discourses. Thus whilst locally inflected language gave a strong sense of belonging to a local community, US dialect was often woven through. Thus one or two words in an update or comment would indicate US pronunciation as opposed to local dialect, e.g. 'Nastaaaaaaaay', 'beeeeeach' (bitch) or 'y'all' (you all'). Drawing on these ways of speaking suggested a local interpretation of global fashions, absorbed from a range of cultures. Their emphasis on trying to re-create the pronunciation of the words suggested to me that they were more interested in the American 'feel' of the words as opposed to the actual meanings here. This playful use of language, moving across Discourses and creating a kind of g/localism (Luke and Carrington 2002) is evident in the spoken English of many British youth, but here it is re-created online, showing a real awareness of the inflections of spoken language with an ironic take. Switching across Discourses in this way created a way of talking that helped delineate the community through Facebook texts as part of a tapestry they wove together. Here we can begin to see the ways in which gender is being explored and held up, tested in different ways through this blended Discourse.

Lines from songs or films, sometimes with one or two words changed for comic effect, were also frequent. Responders might show their knowledge by supplying the next line, or simply name the relevant song or film. These game-like exchanges reflected how expertise in (the right kind of) popular culture is valued and central to their lives. As described earlier, so too are quick wittedness and humour highly regarded. Rhiannon began an exchange which suggested something about gender and foot size (see Table 2). The use of capital letters suggests Rhiannon is shouting; this seems to have attracted Josie's attention as she responds immediately. Josie

Table 2. Lesbian feet.

Name	Comment	Time
Rhi	GET YOUR LESBIAN FEET OUT OF MY SHOES	19.52
Josie	I dont get it	19.52
Rhi	Keira Knightley's Mum says it on bend it like Beckham lmfao	19.55
Josie	No you say it when I try your shoes on	19.58
Rhi	I would do if you could fit your fat toe in them	19.58

realises this is a joke but does not understand, so Rhiannon provides the context – and adds laughter (lmfao = laugh my fucking arse off). This leads to more banter about Josie having big feet and being unable to put Rhiannon's shoes on; again this exemplified how the global was drawn into the girls' local worlds. There is an allusion to folklore or fairy stories here, that girls should have small feet, and that if the feet are not small then perhaps they are not a 'real girl' but a lesbian. They made meanings through both global and local resources, and through their joking make it clear that not only were lesbians outsiders to their group, but that they were less attractive than heterosexual girls. Values came through strongly in such humour and in this particular community of gendered practice, 'lesbian' was not quite within the gender they professed membership to.

Popular culture seemed woven through their interactions and their lives. Other examples of this embedding included referring to television programmes; who they wanted to win popular game shows (especially *Britain's Got Talent*); going to gigs to see celebrities; declarations of wanting to marry particular celebrities; live the lives of particular celebrities; and to look like them. Indeed many of their images seemed not only to be highly fashionable, as one would expect, but also to imitate iconic poses from celebrities. For example, in Figure 1 we see one participant taking on a pose often associated with Britney Spears, a US-based singer – albeit clearly set against a UK urban location.

The video of 'Hit Me Baby One More Time' features Britney dancing in school uniform; stills taken from the video showing similar poses to that shown in Figure 1 are ubiquitous. Similar influences of celebrity poses abound in participants' albums. The women seemed unaware of how their poses echoed those of celebrities; Hannah commented

> I just stand how it feels right or what I think looks good. It's partly to show off your clothes. I like to look back on what I were wearing for things. I stand so that the photo looks nice.

Taylor (2006) has referred to 'postural intertextuality'; and often the poses were imbued with styles from elsewhere so some photo albums had features in common with celebrity magazines, showing lifestyles of well-dressed

Figure 1. Postural intertextuality.

people against a range of domestic and social backgrounds, such as kitchens, nightclubs and bars, etc. Unconscious self-styling in photos is commonplace; conventions in presenting the self, or photographers arranging subjects to display different meanings, are embedded in the process of photography; the traditional arrangement of families at weddings (see Kuhn 1995) or footballers kneeling with balls are examples. We tend to smile directly at cameras – these are learned behaviours. In Figure 1, the adoption of a particular pose highlights a youthful and slim female form – with a sexualised adaptation of the school uniform – a shot that signifies a genre and which the subject just 'naturally' adopted according to her own account. As Read (2011) points out, however, Britney (and others like her) are marketed as if a 'popular girl at school' and this marketing is pervasive and insidious; the adoption of poses similar to hers suggests the absorption of the message that behaving this way is attractive and lucrative. Read, like George (2007), points out that while a girl may be singled out as 'popular' this does not necessarily mean the other girls like her. George's work shows that girls are often in awe or even fearful of popular girls and prefer other girls more; nevertheless they may emulate them to denote loyalty.

Associated with US tradition, the school prom is a new ritual in the UK, very quickly popularised through US television shows; Facebooks abound with albums entitled 'My Prom'. Stretch limousines, huge ballgowns and all the accessories, fill these images. The lavish gown in Figure 2, found through a Google search for 'princess dress', enabled Hannah to locate a Chinese dressmaker with a shop on eBay. The dress arrived from China 'just in time for the prom'. Hannah anxiously anticipated the delivery of the dress but the online search and sourcing of her gown was clearly considered

Figure 2. At the school prom.

to be part of the event itself. Preparations for nights out, so I learned, are as important as the event itself. Apparently the girls in the neighbourhood are commonly helped by friends and family to source dresses, hairdos, limousines and the like. This photograph, along with others, evoking princess fairytale narratives, with popular US television series, signifies a highlight in the local life of girls in this northern UK city. The photographs of the event comprise the Facebook event; providing the evidence to look back on, to talk about and share across multiple Facebooks so that each participant plays a part in building up the accumulated resources forming a collaborative narrative. Facebook, with its ability to display such images for attendees of an event to view together, helps establish events as part of a shared history; tagging images means that groups can see photos displayed together and so a story of what happened is jointly constructed in words and images. Even those who did not attend could comment as onlookers; after a series of comments on one shot, the subject of the image above replied:

:) And Yeah It Wo Gud Actually, :) R88 Posh Tho, :) x

The dress, with its fairytale nuances, its eBay sourcing and international provenance, the prom's US derivation and the sophisticated demeanour of the dress, are brought together ventriloquised through local dialect ('Yeah it was good actually, (smile) Right posh though, smile kiss').

The language and the images, as well as the celebrity fashion and poses, are a blend of local and global discourses reflecting the complex lives in which these young women participate. The fashions they follow, celebrities they imitate and the lives they aspire to, seem to be based on exaggerated forms of femininity; yet these are given a 'local flavour' and it is this I now discuss in the next two sections.

Managing girlishness

While the trainees see hairdressing as serious work, beauty is a key social activity and forms a major component of their identity work. They enjoy working on their own beauty and have pride in creating a 'good look' for themselves and others – rewarding them with social and financial capital. As Paechter (2003, 2006) discusses, benefits of membership to communities of practice can include different types of benefit. These young women carefully balance a range of Discourses to accommodate different styles of femininity at different times. Combining the skills to create stylised versions of femininity with sometimes 'feisty' banter (as exemplified above), they embodied what Read (2011, 2) calls a 'resistance as well as accommodation to dominant discourses of femininity'. They unanimously claimed enjoyment of being 'very very girlie' – despite their banter and satirical use of sexualised terms for each other. I asked for clarification.

Comments included:

> I even love getting ready in the morning. I always get up early and try on clothes and do my hair. In fact when you go out, in the evening. The best thing about it is getting ready. We go round each other's houses, have a little drink and get ready. We take photos at our houses. They are usually the best photos.

> A lot of lads think you try and look good for them but we try and look for ourselves. Sometimes we get all ready [to go out] but then we stay in. We take photos of ourselves and sometimes we just stay in.

> It really matters what you look like. If you think you don't look good you won't go out.

> We plan every detail. It's details that count. Even your nails and your mobile phone. They have to match. You have to think about your phone and 'do I look good using my phone?'

The discussion was animated and fervent; their adamancy suggested that approval from their peers was most important. The importance of belonging to same-sex groups is emphasised; these are the girls who know what each other means when they are 'ironic' on Facebook. They take photos and delete the ones that they do not like and upload them to show on each other's walls. This is about *seeking* female *approbation*; appearance matters and their appearance is evaluated not just in face-to-face scenarios, but much more importantly on Facebook where images will be viewed in their absence and many times over. This was clarified,

> Pictures are everything. I can't wear the same thing twice because of all the photos on Facebook. Even if you are going out with different groups of people – it could be social suicide [laughs]. No you don't want people to think you've not got many clothes.

Indeed the 'bedroom culture' of getting ready together at home was clear from the numerous photos showing them getting ready. This kind of culture is one they value in the workplace too;

> In the salon it's just really girlie. That's what we like. It's mainly women. You do get a few men come in but they don't stay long. They just have quick stuff done. Quick in then out. Then we just chat for ages with girls.

The bedroom seems to be a place where much of the social and identity work gets done; with close conversations, photos edited for Facebook and then a particular version of the group presented online. The salon then seems to be an extension of this, for some of the women at least the workplace continues the joys and the pressures of being forever on show, of being part of a female peer group where popularity is vital.

Whilst this kind of bedroom culture has previously been documented (e.g. Lincoln 2004; McRobbie and Garber 1976), Facebook opens out the private space into the public so that the arena is held up for scrutiny to others. The many posed shots, with similar ones being taken in the ladies toilets of nightclubs, show elaborate transformations taking place using tanning lotion, make up, adjustments to outfits and so on. The public display of before and after photos simulate popular magazine articles and TV transformation shows. The ability to transform oneself is seen as highly valued and whilst in the past looking 'naturally beautiful in an understated way', the cultural move now seems to be more about ability to transform and this is seen as part of the presentation of the self 'as girl'.

Nevertheless, Facebook was a place where the girls could provide another view, in the self-satirising update from Josie, 'Rate annoying when your glasses don't fit over your eyelashes'. There was a sense here of the 'Ugly Betty' situation, where the removal of the glasses would reveal the 'princess' beneath. These women were not dupes; their sense of humour could turn the lens the other way, cutting through the chimera of nail extensions and false eyelashes. I occasionally saw them peep from behind the mask of the feminine stereotype, showing an ironic awareness and a suggestion of criticality.

Awareness of the panopticon

Occasionally Facebook updates would express outrage at others' behaviours. For example Jadie exclaimed:

Deleting this Facebook and making a new one only adding or accepting people I know and like good bye too you FAKES AND STINKING SNAKES!!!!

She received eight likes for the comment and then a few weeks later received five likes and several comments when she declared 'Trust no-one'. This was a clear example of inclusion and exclusion management (George 2007). The liking and affirmative comments indicated those who wished to be included in the next incarnation of Jadie's Facebook. The notion of 'FAKES' suggested that some of Jadie's 'friends' were, according to Jadie, not genuine, while they may have demonstrated specific behaviours to suggest friendship, other behaviours had suggested they contradicted these. The complicated story, involving numbers of people and their offline behaviour as well as Facebook updates, was one that Jadie felt she could resolve through deleting the Facebook and she was tired of being watched and commented upon. Whilst there was much pleasure in being watched and watching others, clearly the women felt strong negatives too and suffered emotional pain in the process.

Conclusions

These trainee hairdressers' Facebook updates needed to be read against the complex contexts, within and beyond Facebook, from which they arose. Facebook itself contained much of the participants' social history but their meanings could only be derived through a connected research approach which traced meanings across spaces and from with insider perspectives. Meanings came through multiple modes and sources. Many of my participants' Facebook activities could be interpreted as participating in gendered communities of practice and I saw how these could be both pleasurable and limiting.

Paechter describes how

> Learning full participation in a community of masculinity or femininity practice is about learning one's identity and how to enact it ... This is an embodied identity; one is not just developing an outlook on life, opinions and judgements. (2006, 17)

I saw how the trainee hairdressers performed gender and friendship through similar styling of the body and hair, posture, language and fashion. This was not just reflected within Facebook but monitored through Facebook and projected beyond it. I saw how the women became both subject and object of their Facebook texts and of the d/Discourses they adopted.

While my participants enjoyed hairdressing and beauty as leisure activities, it was also their route to financial and social capital. Beauty was highly valued not just as a personal attribute, but also as a professional skill associated with hard work, achievement and success. It was the means through which they would gain financial and personal independence as well as acknowledgement as quintessentially feminine; as Paechter argues, becoming a legitimate member of a community of practice is to gain access to both symbolic and material goods.

The way in which Facebook allows friends to monitor each other's profiles, to modify their own and to constantly update in such ways that they can curate their online image, all feed into this process of perpetual evaluation of friends by friends. Facebook allows others to silently patrol friends' Facebook pages and Josie explained to me how she and her friend Rhiannon frequently, 'stalk other people's pages. Checking out if they are fake. Seeing how they lie – and they do lie'. Further, Stacey described how she might 'sarcastically "like" someone's photo; or write something that is not true'. Paechter discusses how being an insider in one community of practice often precludes membership to another group, where boundaries are emphasised by encoding behaviours; Facebook is where much of this work is carried out, explicitly in comments made, and implicitly through the display of images within and without the daily narratives on Facebook walls.

Others have written about how the formation of friendships and how the exclusion and inclusion of individuals in friendships groups are managed (e.g. see Coates 1996; George 2007; Nilan 1991). Read (2011) discusses how twenty-first-century teens and tweens draw on popular culture role models of celebrities to 'perform femininity'. Yet so too there is value in power and influence amongst peers and Read argues this as 'complexly located within the constraints of hegemonic femininity and the dynamics of power relations between girls themselves' (2011, 1–2). In this project, I saw how the many pleasurable discourses in which the young women were involved could also lead them into feeling pressured, constantly under surveillance and needing to participate even when they want 'time out'. Paechter's work proved useful in theorising the Facebook activities; perhaps the gendered Discourses were more so because of the vocational interests of the women in the study. But the data suggested that the communities of practice within which these women were involved were strongly gendered and often limiting. Finally, I saw each of my participants as a kind of text upon which popular Discourses were inscribed so that she becomes both the product and the producer of girl as commodity.

Acknowledgements

This paper would not have been possible without Hannah, Jadie, Josie and Stacey, who gave their time, generosity and friendship. I thank them for their help.

Notes

1. This paper arises from the UK Economic and Social Research Council-funded seminar series 'Young Women in Movement: Sexualities, Vulnerabilities, Needs

and Norms' (ESRC RES-451-26-0715), based at Goldsmiths, University of London, 2009–2011.
2. In this paper I use Gee's (1996) distinction between discourses with a small 'd' and Discourses. The former refers to spoken language, while the latter refers to 'Ways of behaving, interacting, valuing, thinking, believing, speaking ... of being in the world ... that are accepted as instantiations of particular roles ... by specific groups of people ... Discourses are ways of being "people like us"' (Gee 1996, viii).

References

Barton, D., and M. Hamilton. 1998. *Local literacies: Reading and writing in one community.* London: Routledge.
boyd, d., and N.B. Ellison. 2008. Social network sites: Definition, history, and scholarship. *Journal of Computer-mediated Communication* 13, no. 1: article 11. http://jcmc.indiana.edu/vol13/issue1/boyd.ellison.html.
Coates, J. 1996. *Women talk: Conversation between women friends.* Oxford: Blackwell.
Davies, J. 2007. Display; identity and the everyday: Self-presentation through online image sharing. *Discourse: Studies in the Cultural Politics of Education* 28: 549–64.
Davies, J. 2012. Facework on Facebook as a new literacy practice. *Computers and Education* 59: 19–29.
Digital Buzz. 2011. Facebook statistics, stats and facts for 2011. Blogpost. http://www.digitalbuzzblog.com/facebook-statistics-stats-facts-2011/.
Facebook. 2011. Facebook press releases: Statistics 20.12.11. https://www.facebook.com/press/info.php?statistics.
Gee, J. 1996. *Social linguistics and literacies.* 2nd ed. London: Falmer Press.
Gee, J. 2004. *Situated language and learning: A critique of traditional schooling.* London: Routledge.
George, R. 2007. *Girls in a goldfish bowl.* Rotterdam: Sense Publishers.
Goffmann, I. 1959. *The presentation of self in everyday life.* London: Penguin.
Internet World Stats. 2011. Facebook users in the world. Facebook usage and Facebook penetration. Statistics by world geographic regions. http://www.internetworldstats.com/facebook.htm.
Kuhn, A. 1995. *Family Secrets: Acts of memory and Imagination.* London: Verso/Langellier.
Lankshear, C., and M. Knobel. 2011. *Literacies: Social cultural and historical perspectives.* New York: Peter Lang.
Lave, J., and E. Wenger. 1991. *Situated learning.* Cambridge: Cambridge University Press.
Leander, K., and K. McKim. 2003. Tracing the Everyday Sitings of Adolescents on the Internet. *Education, Communication and Information* 3, no. 2: 211–36.
Lemke, J. 2004. Uses of intertextuality in classroom and educational research. In, *Uses of Intertextuality and Educational Research*, eds. D. Bloome and N. Shuart-Faris. Information Age Publishing. December 31, 2011, 3–14. http://www.jaylemke.com/storage/IntertextualityEdResearch-Bloome.pdf.
Lenhart, A., S. Arafeh, A. Smith, and A. Rank. 2008. Writing, technology and teens. Pew Internet & American Life Project. http://www.pewinternet.org/~/media//Files/Reports/2008/PIP_Writing_Report_FINAL3.pdf.pdf.

Lenhart, A., K. Purcell, A. Smith, and K. Zickuhr. 2010. Part 3, Social media: Social media and young adults. Pew Internet and American Life Project. http://www.pewinternet.org/Reports/2010/Social-Media-and-Young-Adults/Part-3/1-Teens-and-online-social-networks.aspx.

Lincoln, S. 2004. Teenage girls' 'bedroom culture': Codes versus zones. In *After subculture: Critical studies in contemporary youth culture*, ed. A. Bennett and K. Kahn-Harris, 94–106. London: Palgrave Macmillan.

Luke, A., and V. Carrington. 2002. Globalisation, literacy, curriculum practice. In *Language and Literacy in Action*, eds. R. Fisher, M. Lewis and G. Brooks London: Routledge Falmer. http://www.education.tas.gov.au/english/word/Global.doc.

Marsh, J. 2011. Young children's literacy practices in a virtual world: Establishing an online interaction order. *Reading Research Quarterly* 46, no. 2: 101–11.

McRobbie, A., and J. Garber. 1976. Girls and subcultures: An exploration. In *Resistance through rituals*, ed. S. Hall and T. Jefferson, 209–22. London: Hutchinson.

Mizen, P. 2005. A little 'light work'? Children's images of their labour. *Visual Studies* 20: 124–39.

Nilan, P. 1991. Exclusion, inclusion and moral ordering in two girls' friendship groups. *Gender and Education* 3: 163–82.

Nutbrown, C. 2011. Naked by the pool? Blurring the image?: Ethical and moral issues in the portrayal of young children in arts-based educational research. *Qualitative Inquiry* 17, no. 1: 3–14.

Paechter, C.F. 2003. Masculinities and femininities as communities of practice. *Women's Studies International Forum* 26, no. 1: 69–77.

Paechter, C.F. 2006. Power, knowledge and embodiment in communities of sex and gender practice. *Women's Studies International Forum* 29: 13–26.

Read, B. 2011. Britney, Beyonce, and me – Primary school girls' role models and constructions of the 'popular' girl. *Gender and Education* 23: 1–13.

Robards, B., and A. Bennett. 2011. My tribe: Post sub-cultural manifestations of belonging on social network sites. *Sociology* 45: 303–17.

Taylor, R. 2006. Actions speak as loud as words: A multimodal analysis of boys' talk in the classroom. *English in Education* 40: 66–82.

Wenger, E. 1998. *Communities of practice*. Cambridge: Cambridge University Press.

'Not girly, not sexy, not glamorous': primary school girls' and parents' constructions of science aspirations[1]

Louise Archer[a], Jennifer DeWitt[a], Jonathan Osborne[b], Justin Dillon[a], Beatrice Willis[a] and Billy Wong[a]

[a]*Department of Education and Professional Studies, King's College London, London, UK;* [b]*School of Education, Stanford University, PaloAlto, California, USA*

> Internationally, there is widespread concern about the need to increase participation in the sciences (particularly the physical sciences), especially among girls/women. This paper draws on data from a five-year, longitudinal study of 10–14-year-old children's science aspirations and career choice to explore the reasons why, even from a young age, many girls may see science aspirations as 'not for me'. We discuss data from phase one – a survey of over 9000 primary school children (aged 10/11) and interviews with 92 children and 78 parents, focusing in particular on those girls who did *not* hold science aspirations. Using a feminist poststructuralist analytic lens, we argue that science aspirations are largely 'unthinkable' for these girls because they do not fit with either their constructions of desirable/intelligible femininity nor with their sense of themselves as learners/students. We argue that an underpinning construction of science careers as 'clever'/'brainy', 'not nurturing' and 'geeky' sits in opposition to the girls' self-identifications as 'normal', 'girly', 'caring' and 'active'. Moreover, we suggest that this lack of fit is exacerbated by social inequalities, which render science aspirations potentially less thinkable for working-class girls in particular. The paper concludes with a discussion of potential implications for increasing women's greater participation in STEM (Science, Technology, Engineering and Mathematics).

Introduction

There have been significant advancements and improvements in gender equity within science over the last 40 years in many countries, with greater numbers of women and girls now taking STEM (Science, Technology, Engineering and Mathematics) qualifications, entering STEM careers and contributing to the wealth of STEM knowledge and research (American Association of University Women (AAUW) 2010; Harding 1998). However, entrenched gender differences still persist, both in terms of students' *attitudes* to science/mathematics and their patterns of *participation* in post-16 science/mathematics, particularly in the physical sciences and engineering, where women remain markedly under-represented (Smith 2010a, 2010b). These inequalities persist despite little, if any, gender differences in terms of pupils' attainment in science (Haworth, Dale, and Plomin 2008; Smith 2011) and mathematics (Boaler 1997; Boaler 2002; Boaler and Sengupta-Irving 2006). Moreover, evidence suggests that boys exhibit consistently more positive attitudes to science than do girls (e.g. Brotman and Moore 2008; Haste 2004; Murphy and Whitelegg 2006; Sjoberg and Schreiner 2005), particularly in relation to the physical sciences (Scantlebury and Baker 2007; Schreiner 2006; Schreiner and Sjoberg 2004), but these are the result of social, not biological, factors (Ceci, Williams, and Barnett 2009).

The reasons for these continued differences between male and female attitudes to and participation in science are complex. For instance, a 2011 report by the English education regulatory body, Ofsted, highlights that although many girls consider that gender is not a barrier to participation and that they will be able to follow 'any' courses and careers in the future, their *actual* choices (of subjects and careers) remain gender-traditional. Indeed, while many interventions aimed at encouraging more girls into science may improve girls' attitudes to science, they frequently have little effect on girls' actual subsequent choices (Darke, Clewell, and Sevo 2002). Hence, while progress is being made (AAUW 2010), undergraduates in the physical sciences remain largely high-achieving, white, middle-class young men (Smith 2010a). These gendered patterns do not reflect differences in achievement or ability (Tytler et al. 2008). Rather, as the review by Osborne, Simon, and Collins (2003) outlines, female under-representation in particular areas of science is the result of an intersecting cluster of social, cultural and structural factors.

The association of science and mathematics with 'masculinity' has long been a concern for feminist theorists (e.g. Burton 1990; Haraway 1988; Harding 1998; Walkerdine 1990) and evidence suggests that most children are aware that mathematics and/or science (but particularly the physical sciences) are 'for boys' (Adamuti-Trache and Andres 2008; Baker and Leary 1995; Breakwell, Vignoles, & Robertson 2003; Calabrese Barton and Tan 2009; Caleon and Subramaniam 2008; Carlone 2003; Farenga and Joyce 1999; Fennema and Peterson 1985; Francis 2000; Greenfield 1996; Jones, Howe, and Rua 2000; Hughes 2001; Lightbody and Durndell 1996; Mendick 2005) and that scientists are male (Baker and Leary 1995; Buck et al. 2008). Indeed, even children as young as six have been found to associate science with masculinity/males (Hughes 2001). Likewise, Haste's (2004) UK survey of 704 young people aged 11–21 years found that those who are 'alienated from science' tend to be female whereas the 'science-orientated' tend to be male. Moreover, evidence indicates that girls tend not to pursue the physical sciences because they see the identities of engineers and physicists as incongruent with their own (Sjøberg and Schreiner 2007).

As Baker and Leary observed, many girls in primary and secondary schools report enjoying science but 'could not imagine themselves as scientists' (1995, 3). Likewise, Carlone's (2003) research in the USA found that girls who do not regard themselves as 'science people' resist the further pursuit of science, even when they are capable of continuing with it. In this paper we explore some of the reasons why girls may not consider science aspirations as 'for me'. We investigate whether there is something about their perceptions of science (and careers in/from science) that renders science 'unthinkable' (undesirable/inconceivable) for them. We do this through an examination of the discourses of those girls in our interview sample who did *not* express science aspirations, based on the assumption that their constructions of (non-science) aspirations may reveal some of the unsaid and unarticulated reasons for why they do not view science-related careers as attractive or desirable aspirations.

To do so, we employ a conceptual framework that draws on feminist poststructuralist theorisations of 'identity' as a means for understanding children's identifications with science and how they reconcile their science aspirations with gendered identity performances. This approach includes Judith Butler's (1990, 1993) theorisations of gender as 'performance' and integrates it with a conceptualisation of gender as intersecting with, and mediated by, other social axes, such as 'race'/ethnicity and social class (Archer and Francis 2007; Calabrese Barton and Brickhouse 2006).

From this perspective, identity is understood as non-essentialised, fluid, contested and produced through discourse (Burman and Parker 1993; Gee 1996). That is, 'identification is an enactment that does not entail fixity or permanence' (Anthias 2001, 633) and identities are 'always in process and always constituted within, not outside, representation' (Hall 1990, 222). Moreover, we treat identities as social products, produced within and through discourse and social relations: they are 'real fictions' that are produced and constructed through social life and relations of power (Foucault 1978; Weeks 1981). Our approach to identity is integrated with the work of Judith Butler, to provide a gender lens for analysing girls' aspirations. Butler (1990) conceptualises gender as performative. That is, gender is not the 'result' of a person's sex – it does not emanate 'naturally' from particular (sexed, racialised, classed) bodies – but is produced through discursive and bodily 'acts'. Gender is, therefore, not something you 'are' or 'have' but rather is something that you 'do' (perform) and continually re-do. Gender is a powerful illusion (Butler 1990, 185–6) that is 'actualized through a series of repetitive performances that constitute the illusion of a "proper", "natural" or "fixed" gender' (Renold 2005, 4). In other words, gender is created through a myriad of verbal and bodily performances in which subjects 'do girl' (or 'do boy') (Butler 1990, 185–6).

We also use Butler's concept of 'intelligibility' to understand the context within which children and adults produce gender identities and the social pressures that they experience to perform particular (normative, socially sanctioned) identities:

> 'Intelligible' genders are those which in some sense institute and maintain relations of coherence and continuity among sex, gender, sexual practice, and desire. (Butler 1990, 23)

Consequently, Butler argues, some gender performances (i.e. those which are more subversive or counter-hegemonic) are rendered 'unintelligible'. That is, 'the cultural matrix through which gender identity has become intelligible requires that certain kinds of "identities" cannot "exist"' (Butler 1990, 24). For instance, children experience considerable pressures to perform particular heterosexualised versions of masculinity and femininity (Renold 2005).

Study details

The ASPIRES project is funded by the UK's Economic and Social Research Council as part of its Targeted Initiative on Science and Mathematics Education (TISME). The study is a five-year, longitudinal exploration of science aspirations and career choice among 10–14-year-olds in England. It comprises a quantitative online survey that was administered to a sample of over 9000 10/11-year-old students in the first phase (students will be tracked and surveyed again in subsequent phases at ages 12 and 14) and in-depth, repeat interviews with pupils (at age 10/11; age 12/13 and age 13/14) and their parents (who are interviewed twice, once when their children are age 10/11 and again at age 13/14).

Over 10,000 students from 279 schools (248 state schools; 31 independent schools) completed the Phase 1 questionnaire between October and December 2009. (The Phase 2 survey took place in autumn 2011 and phase 3 in autumn 2012.) Following data cleansing (including removal of students who were not actually in Year 6 from the sample), 9319 students remained in the sample for analysis. The sample represented all regions of the country and was roughly proportional to the overall national distribution of schools in England by attainment and proportion of students eligible for free school meals. Of the students who completed the survey there were: 50.6% boys, 49.3% girls; 846 (9.1%) in private schools, 8473 (90.9%) in state schools; 74.9% White, 8.9% Asian (Indian, Pakistani, Bangladeshi heritage), 7.5% Black (Black African, Black Caribbean), 1.4% Far Eastern, 7.8% mixed or other (N.B. because the study focuses in part on the impact of ethnicity on students' aspirations, schools with higher populations of ethnic minority students were deliberately over-recruited to ensure sufficient numbers for analysis). The survey itself covered topics such as: aspirations in science; attitudes towards school science; self-concept in science; images of scientists; participation in science-related activities outside school; parental expectations; parental school involvement; parental attitudes towards science; and peer attitudes towards school and towards school science.

This paper is primarily based on analysis of the Phase 1 qualitative dataset, which comprises 170 interviews with 78 parents and 92 children age 10/11 (Year 6), drawn from 11 schools in England. At points throughout the paper, contextual information is provided from the survey as a means for framing the qualitative data analysis, although full details of the survey and its methods, analyses and findings are discussed in separate publications (DeWitt et al. 2010, 2011).

The students and parents who were interviewed were recruited from 11 primary schools in England (one in the Midlands, two in the Eastern region, two in the South East, four in London and one in the South), which were sampled from the 279 schools that responded to the Phase 1 survey as part of the wider study. A sampling frame was constructed to represent six target categories of school (e.g. 'multiethnic urban/inner city schools'; 'working-class suburban'; 'predominantly white, middle-class suburban schools'; 'independent single sex') to ensure a range of school contexts and populations, and prospective schools were purposively sampled from within these target categories. Nine of the schools were state-funded primaries and two were private/independent schools. Students came from a broad range of socioeconomic classes and ethnic backgrounds. Social class categorisations were assigned by the lead author and second author using the National Statistics Socio-economic Classification as a guide to categorise parental occupations. Ethnicity was assigned based on self/parental reported ethnic background.

Following extensive reviews of literature from relevant work within the fields of science education and sociology of education, two topic guides (for use with children and parents) were developed and piloted, covering areas such as: aspirations (and sources of these aspirations); interests in school and out; what they like/dislike about school; attitudes towards and engagement in school science; broader perceptions of science. Parental interviews focused on: family context; perceptions and experience of the child's schooling; involvement in education; child's personality and interests; their child's aspirations, their own perceptions of and relationship with science and engineering, including their thoughts about why so few children pursue science post-16.

Interviews were conducted by four of the paper's authors, with the majority of the interviews being conducted by the second author. Of the interviewers, three (LA, JDW, BW) are White middle-class women (with English, American and French national backgrounds) and one (BWg) is a British-Chinese male PhD student. Interviewees were invited to choose their own pseudonyms, hence the majority of pseudonyms cited in this paper reflect the personal choices of interviewees.

All interviews were digitally audio-recorded and transcribed. In line with the study's conceptual approach outlined earlier, data were analysed using an analysis of discourse approach (Burman and Parker 1993). Initial coding and sorting of the data (on key topic areas, themes and by responses to particular questions) was undertaken by two authors (LA, JDW) using the NVivo software package, with the lead author providing a check on reliability of coded extracts for the specified codes. The lead author then searched coded extracts to identify discursive gender repertoires and patterns of aspirations/relationships with science, which were then tested and refined through successive phases of coding and analysis, iteratively testing emergent themes across the data set to establish 'strength' and prevalence (Miles and Huberman 1994). In line with the stated conceptual framework, the lead author then developed and tested theoretically informed hypotheses to see if they were supported or challenged by the data, for instance to identify interplays of power and practices of power and gendered discourses within respondents' talk. Draft analyses were then fed back to other authors (especially those who conducted fieldwork, BW, BWg) for checking against their readings of the data.

'I like science … but it's not for me'

Our survey of over 9000 10- and 11-year-olds indicated that the majority (over 70%) of children reported enjoying science, held positive views of scientists, took part in science-related activities in their spare time and felt that their parents valued science. However, a much smaller proportion (under 17%) aspired to careers in science. There was no notable gender difference within the 648 children who were classified as 'uninterested in science' (i.e. those who recorded the lowest scores on all the five science aspirations items), but notably fewer girls ($n = 92$, 37%) than boys ($n = 159$, 63%) were classified as being 'science keen' ($n = 251$) (i.e. those scoring very highly on all five science aspirations items). That is, of the overall sample, 3.4% of the boys were classified as 'science keen' and 2.0% of girls. Moreover, our data suggest that children from 'middle-class' backgrounds are more likely to develop and sustain science aspirations which, as we discuss elsewhere, reflects differences and interactions between family practices, values and science capital. Science capital is defined as the material and cultural science-related resources that a family may be able to draw on, such as science-related qualifications, knowledge, understanding ('scientific literacy') and social contacts and, as we discuss elsewhere, interacts with family habitus to shape the likelihood of children developing science aspirations (see Archer et al. 2012a). For instance, of the 92 'science-keen' girls who completed the survey, only 10.9% ($n = 10$) were classified as having very low/low cultural capital (cf. 25.3% of the total sample with very/low cultural capital) whereas 59.7% ($n = 55$) of science-keen girls had high or very high cultural capital (cf. 40.6% of the total sample with very/high cultural capital). Analysis of the qualitative data also indicated that those girls who did express science aspirations tended to be middle class and undertook considerable identity 'work' to reconcile their science aspirations with acceptable discourses of femininity (Archer et al., 2012b).

In this paper, we attempt to explore why many girls did not aspire to careers in science, even though most of these girls also reported enjoying science in and out of school. In particular, we try to understand why the working-class girls in our sample were proportionally less likely to express science aspirations than their middle-class counterparts and we discuss the reasons why science aspirations may be less 'thinkable' for these girls.

Of the 55 girls in the interview sample, 17 expressed science aspirations, 13 identified science-related aspirations and 25 expressed aspirations unrelated to science. The discourses of girls who aspired to careers in/from science (and their constructions of femininity) are discussed elsewhere (Archer et al., 2012b), and in this paper we focus on the 25 girls who did *not* aspire to science-related careers. Of these 25 girls, nine were categorised as working class, eight middle class, six were on borders of working/middle class and two were unassigned due to lack of data.[2]

As detailed in Table 1, while these girls expressed a range of aspirations (often holding more than one aspiration at a time), these tended to coalesce around traditionally gendered careers in the fields of the nurturing/caring professions, expressive/artistic/glamorous jobs and sports/active jobs – although other areas such as law, business and the police were also mentioned.

As Francis (2000) discusses, vocational career motivations ('to help others') are among the most common concerns that girls express when discussing their career aspirations – and are consistently found among girls

Table 1. Classification of aspirations expressed by 25 girls who did not hold science-related aspirations.

Coding of job type	No. of girls expressing aspiration
Nurturing jobs (e.g. teacher, childcare)	15
'Glamorous' and 'girly' jobs (e.g. show business, fashion designer, model, hair and beauty)	14
Active/sporty (e.g. athlete; swimming instructor)	11
Other professional (e.g. psychologist, architect, lawyer)	5
Businesswoman (e.g. own business)	2
Other (shop work)	1

Note: Most girls expressed more than one aspiration.

irrespective of their ethnic and/or social class backgrounds (e.g. see also Archer and Francis 2007). Indeed, notions of care (of others and of the self) are integral to 'traditional' (dominant) constructions of femininity (Francis 2005) and tend not to be voiced by boys to the same extent. As noted in Table 1, the girls' aspirations also reflect high levels of interest in the body and appearance, which also resonate with dominant discourses of hetero-femininity (Renold 2001), although as we shall discuss, these also intersect with classed discourses (e.g. see Skeggs 1997; Skeggs 2004).

In the analyses that follow, we suggest that science aspirations are largely unthinkable for these 25 girls because they do not see science as fitting with either (1) their constructions of desirable/intelligible femininity or (2) their learner identities and student self-concept. Moreover, we shall suggest that this lack of fit appears to be exacerbated by social inequalities, which render science aspirations less thinkable for working-class girls in particular.

Tensions between girls' constructions of science and their constructions of desirable femininity (science as not 'caring' and not 'girly')

As detailed in Table 1, the two categories of aspiration most commonly cited by the non-science aspirant girls were for 'nurturing' ($n = 15$) and 'glamorous/girly' ($n = 14$) jobs. The most popular 'nurturing' aspirations were to work in teaching and/or childcare, which were widely recognised by girls and their parents as 'good jobs'. When asked to explain why they aspired to these jobs, the girls' responses evoked dominant discursive associations between femininity and 'caring' and they frequently named specific female family members and teachers (who had nurturing roles) as the people that they most admired and wanted to emulate in the future. For instance, Celina (white English, working class, Metropolitan School) explained that she wanted to become a primary school teacher because of her positive experiences of school, her desire to nurture children ('I just want to help children learn for the future, like the teachers are doing for us now") and because she admires her mother's nurturing femininity:

> Because she [mum] has a way with children, like when my sister is crying and I can't stop her, like she can stop her and she can calm her down and that when she's really angry, yeah and she gets me to calm down when I'm really angry and I just wish I could be like her.

Likewise, Mary (Pakistani, working class, Metropolitan School) explained her rationale for wanting to become a primary school teacher as: 'I like it because you're teaching someone else education and that's a good thing. And when someone needs help you're teaching them what they need to know for when they grow up'. Mary also named her sister (who works in childcare) as the person she most looks up to and wants to emulate in the future ('cos she's [working] at a nursery so she would be a role model to me when I grow up because she wants to be a primary teacher as well').

In line with dominant societal gendered constructions of femininity (Francis 2000), these girls' visions of 'good' (desirable) femininity were characterised by nurturing and caring for others. We might infer from the absence of science aspirations among these girls that they did not perceive science to offer an obvious arena for performing this interpersonal caring role. Moreover, a small number of these girls explained their reasons for not aspiring to science-related careers as due to a perception of science as *not* nurturing. For instance, Flower (White Eastern European, working class, Metropolitan School), who aspired to become a teacher, explained that she would not want to become a scientist 'because I love animals and I don't want to harm them'. This view seemed to derive from her sister's account of dissection at secondary school ('because my sister said when she was in school she used to do science in secondary school, they used to have to cut frogs and mouses [*sic*] and she loves animals and she doesn't want to harm them').

The second most popular category of career aspirations was for 'girly' and 'glamorous' jobs ($n = 14$). Although an interest in fame was common across both boys and girls in the survey sample (with 64.8% of all children replying that 'being famous' is very or fairly important to them), analysis of the interview transcripts revealed a stereotypically feminine flavour to girls' aspirations for 'glamorous' careers (notably in acting, dancing and singing). Of the non-science aspirant girls, these were the most likely to say that they would definitely not want to work in science in the future and were more likely to be preoccupied with celebrity culture. For instance, as Louise (white English, working class, Woodstock School) reflected:

> Actually I don't know what I'd like to be if I didn't get into show business. I'd have to like figure it out ... Like I'm obsessed with Cheryl Cole[3] at the minute. I've got her biography, her book. Um, I'm just obsessed with her at the minute.

Similarly, Celina2 (white, working class/lower middle-class, South Coast School) explained how 'when I'm older I want to be an actress and, um, I've got loads of role models that are actresses'. Celina2 was adamant that she did not want to continue with science or pursue a science-related career when she grows up. Instead, her aspirations were firmly entrenched within a clear gendered, classed trajectory ('I really want to do beauty, as well as acting'). Pop stars such as Lady Gaga were also mentioned as being the inspiration for girls' aspirations to become celebrity fashion designers. For instance, Lucy (white English, working class, Midlands School) shared how 'I've got a book which is just little sketches and I've got – there are loads of Hollywood starlets and all the dresses'.

Some mothers recognised that science does not fit easily with girls' performances of 'girling'. As Sandra (mother of Danielle, white, lower middle class, Midlands School) put it, 'girls are more interested in fashion usually and things with peers. You know and it seems to be a bit geeky to be into science', although Sandra also stressed that she was very concerned that Danielle should not get the impression that science is 'all geeks' ('I don't want [Danielle] to get that impression. I don't want you thinking it's geeks'). She continued:

> I said so how do you feel about science? And she said it's really interesting, I love it, but don't only geeks do it? [Int: Oh did she?] I know and this is why I wanted to get away a bit from her thinking that science is only for people I don't know who ... because she's got this impression that only people who don't have a life do science, which is terrible.

Sandra felt that TV was largely to blame for promulgating these stereotypes:

> I have to blame TV ... Oh she watches these things, you know on TV if somebody is good at something like science don't they always say they're a boffin and they just sit at the computer or they do something and they don't have a life. They're like geeks. [I: Yeah] They put them with big heads and glasses. [I: Yeah] It's just stereotyping.

Danielle herself explained her aspirations as 'I'd like to be either a hairdresser or, um, like someone who works with children, you know like a teacher. I just really like making people's hair and I enjoy doing my own hair and I like to do my mum's'. Likewise, another mother, Ella, felt that girls are often put off science because 'it's not very girly ... it's not a very sexy job, it's not glamorous'. While the above girls' interests in fashion, appearance and celebrity culture can be found among girls from different social class backgrounds, research indicates that such interests can assume particular significance for working-class girls. Since the 1980s, feminist academics have drawn attention to how working-class girls may resist education through hyper-heterosexual femininities that are organised around themes of heterosexuality, appearance and romance (e.g. Griffin 1985; Hey 1997; McRobbie 1978; Skeggs 1997).

The girls' interest in 'glamorous' jobs (focusing on clothes and appearance, as exemplified by the fashion and beauty industries) was also clearly rooted within their interest in performing desirable hetero-femininity within their daily lives. For instance, Rachel (British Indian, middle class, Midlands School) was interested in becoming a fashion designer, which seemed to reflect her everyday performance of femininity ('I just like shopping with loads of clothes and that. I like accessorising and all that'). Against this, science did not seem to be popularly perceived as congruent with performances of ('girly') popular hetero-femininity. As feminist theorists (e.g. Francis 2000;

Paechter 2000) argue, femininity and masculinity are inherently relational concepts, such that a characterisation of science as 'not feminine' implies a construction of science as masculine. In this way, we suggest that an underlying association of science with masculinity can be detected in these girls' constructions of their preferred career aspirations as caring and/or expressive and 'girly'. That is, science appears by default as an imagined space that is incompatible with girls' performances of popular/desirable hetero-femininity.

The disconnect, between these girls' constructions of science aspirations and their performances of femininity may reflect a wider popular public discourse in which science careers (especially in the physical sciences) are aligned with masculinity. The majority of parents in our study felt that science careers are associated with masculinity and held a perception of science as being an area that more men than women study and work in (as one mother, Shelley, put it: 'it's always seen as men, isn't it? But geeky men – sorry!'). Although most parents did not subscribe to Shelley's characterisation of scientists as 'geeks', over half did view the sciences as dominated by men, although views differed considerably among parents as to the reasons for this imbalance, being divided between biological/genetic arguments (in which boys are assumed to be 'naturally' more interested in and inclined towards the sciences) and socio-cultural/structural arguments (which saw imbalances as the result of socialisation and structural inequalities).

Pupils tended to express slightly less clear-cut views of the gendered nature of science than parents although there was still a widespread recognition that popular discourses align science with masculinity (for instance, even those children who did hold science aspirations recognised that they were unusual among their class mates – such as Demi (White English, middle class, South Coast School) who said that although she personally held science-related aspirations, most of the girls in her class do not like science and prefer 'girly stuff': 'they just like ... all like girly stuff, like singing and hairdressers'). Thus, it might be noted that although Demi is able to negotiate femininity in such a way as to be congruent with holding personal science aspirations, she is still subject to patriarchal norms and discourses, as demonstrated by her dismissal of other girls' 'non-science' aspirations and interests, as 'girly stuff'.[4]

This association of science with masculinity was both representational and experiential, with some parents and girls recounting experiences of having felt outnumbered or excluded in particular science spaces. For example, Sandra described how her daughter, Danielle, had stopped attending an after-school science club because 'it was all boys' and how this had impacted on Danielle's perception that science is 'a boy thing':

> Sandra: I said why can't you do science? She [Danielle] said well, 'oh no it's a boy thing'. And I said 'it's not'. They had [science club name] at school. It's an after-school club on Monday and she said 'I'm not going because it's

all boys'. You can see what I mean when you're fighting against it aren't you? I said 'well you should at least go along and see if you enjoy it. It's all these experiments' and she said 'oh, it's fun, we did all this'...

Int: Sorry, is she going to this science after-school club?

Sandra: She went twice [Int: She went twice] and then she stopped going because it was all boys and she had no girls to talk to.

The gendered construction of science as masculine was further reinforced by a popular discourse in which the arts and sciences are perceived as being dichotomous (as encapsulated by C.P. Snow's (1959) famous reference to the 'two cultures' of the arts and sciences). This dichotomy was realised through the notion that children who are creative/arty are, therefore, not likely to also aspire to science careers) and was brought up mostly (although by no means exclusively) by girls and/or by parents in relation to their daughters. For instance, Mary (mother of Amy, white English, middle class, Clover School) explained that her daughter's aspiration to be a teacher reflected her 'creative' nature and Sally-Ann (the mother of LemonOnion, South Coast School) described her daughter (and friends) as being into the 'arty side of things' rather than science. As a comment by Lucy (White English, working class, Midlands School), that 'girls are more into literacy and boys more into science') illustrates, a number of parents and children were generally aware of a popular societal discourse that aligns femininity with the arts and masculinity with science, reflecting the historical alignment of science with masculinity and continuing gendered differences in science and arts participation.

Research has found that young people in advanced Western societies generally express less positive attitudes to science than their counterparts in the less-economically developed world (Schreiner and Sjoberg 2004). One contributing factor to this pattern may be that the arts and creative industries appear to offer a closer fit with the current 'age of desire' (Kenway and Bullen 2001, 7) that is prevalent in capitalist developed economies, where consumerism has become a key aspect of identity (Bauman 2000). In such societies, consumer-media culture plays a key role in young people's lives, the ways they see themselves and even their dis/engagement with education (Archer et al. 2007, 2010) and some tenets of this were already evident in these (young) girls' descriptions of their aspirations and interests (for instance in fashion and celebrity culture).

The disconnect between science and girls' constructions of their learner identities and competencies (science as 'clever'/'brainy')

Across the survey and interview data, children strongly associated science with 'cleverness'. For instance, over 81% of the 9000+ survey respondents agreed or strongly agreed that 'scientists are brainy' and an association between science and 'cleverness' was evident across both parent and child interviewees. The association between science and cleverness/braininess was voiced both by those who personally aspired to science-related careers and by those who resisted science aspirations, reflecting a historic discourse of the sciences as 'hard', difficult and high-status subjects. Consequently, those expressing science aspirations also performed (and were required to negotiate) 'clever' student identities (see Archer et al., unpublished manuscript) – identities which can be difficult to occupy comfortably (see also Mendick 2005 in the context of mathematics). Moreover, as we now move to discuss, this popular association of science with cleverness played an influential role in rendering science aspirations 'unthinkable' for many of the girls in our study.

As discussed earlier, analysis of the survey data suggested that a relatively small proportion of children were not at all interested in science, which was similarly reflected in the interviews, with just a handful of children claiming to strongly dislike science and/or the idea of a future job that might use science in some way. However, children from working-class backgrounds (who constituted a minority of study participants overall) were over-represented among the 'uninterested' category. Moreover, within the interview sample, those from working-class backgrounds were much more likely to not identify themselves as 'clever' – those who identified themselves as clever and/or who were identified by parents as being clever/bright were more likely to express science aspirations. For example, Louise (White English, working class, Woodstock School) expressed some of the most resistant views of science within the interview sample. When asked by the interviewer 'who is into science?', Louise replied 'Well the clever ones are. Like the ones that are going to the grammar school are into like every subject ... They don't mind having lessons'. She continued 'its just strange how all the clever ones are into science'. Likewise, Victoria2 (white Eastern European, working class, Metropolitan School) gave her reasons for not wanting to become a scientist as 'cos most scientists are brainy and I don't want to be brainy'. Interestingly, Victoria2 did like some areas of science (notably animals and biology) but did not enjoy what she called 'the normal subject' of science. Despite her resistance to being 'brainy', she also held some more general, positive views of science, describing it as 'awesome' – suggesting a disconnect between her interest and respect for (some areas of) science and her view of herself as a learner and the capacity to see herself as a 'science person'. Flower (White, Eastern European, working class, Metropolitan School) also agreed that you have to be clever to be into science and was adamant that personally she would not want to follow a science career 'because I'm not that smart'. Likewise, Celina (white, working class, Metropolitan School) described those who are 'really into science' as 'brainiacs, because they just want to do science, they don't want to do anything else in their life'.

In other words, the popular association of science with cleverness means that science aspirations are not experienced as viable or appropriate for all students – and can be notably problematic for those who do not perform (and/or who do not consider themselves as performing) academic success and 'cleverness'. Even where parents attempted to encourage their daughters' science interests and challenged negative stereotypes of science (e.g. as being 'geeky' or 'for boys'), the dominant association of science with cleverness remained as a fundamental, taken-for-granted inherent feature of science by most of those interviewed. This is exemplified by the case of Danielle and her mother, Sandra. Danielle describes herself as a 'middle' student, a view that her mother, Sandra, concurs with ('Um, I think she's more of a middle of the range child. There's nothing really that she excels in') but among her various interests, Danielle does enjoy science and says it is one of her favourite lessons ('I'm not being a kiss-up[5] but my favourite lesson is actually science), her mother is strongly supportive and her father works as a mechanical engineer. Yet, science aspirations are unthinkable for Danielle, who feels 'I'm not clever enough to be good at science'. As Sandra explained:

> Sandra: Yeah, that's what she said to me. I said why? She said oh, you have to be really clever, you have to be a geek.
>
> Int: Mmm, how did you respond?
>
> Sandra: [I said] 'What do you mean, what do you mean you have to be really clever and be a geek?' She said 'well, you do don't you? Everybody sees it. You have to … you see it on TV and [scientist character], she's a geek, no friends, got glasses'. … She said 'well, you have to be really clever and I'm not'. I said you are clever. You could do anything you want.

We suggest that the disconnect that Danielle feels between her construction of science (as 'clever') and her own self-concept as a 'middling' pupil plays an influential role in preventing her from seeing science aspirations as 'for me'.

Other work that has sought to interrogate and deconstruct dominant educational discourses highlights how the characteristics commonly associated with the 'ideal pupil' tend to be gendered, racialised and classed in particular ways (Archer 2008; Archer and Francis 2007), such that notions such as 'natural brilliance' tend to be associated with masculinity. Carlone's (2003) US research suggests that the popular association of science with 'cleverness' (and 'natural' academic brilliance) is often reinforced in particularly gendered ways by science teachers. She found that teachers in an Advanced Physics class made unconscious but stark gendered attributions of student aptitude, perceiving boys as more naturally able in physics than girls, despite girls tending to achieve higher marks. Echoing wider gender and education research (e.g. Francis 2000), girls' achievement was attributed to their plodding diligence and 'hard work' whereas boys' lower achievements were explained as due to a lack of application (rather than a lack of aptitude). The study of Carlone et al. (2008) found that teacher approaches can make a difference to the extent that some students, but notably poor, minority ethnic girls, feel they can identify with science and be a good science student – irrespective of their actual attainment in the subject.

Moreover, as others have written, gender is a relational construction in which intelligence and 'the mind' have been historically configured as masculine, against which femininity has been associated with 'the body' (e.g. Paechter 2000). Consequently, as the sciences (and mathematics) are associated with cleverness which is linked to masculinity, so a sustainable science identity may be 'more challenging for girls than it is for boys' (Carlone and Johnson 2007; Ong 2005). We suggest that this relationship is further exacerbated in the case of working-class girls due to the intersection of classed discourses which align middle-class students with achievement/the mind and working-class students with the body/underachievement (see Archer 2008), resulting in the exclusion of working-class girls not only from the identity of the ideal student but also, in particular, from science-related future aspirations.

For instance, a number of pupils distinguished between those who are 'academic' and those who are 'practical', reflecting a discourse of the 'academic–vocational divide, which is long-standing within UK education (e.g. see Leathwood and Hutchings 2003 for discussion and critique). Within this discourse, working-class learners have traditionally been associated with 'practical' and vocational subject routes (as preferences and as fitting their assumed skills and aptitudes). Girls' preferences for 'hands-on' jobs in show-business, the beauty industry and sports-related careers (see Table 1) can all be understood as reflecting this longstanding discourse of the academic–vocational divide. For instance, LemonOnion described how she generally liked science classes at school but felt that science played little role in her wider life or aspirations. Instead, she and her friends identified with artistic/creative subjects, which SallyAnn (her mother) attributed to the girls not being 'academic' ('I wouldn't say they are all academic. I think most of the children she likes to mix with, like the arts – drama, singing, drawing, making, doing. I think that's more where they are').

Consequently, we would argue that the powerful popular association of science with 'cleverness' (and its perception as being a highly academic subject) means that identifying with science (seeing oneself as a potential 'science person') requires taking up (and being recognised by others for occupying) a 'good student' identity. Research suggests that this can be more difficult for working-class learners, girls and those from some minority ethnic backgrounds due to dominant educational discourses that construct the 'ideal learner' as white, male and middle class (Archer 2008). Moreover, we would suggest that the popular association of science with cleverness constructs science as an exclusive, distinct and exceptional field – something that is for the 'clever' few, and is not seen as 'for me' by the majority of students.

The girls' non-science aspirations tended to be rooted within those areas of their life in which they felt they had (or were developing) practical competencies, and which they were reinforcing and developing through their everyday activities. For instance, those girls who saw themselves as 'good at sport' often named sports-related aspirations and those who aspired to work with children tended to have younger siblings or extended family members who they looked after regularly. Moreover, the girls described receiving considerable support and reinforcement of their capabilities from their parents, which bolstered their sense of being competent and well suited for this particular area (e.g. as 'good with children'). Parents concurred with these views, for instance, Celina's mother (Leah2) describes her daughter as 'good with children' and emphasised that she felt Celina would make a good teacher. Many girls recounted the explicit encouragement and reinforcement they received from home in this respect. As Charlie, who aspired to be a teacher, explained:

> When I go round my nan's and my cousins, mum and dad come in and all that and they go 'oh you're so good with babies ... they say you're really good with babies and you should be like someone who looks after children ... like a childminder or a babysitter or something. (Charlie, white English, middle class)

Elsewhere we have discussed the importance of science capital (science-related qualifications, resources, knowledge/literacy and contacts) for 'growing' children's science aspirations, outlining the ways in which capital interacts with family habitus to make science aspirations more, or less, thinkable for children (Archer et al., forthcoming) and how a lack of science capital can hinder the development of science aspirations. The data from the girls without science aspirations reinforce the importance of capital in that their stated aspirations are clearly rooted within particular forms of social and cultural capital (family contacts, everyday experiences of e.g. babysitting/childcare, fashion and sport). The absence of science capital within their daily lives renders science aspirations less conceivable (and achievable), not only reducing their opportunities for developing a practical 'feel' for science but also of being able to see science as a 'thinkable' performance of femininity. Although only a small minority of children in the survey and interviews reported unambiguously negative attitudes to science, that these children tended to be girls from working-class or lower-middle-class backgrounds is noteworthy and underlines the 'distance' between science (as male and middle class) and working-class femininity. As discussed elsewhere, that science capital is unevenly spread across families and tends to be concentrated in the middle classes (Archer et al., forthcoming), means that other girls are particularly likely to lack opportunities to see science as fitting with their constructions of femininity and everyday lives. In short, for many girls – even those in primary school who tend to enjoy science – science aspirations are already undesirable and 'unthinkable'.

Discussion/conclusion

In this paper we have explored possible reasons for why many girls in our sample liked and enjoyed science but did not consider science aspirations as 'for me'. By looking at some of the reasons they gave for their non-science aspirations, we have sought to understand the 'unsaid' aspects of their constructions of science, probing in particular the ways in which these are inflected by gender.

Our analysis suggests that the highly gendered nature of these girls' alternative aspirations is not coincidental or by chance but rather indicates their underlying constructions of science careers as 'masculine'. Their discourses reveal the extent to which science careers are imagined (and/or experienced) as being incompatible with girls' performances of popular femininity. Indeed, we might argue that science aspirations are 'unthinkable' for these girls due to their perceptions of science as not nurturing, not glamorous/girly and not 'practical' (being too 'clever' and academic). Moreover, these perceptions appear to be exacerbated by social class inequalities and may be amplified for working-class girls, given the resonance between discourses of 'glamour', 'girliness', 'hands on' (vocational) education and popular performances of working-class femininity. Notably, we suggest that those girls and boys who feel excluded from high academic achievement will learn from an early age that science aspirations are 'not for me', even if they otherwise enjoy science in and out of school.

Given that existing research shows that hetero-femininity continues to be a defining feature of many girls' sense of self and their ways of 'doing girl' (Ali 2003; Renold 2005), we might anticipate such constructions of identity continuing to intensify with age as these 10/11-year-old girls progress through secondary school. Moreover, popular constructions of science, as aligned with 'cleverness' and 'the mind' (abstract/academic, cerebral) do not fit easily with many of our girls' interests in the body, appearance and celebrity culture, nor with their 'non-academic' learner identities. Indeed, some research indicates that highly feminised ('girly') STEM role models can actually decrease non-STEM interested girls' STEM interests and aspirations because they are perceived by these girls as particularly unobtainable (Betz and Sekaquaptewa 2012). We might similarly speculate that for some of our girls, science is an 'unthinkable' identity due to its profound incongruence with key elements of popular femininity.

Our analysis of the girls' discourses indicates an underlying binary construction of science and non-science aspirations (see Table 2), in which science aspirations are constructed relationally to the three main categories of non-science aspirations (nurturing, girly and sports-related aspirations). That is, key elements within each set of constructions (of science versus non-science aspirations) can be configured in oppositional terms (what one 'is' illuminates and implies what the other 'is not').

We suggest that there is a close alignment between the right-hand column of Table 2 (of non-science aspirations) and these girls' everyday performances of hetero-femininity, which renders such aspirations 'obvious'/thinkable. Against this, science is constructed as an undesirable and unthinkable aspiration – it simply does not 'fit' with these girls' sense of identity. Moreover, the prevalence of popular discourses that align the qualities within the left-hand ('science') column with masculinity and middle-classness (and conversely the right-hand column with femininity and working-classness) would imply that science aspirations are less likely to be experienced as a conceivable and achievable option for working-class girls in particular – who may need to engage in considerable identity work if they are to come to see science aspirations as 'for me'.

The discursive mapping in Table 2 indicates potential opportunities for opening up and challenging popular representations of science (including those promulgated by the scientific community). For instance, our analyses suggest that work might usefully be undertaken to open up popular perceptions of the sciences, and the cultures that operate within the sciences, to render them more accessible for 'non-traditional' groups. In particular, careful attention might be paid to how the sciences might encourage and value broader forms of participation and engagement, such that children can see that careers in/from science welcome and embrace a wide range of identity performances (e.g. not just being 'clever' and geeky).

It would also appear valuable to increase the potential for (and/or families' awareness of) more diverse forms of participation in post-compulsory science. The children and parents in our study largely saw science jobs only in terms of becoming a scientist (or doctor or science teacher), suggesting little public awareness of either the diversity contained within 'being a

Table 2. Binary constructions of science and non-science aspirations.

Science	Non-science aspirations
Academic, 'clever', 'brainy', cerebral/'the mind'	Practical/*vocational*, 'normal', 'hands-on', active, *'the body'*
Not nurturing/*dispassionate*	Nurturing
Geeky	Glam, fashionable
Other, unknown, distant	*Known, everyday*

Note: Inferred attributes are in italics.

scientist' (e.g. see the Science Council's campaign on 'Ten Types of Scientist), nor of the immense diversity of jobs from science (e.g. jobs that are science-related or that are informed by science). Work to increase teachers', families' and children's awareness of the wide diversity of careers in/from science would seem important for increasing future participation. Indeed, it is particularly ironic that the KS4[6] programme of science study in England contains not a single reference to the need to educate students about possible future careers in/from science, even though one of the main rationales given for the importance of science to the UK curriculum is the preparation of the next generation of future scientists. Yet changing perceptions of the value of science for future careers is not only a matter of increasing public awareness of diverse routes – there is also a case for increasing the actual diversity of available routes in/from science that go beyond the 'gold standard' of A level and university degree routes in order to broaden participation in the sciences. This is not only a STEM 'pipeline' issue but, in our view, is an important social equity issue. Currently, the potential material and cultural benefits that are offered by post-16 science qualifications and/or careers are largely the preserve of particular, privileged social groups (notably white, middle-class men).

We do not see the challenge, however, as merely an issue of changing students' (and parents') perceptions: there is also a need to ensure that the cultures operating within post-16 science (in colleges, universities and workplaces) are indeed equitable and do not alienate or disadvantaged 'non-traditional' participants. Existing evidence suggests that there are still a number of challenges on this front (e.g. Carlone 2004; Ong 2005). This will require scrutinising the cultures that currently operate within the sciences, to make sure that they are fair and inclusive.

Finally, we feel there is a strong case to be made for the implementation of strategies designed to increase science capital (Archer et al., forthcoming) within UK families, to help make science (and hence science aspirations) more 'known' and familiar within families' everyday lives. In other words, there is still a considerable challenge facing the science education community to enable and encourage more girls to see science aspirations as desirable and 'thinkable' for them. As Pamela (Black Caribbean girl at Chestnut Junior School, who aspires to be an actress, dance teacher or sports teacher) explained, although she enjoys science and does well in it, a science-related future career would be 'good for some people but not for me'.

Notes

1. This paper arises from the UK Economic and Social Research Council-funded seminar series 'Young Women in Movement: Sexualities, Vulnerabilities, Needs and Norms' (ESRC RES-451-26-0715), based at Goldsmiths, University of London, 2009–2011.

2. Cf. the science-aspirant girls who were predominantly middle class (only one working-class girl) – see Archer et al. (forthcoming).
3. Cheryl Cole is a very popular English pop star and celebrity. She rose to fame through a reality pop competition and joined the manufactured girl band Girls Aloud. She has since enjoyed success as a solo artist, TV personality, model and as the face of international cosmetics company L'Oreal. She is frequently featured in the tabloid press and fashion/ lifestyle magazines.
4. We are grateful to the anonymous reviewers for suggesting this point.
5. Kiss up' means to falsely flatter or in this case, to express a false opinion in order to curry favour with the interviewer.
6. The two years of schooling in England for pupils between the ages of 14 and 16, which incorporates GCSEs, the national examinations taken by pupils at the end of this period.

References

Adamuti-Trache, M., and L. Andres. 2008. Embarking on and persisting in scientific fields of study: Cultural capital, gender, and curriculum along the science pipeline. *International Journal of Science Education* 30: 1557–84.

Ali, S. 2003. To Be A Girl: Culture and Class in Schools. *Gender and Education* 15, no. 3: 269–83.

American Association of University Women (AAUW). 2010. *AAUW annual report*. Washington, DC: AAUW.

Anthias, F. 2001. New hybridities, old concepts: The limits of 'culture'. *Ethnic and Racial Studies* 24: 619–41.

Archer, L. 2008. The Impossibility of Minority Ethnic Educational 'Success'? An Examination of the Discourses of Teachers and Pupils in British Secondary Schools. *European Educational Research Journal* 7, No. 1: 89-107.

Archer, L., and B. Francis. 2007. *Understanding Minority Ethnic Achievement*. London: Routledge.

Archer, L., J. DeWitt, J. Osborne, J. Dillon, B. Willis, and B. Wong. 2012a. Science Aspirations and family habitus: How families shape children's engagement and identification with science. *American Educational Research Journal* 49, no. 5: 881–908.

Archer, L., J. DeWitt, J. Osborne, J. Dillon, B. Willis, and B. Wong. 2012b. "Balancing acts": Elementary school girls' negotiations of femininity, achievement, and science. *Science Education* 96, no. 6: 967–89.

Archer, L., S. Hollingworth, and A. Halsall. 2007. University's not for me – I'm a Nike person: Urban, working class young people's negotiations of 'style', identity and educational engagement. *Sociology* 4, no. 2: 219–37.

Archer, L., S. Hollingworth, and H. Mendick. 2010. *Urban Youth and Schooling*. Maidenhead: Open University Press.

Baker, D., and R. Leary. 1995. Letting girls speak out about science. *Journal of Research in Science Teaching* 32, no. 1: 3–27.

Bauman, Z. 2000. *Liquid Modernity*. London: John Wiley & Sons.

Betz, D.E., and D. Sekaquaptewa. 2012. My fair physicist? Feminine math and science role models demotivate young girls. *Social Psychological and Personality Science*. Published online March 2, doi: 10.1177/1948550612440735

Boaler, J. 1997. Reclaiming school mathematics: The girls fight back. *Gender and Education* 9: 285–305.

Boaler, J. 2002. Paying the price for 'sugar and spice': Shifting the analytical lens in equity research. *Mathematical Thinking and Learning* 4, no. 2: 127–44.

Boaler, J., and T. Sengupta-Irving. 2006. Nature, neglect & nuance. Changing accounts of sex, gender and mathematics. In *The Sage handbook of gender and education*, ed. C. Skelton, B. Francis, and L. Smulyan, 207–20. London: Sage.

Breakwell, G.M., V.L. Vignoles, and T. Robertson. 2003. Stereotypes and crossed-category evaluations: The case of gender and science education. *British Journal of Psychology* 94: 437–55.

Brotman, J.S., and F.M. Moore. 2008. Girls and science. A review of four themes in the science education literature. *Journal of Research in Science Teaching* 45: 971–1002.

Buck, G.A., V.L. Plano Clark, D. Leslie-Pelecky, Y. Lu, and P. Cerda-Lizarraga. 2008. Examining the cognitive processes used by adolescent girls and women in identifying science role models: A feminist approach. *Science Education* 92: 688–707.

Burman, E., and I. Parker, eds. 1993. *Discourse analytic research: Repertoires and readings of texts in action*. London: Routledge.

Burton, L. 1990. *Gender and mathematics: An international perspective*. London: Cassell Educational.

Butler, J. 1990. *Gender trouble: Feminism and the subversion of identity*. London: Routledge.

Butler, J. 1993. *Bodies that matter: On the discursive limits of sex*. London: Routledge.

Calabrese Barton, A., and N.W. Brickhouse. 2006. Engaging girls in science. In *The Sage handbook of gender and education*, ed. C. Skelton, B. Francis, and L. Smulyan, 221–35. Thousand Oaks, CA: Sage.

Calabrese Barton, A., and E. Tan. 2009. Funds of knowledge and discourses and hybrid space. *Journal of Research in Science Teaching* 46: 50–73.

Caleon, I.S., and R. Subramaniam. 2008. Attitudes towards science of intellectually gifted and mainstream upper primary students in Singapore. *Journal of Research in Science Teaching* 45: 940–54.

Carlone, H.B. 2003. (Re)producing good science students: Girls' participation in high school physics. *Journal of Women and Minorities in Science and Engineering* 9, no. 1: 17–34.

Carlone, H.B. 2004. The cultural production of science in reform-based physics: Girls' access, participation, and resistance. *Journal of Research in Science Teaching* 41: 392–414.

Carlone, H.B., M. Cook, J. Wong, W.A. Sandoval, A.C. Barton and E. Tan. 2008. Seeing and supporting identity development in science education. Paper presented at the Proceedings of the 8th international Conference on the Learning Sciences, Volume 3.

Carlone, H.B., and A. Johnson. 2007. Understanding the science experiences of successful women of color: Science identity as an analytic lens. *Journal of Research in Science Teaching* 44: 1187–18.

Ceci, S.J., W.M. Williams, and S.M. Barnett. 2009. Women's underrepresentation in science. Sociocultural and biological considerations. *Psychological Bulletin* 135: 218–61.

Darke, K., B. Clewell, and R. Sevo. 2002. Meeting the challenge: The impact of the National Science Foundation's Program for Women and Girls. *Journal of Women and Minorities in Science and Engineering* 8: 285–303.

DeWitt, J., L. Archer, J. Osborne, J. Dillon, B. Willis, and B. Wong. 2010. High aspirations but low progression: The science aspirations-careers paradox among minority ethnic students. *International Journal of Science and Mathematics Education* 9, no. 2: 243–71.

DeWitt, J., J. Osborne, L. Archer, J. Dillon, B. Willis and B. Wong. 2011. Young children's aspirations in science. The unequivocal, the uncertain and the unthinkable. *International Journal of Science Education.* published August 2011, iFirst.

Farenga, S.J., and B.A. Joyce. 1999. Intentions of young students to enroll in science courses in the future: An examination of gender differences. *Science Education* 83: 55–75.

Fennema, E., and P.L. Peterson. 1985. Autonomous learning behavior: A possible explanation of sex-related differences in mathematics. *Educational Studies in Mathematics* 16: 309–11.

Foucault, M. 1978. *The history of sexuality: An introduction.* New York: Pantheon.

Francis, B. 2000. The gendered subject: Students' subject preferences and discussions of gender and subject ability. *Oxford Review of Education* 26: 35–48.

Francis, B. 2005. Not knowing their place. Girls' classroom behaviour. In *'Problem' girls: Understanding and supporting troubled and troublesome girls*, ed. G. Lloyd, 9–21. London: Routledge.

Gee, J.P. 1996. *Social linguistics and literacies: Ideology in discourses.* London: Routledge.

Greenfield, T.A. 1996. Gender, ethnicity, science achievement and attitudes. *Journal of Research in Science Teaching* 33: 901–33.

Griffin, C. 1985. *Typical Girls.* London: Routledge.

Hall, S. 1990. Cultural identity and diaspora. In *Identity: Community, culture, difference*, ed. J. Rutherford, 392–403. London: Lawrence & Wishart.

Haraway, D. 1988. Situated knowledges: The science question in feminism and the privilege of partial perspective. *Feminist Studies* 14: 575–99.

Harding, S. 1998. Women, science, and society. *Science* 281, no. 5383: 1599–600.

Haste, H. 2004. *Science in my future: A study of values and beliefs in relation to science and technology amongst 11–21 year olds.* London: Nestle Social Research Programme.

Haworth, C.M.A., P. Dale, and R. Plomin. 2008. A twin study into the genetic and environmental influences on academic performance in science in nine-year-old boys and girls. *International Journal of Science Education* 30: 1003–25.

Hey, V. 1997. *The company she keeps: An ethnography of girls' friendship.* Buckingham, UK: Open University Press.

Hughes, G. 2001. Exploring the availability of student scientist identities within curriculum discourse: An anti-essentialist approach to gender-inclusive science. *Gender and Education* 13: 275–90.

Jones, M.G., A. Howe, and M.J. Rua. 2000. Gender differences in students' experiences, interests, and attitudes toward science and scientists. *Science Education* 84, no. 2: 180–92.

Kenway, J., and E. Bullen. 2001. *Consuming Children.* Maidenhead: Open University Press.

Leathwood, C., and M. Hutchings. 2003. Entry routes to Higher Education: pathways, qualifications and social class. In *Higher Education and Social Class*, ed. L. Archer, M. Hutchings, and A. Ross. London: RoutledgeFalmer.

Lightbody, P., and A. Durndell. 1996. Gendered career choice. Is sex-stereotyping the cause or the consequence? *Educational Studies* 22: 133–46.

McRobbie, A. 1978. *Jackie: An Ideology of Adolescent Femininity*. University of Birmingham.
Mendick, H. 2005. Mathematical stories: Why do more boys than girls choose to study mathematics at AS level in England? *British Journal of Sociology of Education* 26: 235–51.
Miles, M.B., and A.M. Huberman. 1994. *Qualitative data analysis: An expanded sourcebook*. Newbury Park, CA: Sage.
Murphy, P., and E. Whitelegg. 2006. *Girls in the physics classroom: A review of the research on the participation of girls in physics*. London: Institute of Physics.
Ofsted. 2011. *The annual report of Her Majesty's Chief Inspector of Education, Children's Services and Skills*. Norwich, UK: Ofsted.
Ong, M. 2005. Body projects of young women of color in physics: Intersections of gender, race, and science. *Social Problems* 52: 593–617.
Osborne, J., S. Simon, and S. Collins. 2003. Attitudes towards science. A review of the literature and its implications. *International Journal of Science Education* 25: 1049–79.
Paechter, C. 2000. *Changing school subjects: Power, gender and curriculum*. Buckingham, UK: Open University Press.
Renold, E. 2001. 'Square-girls', femininity and the negotiation of academic success in the primary school. *British Educational Research Journal* 27: 577–88.
Renold, E. 2005. *Girls, boys and junior sexualities: Exploring childrens' gender and sexual relations in the primary school*. London: Routledge.
Scantlebury, K., and D. Baker. 2007. Gender issues in science education research: Remembering where the difference lies. In *Handbook of research on science education*, ed. S. Abell and N. Lederman, 257–86. Mahwah, NJ: Lawrence Erlbaum.
Schreiner, C. 2006. *Exploring a ROSE-garden: Norwegian youth's orientations towards science – Seen as signs of late modern identities*. Oslo: University of Oslo.
Schreiner, C., and S. Sjoberg. 2004. *Sowing the seeds of ROSE: Background, rationale, questionnaire development and data collection for ROSE (The Relevance of Science Education) – a comparative study of students' views of science and science education*. Oslo: University of Oslo.
Sjøberg, S., and C. Schreiner. 2005. How do learners in different cultures relate to science and technology? Results and perspectives from the project ROSE (the Relevance of Science Education) *Asia-Pacific Forum on Science Learning and Teaching* 6, no. 2: 1–17.
Sjøberg, S., and C. Schreiner. 2007. Perceptions and images of science and science education. In *Communicating European Research 2005*, ed. M. Claessens. Dordrecht: Springer.
Skeggs, B. 1997. *Formations of class & gender: Becoming respectable*. Thousand Oaks, CA: Sage.
Skeggs, B. 2004. *The re-branding of class: Propertising culture*. Basingstoke, UK: Palgrave Macmillan.
Smith, E. 2010. Do we need more scientists? A long-term view of patterns of participation in UK undergraduate science programmes. *Cambridge Journal of Education* 40: 281–98.
Smith, E. 2010. Is there a crisis in school science education in the UK? *Educational Review* 62, no. 2: 189–202.
Smith, E. 2011. Women into science and engineering? Gendered participation in higher education STEM subjects. *British Educational Research Journal* 37: 993–1014.

Snow, C.P. 1959. *The two cultures*. Cambridge: Cambridge University Press.
Tytler, R., J. Osborne, G. Williams, K. Tytler, and J. Cripps Clark. 2008. *Opening up pathways: Engagement in STEM across the Primary–Secondary school transition*. Australian Department of Education, Employment and Workplace Relations, Canberra, A.C.T.
Walkerdine, V. 1990. *Schoolgirl fictions*. London: Verso Books.
Weeks, J. 1981. *Sex, politics and society: The regulation of sexuality since 1800*. New York: Longman.

Index

'A Girls' Work Manifesto' 43, 45, 47, 50–52
academic knowing 101
acceptance 64–5
accomplishment 78–9, 83–91
Adkins, L. 107
affect amplification 11
affective turn 97–8
Aftermath of Feminism 38
agency 5–6, 98–9, 107
agnosticism 97
Ahn, J. 113–14
airbrushing 36
alienation 172
'Alpha Girl' 48, 60, 100
Alte Molkerei Frille 43–5, 52–3
Althusser, Louis 134
ambivalent success 103–4
anonymisation 151
anorexia 16, 119–24
anorexic tricks 120
anti-obesity discourse 7, 16
anti-racism 50
anti-sexism 44
anti-social behaviour 26
anti-social behaviour orders 27
antiracism 61
apprenticeships 89
appropriation of body 9, 34
aptitude 185
art of conversation 31
ASBOs see anti-social behaviour orders
ASPIRES project 174–6
assuredness 76
attachment 98
attending Girls' Club 67–8
attitude 36, 44
austerity 23–5, 102–3
authenticity 120–23, 148–9
autonomy 20, 31, 48, 61, 132, 141
awareness of panopticon 165–6

Baker, D. 173
Ball, S.J. 75–6, 98–9
Barton, D. 148
Batsleer, J. 28, 30, 34
Beck, U. 96, 104
Beck-Gernsheim, E. 96
becoming accomplished 75–93; conclusion 90–91; current study 77–9; findings 79–89; introduction 75–7
bedroom culture 131–2, 165
being a 'nice' girl 120–21
Bennett, A. 149
Bielefeld Girls' Club 62–3, 67–8
Bitzan, Maria 60
blogging 25, 118–20
Bochner, A.P. 101
body knowledge 9–10
body modification 122
body pedagogies 10
Bourdieu, Pierre 106–7
boyd, d. 115, 150
boyishness 137, 141
Bradford, S. 24–5, 28
BRAVO GIRL 60
breast augmentation 122
Britain's Got Talent 161
Broken Britain 27
Brotsky, S.R. 120
bulimic identity 119–20
bullying 16, 35–6
Bundes Republik Deutschland 45–7
burden of health 10–12
Butler, J. 31, 48–9, 59–60, 98–9, 173–4
buying private education 79–89; choosing between schools 81–2; effortless accomplishment 86–7; expectation of accomplishment 82–6; going private 79–81; reproduction of privilege 87–9

Carlone, H.B. 173, 185
carnivalistic making of gender 50–51

INDEX

catch-22 43–5
celebratory discourses 6
challenging personality 129–45
changing times 5–22; conclusion 19–20; healthy girlhood 12–16; introduction 5–7; new girlhood 16–19; new pedagogies of health 7–9; research design 9–10; stories of future health 10–12
child perspective of media commerciality 139–43
children's gender and sexuality norms 129–45
child's knowledge of media services 142
Chittenden, T. 118
choosing between schools 81–2
civil disturbance 27
Clarke, B. 115
class inheritance 95–110
co-education 44–6, 62, 69–70
Coalition 25, 27–8, 30
Coates, J. 148, 155
Coburn, A. 30
Cohen, N.S. 115
collaborative identity construction 111–27
Collins, S. 172
commerciality of new media 139–43
community of gendered literacy practice 147–69
competing with boys 64–5
concept of girls' work 61–2
concerted cultivation 75–93
conformity 26
congruence of experience 47
Connexions 29–30
consciousness raising 30–31
constraints 1
constructing identity 111–27; authenticity 120–23; conclusion 123–4; identity communities 118–20; introduction 111–12; online privacy 114–18; SNS interaction 112–14
construction of science aspiration 171–94
constructions of science 178–82
consumerism 95–6
contemporary youth work 23–42
contextualisation of topic-related research 129–31
cosmetic surgery 122
crime prevention 24–5
crisis of the boys 67
critical girls' work 30–33
cross-generational conversation 34
Crozier, G. 75
cultivatedness 75–93
cultural omnivores 76
current pedagogical challenges 66–7

Danowski, J. 122
Davies, Bronwyn 32
Davies, J. 115, 118–19, 123
deconstructivism 31, 47–50, 52–3, 57–8
deficit approach 46–7
demonstrating thinness 14–15
denigration of women 159
Department for Children, Schools and Families 7
Department of Health 7
deprivation 103–4
desirable femininity 178–82
desire for accomplishment 82–6
Deutscher Presserat 60
dichotomy of gender 51–4
Die Tageszeitung 57–8
diet 6–8, 119–20
digital literacies 148
diligence 35
disaffection 18, 26, 106
disconnect between science and learner identity 182–7
dissidence 95–110; affective turn 97–8; context 96–7; immediate context 102–3; implications 106–8; introduction 95–6; research data 101–2; subjectification 98–9; triumph of desire 104–6; welfare and wanting 103–4; world in question 100
diversification 51–3
DIY *see* do-it-yourself
do-it-yourself 23–42
doing girl 60, 187
doing without 103–4
Dolar, Mladen 130
down classing 96, 98–9
Dribbusch, Barbara 57–8
drug taking 26–7, 29
Duke of Edinburgh awards 88
dynamic tension 100
dysfunction 26

e-zines 116
E2E *see* Entry to Employment programme
eating disorders 26–7, 120
Economic and Social Research Council projects 9–10, 77–9, 95–6, 174–6
educational failure of boys 25–8
effects of 'strong girl' ideology 60–61
effortless accomplishment 86–7
elite identification 76–7
Ellesworth, E. 31
Elley, S. 75, 89–90
Ellis, C. 101
Ellison, N.B. 150
emancipation of girls 45–7, 60–62
emotional engagement 114–15

INDEX

empowerment 30–31, 33
English youth work 23–42; conclusion 37–8; failing boys, problem girls 25–8; 'girls' work' 28–30; introduction 23–5; modern critical girls' work 30–33; moments of resistance 33–7
enjoying science 176–8
Entry to Employment programme 28–9
epistemic contextualisation 129–31
eroticism 139–40
ethnicity 9, 16, 51, 61, 174
Evans, M. 100
exclusion 77
exercising 6–8, 11–13
exigencies of capitalism 107
expectation of accomplishment 82–6
explaining attendance 67–8
external opinions 67–8

Facebook 53, 113–14, 147–69
failing boys 25–8
'fallen girls' 46
fashion blogging 118–20
fated individualisation 96
Faulstich-Wieland, Hannelore 69–70
fear of fatness 10–11
Fegter, Susann 67
feisty banter 164
felt authenticity 99
female inferiorities 48
feminisation of normality 46
feminism 23–42
feminist traditions 28–30
Feministwebs 23–4, 33–7
'5-a-day' 14, 18
fixing transgression 17, 27
forms of being 49
Foucault, M. 8, 130, 139
Fox, N. 119
Francis, B. 177–8
Freire, Paulo 24, 30–31
friends vs. haters 156–7
future bodies 5–22

Gaztambide-Fernández, R. 76–7, 90–91
GDR *see* Bundes Republik Deutschland
Gee, J. 151
geekiness 184
gender deconstruction 57–8
gender equality 33–4, 171–4
gender hierarchy 47, 62, 131
gender norms 129–45
gender stereotypes 60–61, 179–80
gendered language of risk 29–30
gendered literacy practice 147–69; approaches to the research 152–4; conclusion 166–7; discussion of data 154–66; introduction 147–8; social, gendered practices 148–50; what can be done on Facebook 150–51
gendering 'internet risks' 133–8; individualised media harms 136–8; Kids Online 134–6; responsible grand quantitative survey research 138
geo-tagging 151
geopolitical uniformity 131–3
George, R. 98, 102, 149–50, 156, 162
German feminist girls' work 45–7, 62–3
Giardina, N. 113
Giddens, Anthony 100, 104
Giles, D. 120–21
Girl Guides 33, 37
'Girl Power' 36
Girlguiding UK 33, 35–6
Girls Friendly Society 29
girls today 58–60
girls' views on self-determination 62–3
girls' work 23–33, 45–54, 61–2; after queer theory 47–50; queer spaces in 51–4
girly stuff 181
Giroux, H. 30
girrls 131
glamour 171–94
glass bedroom 116, 123–4
globalisation 131–3
glocalism 160, 164
Glücks, E. 47
Goffman, I. 148–9
going private 79–81, 87–9
Google search 162
governance of the soul 106
Greenham Common 34
grooming 137, 141
growing up 129–33
growing-up challenged 129–45
gymslip mums 27

habitus 18, 107
Hageman-White, Carol 61
Haltung 44
Hamilton, M. 148
Haraway, Donna 131
Hargittai, E. 115
Harris, A. 5–6, 10, 18, 20, 116
haters *see* friends vs. haters
health issues 5–22
health promotion 6–7
healthism 16–19
healthy girlhood 12–16
Herring, S.C. 115
heterofemininity 28, 180–81, 187–9
heteronormativity 37
heterosexuality 51, 133, 141, 157, 180

INDEX

Hey, V. 31–2, 99, 102
Hills, R. 26
Hirschauer, Stefan 62
Hodkinson, P. 116–17
hollowed-out girls' work 28
homosexuality 51, 61–2
Howard, A. 76–7, 90–91
Humboldt, W. von 61
hyper-heterosexuality 180
hyper-reality 133, 137, 144

identity attributions 48
identity communities 118–20
identity construction 2–3, 111–27
identity work 98–9
ideology of 'strong girl' 60–61
imagined futures 5–22
immigration society 50–51
independence 1
individualised media harms 136–8
individualism 20
inequality 8, 333
informal learning 44
inheritance 95–110
insiders vs. outsiders 156–60; friends and haters 156–7; risky talk 157–60
institutional habitus 18
institutionalisation 47–50
insufficiency of research norms 143–4
intelligible sexuality 141
internalisation of elite status 77
internet pornography 2
internet risks 129–45
intertextuality 160–64
Irwin, S. 75, 89–90
Ivy League universities 85, 89

Jackson, C. 30, 123
James, D. 75
Jeffs, T. 26, 31
Jimenez, L. 97
junk food 10–11, 18

Kapidzik, S. 115
Kids Online 3, 133–8
Knobel, M. 148
knowing what you want 65–6
knowledge of media content 142
KS4 programme 189
kudos 150

Lacanian lack 103–4, 136
lack of aspiration 100
ladettes 27, 141
Lady Gaga 179
Ladyfest 53

Landesarbeitsgemeinschaft Mädchenarbeit 60–61
Lankshear, C. 148
Lareau, Annette 75–7, 90–91
Larsen, M.C. 121
Lash, S. 104
late developer education 102
Lave, J. 149
Lawler, S. 100
learning in processes 43–5
Leary, R. 173
Lemke, J. 160
Leonard, Diana 70
lesbianism 47
Levi-Strauss, C. 130
LGBTQ youth 31, 69
'liking' 151
liminality of youth work 24
Lincoln, S. 116–17
liposuction 122
Livingstone, S. 113, 115, 121
London School of Economics 89
looking at young women 58–60
losing weight 6–13
LSE *see* London School of Economics
Lucey, H. 107
Lütgert, Heike 61

McCabe, J. 34
McLeod, J. 6, 8–10
McNay, L. 100
McRobbie, Angela 6, 28, 34, 38, 60, 137, 139
making the self 87–9
making sense of diversity 96–7
Mallan, K. 113
managing girlishness 164–5
marginalisation 29, 31–2
Marxism 106
masturbation 141–2, 159
Mecheril, P. 62
media commerciality 139–43; children's knowledge of media content 142; what children should (not) know 142–3
mediated life contexts 19–20
melancholia 23–42
Mill Lane youth club 28
mimesis 98
Mizen, P. 153
modern critical girls' work 30–33
moments of resistance 33–7
Momus technologies 115, 117
monopolisation 28
moral panic 2, 6–8, 26–8
mortality rates 6–7
mutual disciplinary gaze 117

INDEX

narrowcast communities 118–20
narrowing gender perspective 134–6
National Citizenship service 27–8, 33
National Occupational Standards for Youth Work 24
naturality 48
need 103–4
negative media imagery 15
neo-managerialism 29, 38
neoliberalism 5–6, 8, 10–16, 30, 34, 65
neuroscience 97
new authoritarianism 27
new girlhood 16–19
New Labour 25, 27, 29
new media 129–33
new pedagogies of health 7–9
niceness 121, 124
non-obesity 10
'not girly, sexy or glamorous' 171–94
'nurturing' aspirations 178–82
Nutbrown, C. 153

obesity 6–13, 17
obesity epidemic 11
Oedipal version of family 107
OFSTED 34
one size fits all policies 16
online identities 120–23
online privacy 114–18
online text making 147–8
oppression 31, 37, 107
O'Rourke, A. 119
Osborne, J. 172
'Others' 77
Ottemeier-Glücks, F.-G. 47
'Out of the Ruins: Feminist Pedagogy in Recovery' 58
outsiders *see* insiders vs. outsiders
Oxbridge 85, 88–9

Paechter, C.F. 149, 152, 164, 167, 181, 185
paedophilia 141
panoptic mechanisms 149
panopticon 165–6
paradoxes of topic 1–3
paradoxical intervention 62
paralysing perplexity 96
parental construction of aspiration 171–94
Parsell, M. 119
partiality 46
participating on social networking sites 112–14; *see also* using Facebook
passivity 26
patriarchy 46
Pearson, E. 114, 116
pedagogical challenges 57–73

Pedagogy of Diversity 62
performativity 48–9, 53
performing femininity 167
performing identity 112–14
peripheral participation 149
'phallic girls' 29, 136
phatic performances of friendship 154–66; awareness of panopticon 165–6; insiders and outsiders 156–60; intertextuality 160–64; managing girlishness 164–5; sharing life rhythms 154–6
physical perfection 118, 122
Platform 51 36
Plößer, M. 62
'poking' 151
political talk 101–2
polyphonous meanings 155
pornification 122
porno-chic material 133, 140
pornographisation 131, 136, 138, 142–3
pornography 2, 133–43
pornosexuality 142
Positive for Youth 25
post-feminism 35, 95–6, 107–8
post-queer theory 43–56
post-welfare 104–6
poststructuralism 31, 37–8, 98
postural intertextuality 161–2
power relations 111–12
practices of middle-class parents 90–91
Prengel, Annedore 62
prettiness 57–73
private education 75–93
privilege 75–7, 87–9; as identity 76
privileged relation 129–33; contextualisation of topic-related research 129–31; thematic issues/hypothesis 131–3
pro-ana sites 119–21, 123–4; *see also* anorexia
problem girls 25–8
Probyn, E. 11
psychic life of inheritance 95–110
psychoanalysis 97
psychosocial 97
psychosocial complexity 101

queer spaces 51–4
queer theory 43–56; deconstructivism 47–50; feminist girls' work in Germany 45–7; and girls' work 43–56; introduction 43–5; perceptions of reality 50–51; queer spaces 51–4

Rail, G. 8
rampant individualisation 106
rape 61
Rauw, Regina 61

INDEX

Read, B. 162, 164
Reay, D. 75
referential research on internet risks 129–45
reflexive co-education 44, 69–70
reformed burdens 16–19
Renold, Emma 139, 141
reproduction of privilege 78–9, 87–91, 104–5
resistance 33–7, 107–8, 164
responsible grand quantitative survey research 138
rhinoplasty 122
Rich, E. 119–20, 123–4
Ringrose, J. 115, 118, 121–2, 124
risk society 19–20
'Risks and Safety on the Internet' 143–4
risky talk 157–60
Robards, B. 149
role deviances 47
role models 57–8, 131
Roof, J. 107
rounded accomplishment 91

Safer Internet Programme 133–4
sanctum of justice 68–9
school exclusion 77
science aspirations 171–94; aspiring to career in science 176–8; conclusion 187–9; construction of desirable femininity 178–82; disconnect between science and learner identity 182–7; introduction 171–4; study details 174–6
Science Council 189
scientific literacy 176
Second World War 44
second-wave feminism 28, 34–5, 37–8, 61
self-authored e-zines 116
self-care 7, 10, 12
self-commodification 115
self-confidence 59–60, 88–9, 137
self-determination 57–8, 61–3, 66, 69
self-esteem 122
self-expression 59
self-fulfilment 48
self-identification 141
self-organisation 1
self-pornographisation 131, 136
self-responsibility 1, 10
self-restriction 57–8
self-satire 159, 165
self-serving rampant individualisation 106
self-styling 162
sex–gender mutability 31, 34, 38
sexting 134–5, 142–3
sexual assertion 115
sexual deviance 26
sexual precocity 26–7, 29

sexualised hyperfemininity 100–101, 104
sexuality norms 129–45; conclusion 143–4; gendering of 'internet risks' 133–8; introduction 129–33; new media commerciality 139–43
sexually transmitted diseases 2
Shade, L.R. 115
shame 103–4
sharing life rhythms 154–6
significance of health 5–22
Simons, S. 172
sincerity 121; *see also* authenticity
single-sex youth work 28–30, 57–8, 69–70
Skeggs, B. 100
Smith, M. 26, 31
Snow, C.P. 182
SNSs *see* social networking sites
social bonds 95–6
social cohesion 155
social interaction 116–17
social isolation 10
social networking sites 111–27
social practices 148–50
socialisation 27–8, 46–7
socio-cultural capital 9–10
Spears, Britney 161–2
Spence, J. 28
spiralling individualisation 96
statistically individualised harms 136–8
STDs *see* sexually transmitted diseases
STEM qualifications 171–4, 187–9
stigmatisation of boys 44
stories of future health 10–12
street politics 106
'strong girl' ideology 60–61
structured individualisation 100–101
subject positions 9
subjectification 6, 8, 98–9, 107–8
subordination 1
subversion 28, 36, 38
success levels 106–7
sureties in making self 87–9
surveillance 20
synchronic signs 131–2

talking personally 101–2
taste of freedom 57–8
Taylor, R. 161
techno–human contact 133
teen pregnancy 2, 23–42
'Ten Types of Scientist' campaign 189
theory of late modernity 100
third-wave feminism 37
Thompson, J.B. 77
thuggishness 26
Tinkler, P. 30

INDEX

'too pretty to do math' 57–73
'top girls' 60
topic-related research 129–31
trainee hairdressers 147–69
transformation of intimacy 100
transgression 17, 27, 29
transition 5–7
triumph of desire 104–206

ubiquity of Facebook 150–51
'Ugly Betty' situation 165
UK Youth 23
underperformance 26
unintentional lessons 90–91
unsaid aspects of science construction 187–9
up classing 98–9
updating Facebook 166–7
using Facebook 113–14, 147–69; *see also* participating on social networking sites

van Manen, M. 115–16
vanguard of new subjectivity 5–7
verbal dexterity 159
vernacular literacy practices 152–4
Vincent, C. 75–6
Vinke, Beate 60–61
virtual care community 119
'virtual experience of present absence' 115
visibility of bad behaviour 28–30

Walkerdine, V. 97, 107
Walther, J.B. 114
Walzer, Michael 68–9

Ward, K. 119
Warin, M. 8
weight 6–13
Weiler, K. 31
Weiner, Gaby 58
welfare 103–4
Wenger, E. 149
westernisation 5–6, 16
what children should (not) know 142–3
Wiccanism 118–19, 123–4
'wikidentities' 113
women cyborgs 131
women's imagined futures 5–22
Women's Liberation Movement 25, 28, 35
working-class femininity 186–8
world in question 100
Wright, J. 11

Yates, L. 6, 8–10
Youdell, D. 31
Young Enterprise schemes 83
young women in movement 57–73; acceptance 64–5; co- vs. single-sex pedagogy 69–70; concept of girls' work 61–2; current pedagogical challenges 66–7; external opinions 67–8; Girls' Club Bielefeld 62–3; introduction 57–8; knowing what you want 65–6; 'strong girl' ideology 60–61; young women today 58–60
young women online 111–27
Youth & Policy 23
YWCA 29, 33

Zywika, J. 122